FROM ROME TO BYZANTIUM

FROM ROME TO BYZANTIUM

The fifth century AD

Michael Grant

London and New York

First published 1998
by Routledge
11 New Fetter Lane, London EC4P 4EE

Simultaneously published in the USA and Canada
by Routledge
29 West 35th Street, New York, NY 10001

Typeset in Garamond by
J&L Composition Ltd, Filey, North Yorkshire
Printed and bound in Great Britain by Biddles Ltd, Guildford and King's Lynn

British Library Cataloguing in Publication Data
A catalogue record for this book is available
from the British Library

Library of Congress Cataloging in Publication Data
A catalogue record for this book has been requested

ISBN 0–415–14753–0

CONTENTS

ILLUSTRATIONS

Figures

The author and the publisher wish to thank the following for their help in acquiring permissions; the Bibliothèque Byzantine, Paris, the Warburg Institute, London, the Conway Library, the Courtauld Institute, London, the Classical Institute, London and Thames & Hudson Ltd. Every effort has been made to contact copyright holders and we apologise for any inadvertent omissions.

Maps

INTRODUCTION

Byzantium figures very little in our own talking points. It was dismissed by Gibbon and his Victorian successors as a decadent, dark, oriental culture given up to intrigue, forbidden pleasure and refined cruelty.[1] While most schoolboys of my generation knew the key figures in republican or imperial Rome, we would have a hard time saying much about Byzantium other than that Constantine was its re-founder, and had a vision which inspired him to make Christianity the empire's official religion. See also the Epilogue for more on this subject. But meanwhile it may be added that the fifth century AD, with which this book is concerned, is one of the least and most imperfectly known of all history. We are often told that the western Roman empire ceased to exist during that period. But who can explain, although some have tried, why the eastern empire did not cease to exist, but on the contrary, continued to exist, governed from Constantinople, as the Byzantine empire, for nearly a thousand years to come (with an intermission during the thirteenth century)?

Despite the determined efforts of experts since the late 1920s, the Byzantine empire is still not sufficiently appreciated or understood in western countries. This is partly because of chauvinist biases, which lay great emphasis on petty western states and statelets, and ignore the fact that the empire ruled from Constantinople was infinitely more powerful, and was, indeed, by far the most important state in the world west of India and China. This situation is reflected in the educational system today, which says hardly anything about the Byzantine empire. Our pro-western prejudice is paramount.

If the Byzantine empire as a whole is neglected, how much greater is the neglect of the fifth century, when that empire survived the fatal threats to the west and set itself up as the most impressive unit in Europe and western Asia? Virtually nothing, except about the fall of Rome, is said about the fifth century, and yet that was the period when this great eastern empire survived its birth pangs and continued to flourish.

One of the reasons why so comparatively little is known about the eastern empire is our ignorance of Asia Minor.[2] On the map (p. 33), that seems a single unit, whereas in reality it is as complex and diverse as a whole continent, and had already been complex and diverse for centuries, including the fifth, in which Asia Minor was unscathed by Rome's fall, remaining the heart of the eastern empire and the core of Byzantine rule. Here, then, is a further, special reason why this latter is misunderstood and underestimated, because so little is known about Asia Minor today.[3]

Ancient Asia Minor was full of rich, fine and stable commercial cities. This is what Pausanias, in the second century AD, had to say about its west coast, centred upon Ionia: 'Ionia enjoys the finest of climates, and its sanctuaries are unmatched in the world. . . . The wonders of Ionia are numerous and not much short of the wonders of Greece itself.'[4]

The Ionian cities played a considerable part in the dawn of the imperial Christian faith. For example, Pergamum (Bergama) maintained its intellectual leadership and became an important missionary centre. The Aegean coastlands were at first dependent on Constantinople, but their long tradition enabled them to strike out for themselves, in very varied fashion.

Elsewhere in Asia Minor, too, there was considerable activity. Perga (Murtana) in Pamphylia was still prosperous, and Myra (Kale) was the capital of the independent province of Lycia at the time of Theodosius II (408–50). Side ('Pomegranate'; Selimiye) revived in the fifth century. Prusias ad Hypium (Prusa, Brusa) in Bithynia was prosperous. But there was also a good deal of individual activity in the central, inland part of the peninsula. The employment by Leo I (457–74) of officers and soldiers from the bandit country of Isauria is particularly famous, and led to the creation of important churches and monasteries in the region. Angora (Ancyra) in Galatia, too, enjoyed a good deal of wealth. Cappadocia had already given the world talented bishops, the 'Cappadocian Fathers', in what was a productive but traditionally backward area[5] (now the territory of Cappadocia had been divided into two provinces, Prima and Secunda).

'I am convinced', said Norman Baynes quite rightly, 'that the essential condition of the prosperity of the later Roman empire was its possession of Asia Minor – that reservoir alike of money and of men.'[6]

Let us consider what in fact happened during this period. In 395 Theodosius I, having gained control of the whole empire, died, leaving the west to his son Honorius and the east to Honorius's elder brother Arcadius, both very young. In the west, Honorius ruled until 423, moving from Mediolanum (Milan) to Ravenna in 402, and suffering the sack of Rome by the Visigoth Alaric in 410. Thereafter, following a brief interlude, Valentinian III, the son of Constantius III and Galla Placidia, was western emperor from 425 until 455, during the latter part of which time there was a grave danger from the Huns, whose king Attila was, however, defeated in 451 by the Roman general Aetius, subsequently murdered by Valentinian III (454), who paid for the crime with his life. Then followed, with the support of the German commander of the day, a rapid succession of short-lived western emperors, terminating in Romulus Augustulus, who was deposed in 476 by the German Odoacer (Odovacar), whereupon the western empire ceased to exist. Odoacer became king of Italy, and was succeeded by the Ostrogoth Theoderic (or Theodoric) (493–528).

Meanwhile, the eastern empire had managed to evade external threats, under Arcadius (395–408), Theodosius II (408–50), Marcian (450–7), Leo I (457–74), Zeon (474–91) and Anastasius I (491–518). It is worth while to investigate why this eastern empire did not fall, while its western counterpart did.[7]

One difficulty that we are bound to experience in considering that question is that the fifth century was a deeply religious period. People were very much concerned with what the true, defensible character of Christian belief was, and this is reflected in the events that occurred. The resultant situation has been described by A.H.M. Jones:

> It is difficult to make any generalisation which is both true and significant about the religious temper of an age, but it may at least be asserted with some confidence that the later Roman empire was intensely religious. Sceptics and rationalists, if they existed, have left no mark on history and literature. All, pagans and Christians alike, believed, and it would seem believed intensely, in supernatural powers, benevolent and malign, who intervened actively in human affairs. All were anxious to win their aid and favour, or to placate and master them, as the case might be.[8]

The same point was made by Averil Cameron: 'Christian doctrines themselves, together with the many permutations on which Christians were divided, aroused the passionate feelings of contemporaries in just the same way as social and political issues do today.'[9]

This makes the period hard for us to comprehend, because such an attitude is inconceivable, and not easy to understand, in our own time. In those days, however, religious beliefs had great dynamic force: even if they mean little now. Indeed, religion seemed the only source of stability and permanence in an unstable world.

The writer Procopius (born c. 500) was one of the few people who thought it best to avoid Christological debate: 'I hold it to be a sort of mad folly', he said,

> to research into the nature of God. Even human nature cannot, I think, be precisely understood by man; still less so can the things that appertain to the nature of God. So let us shun the peril and pass these questions by in silence, if only to avoid casting doubt

on things revered. For I personally will say nothing whatever about God except that he is altogether good and holds things in his power.[10]

As against this view, consider how St Gregory of Nyssa (c. AD 330–95) had found the public – much more typically:

> Every corner of the city is thronged with men arguing on incomprehensible subjects. Ask a man how many obols a thing costs, and he dogmatises on generated and ungenerated Essence. Enquire what is the price of bread, and you are answered, the Father is greater than the Son, and the Son is subordinate to the Father. Ask about your bath, and you are told, the Son was created out of nothing.[11]

That sort of conversation would certainly not happen today, and the fact that it happened then creates a gulf between the fifth century and ourselves which is virtually impossible to bridge. The people of that time seem quite different from ourselves, or from anyone we meet or know. And the rulers were correspondingly pious; agnosticism practically did not exist, as we have seen.

For these various reasons it is hard to reconstruct what really happened during the fifth century AD.[12] The present book is an attempt to rectify this situation, and to look behind the smog-corroded urban blight of the present Constantinople to locate its early soul. This is not an easy task. For one thing, as W.B. Anderson observed, 'the sources available for our knowledge of the fifth century are meagre and often obscure, and the attempts of modern historians to reconstruct the facts show marked divergencies'.[13] Yet there is little doubt that during the fifth century the emperor at Constantinople was the richest monarch in the world – and therefore worth studying.[14]

Yet, as we have seen, that century is not a readily accessible period, being remote from our consciousness and grasp of events, preoccupied with matters that scarcely concern us now, badly served by our existing sources, and seen lopsidedly, when seen at all, because of our preference for the west. Yet the fifth century is worth persevering with, not only for its own sake but because it lies at the heart and origins of our modern civilisation, which would not have been at all the same without it.

Finally, may I add one or two personal notes. I have allowed myself some repetitions. I have inserted these deliberately, because the subject is complicated, and I felt my readers would be helped if I said certain things more than once. And I have introduced a good many quotations from modern sources. I have done this because, although Byzantium, as I have said, is underestimated in the west today, a certain amount has nevertheless been said about its early years: and it would be a pity if this were forgotten. Among other things, the actual course of events has been narrated by earlier writers. And I have not attempted to do so once again. This book is rather a series of comments on some of the situations that existed and arose.

I am very grateful to Mr Richard Stoneman of Routledge and his colleagues and staff, especially Leigh Wilson, Coco Stevenson and Sarah Brown, for their help. I also owe thanks to Mrs Maria Ellis and Dr James Crow and Mr Paul Jackson, of the Library of the Hellenic and Roman Societies and the Reader Services of the British Library, for very useful assistance. And, as always, I appreciate very warmly the aid I have received from my wife.

I also want to thank the following publishers for the quotations from books published by them which I have included: Barnes & Noble; British Museum Publishers; Holt, Rinehart & Winston; Meridian Books; Methuen; Murray (John); Johns Hopkins University Press; Oxford University Press; Princeton University Press; Redman (Alvin); Routledge; Ullstein Bücher; University of Oklahoma Press (Norman); Unwin (L. Fisher); Variorum; Weidenfeld & Nicolson.

Michael Grant
Gattaiola, 1997

1

ROME AND OTHER CITIES

It was nothing new for emperors to consider and decide that Rome would not do any longer as the political and military centre of the empire. Panegyrists plaintively felt that Rome should once again become the imperial capital[1] but there was no chance that this would happen. In consequence, there was a long pre-Constantinian history of the planting of imperial headquarters in other cities. As Herodian had already observed in the second century AD, 'Where Caesar is, there Rome is.'[2]

Yet Rome was still all-powerful at that epoch. In the third century, however, Gallienus had established his headquarters at Mediolanum (Milan), when his father Valerian had gone east to fight the Persians.[3] Mediolanum was conveniently equidistant from the northern frontier and Rome – and the location of major road crossings from the provinces – and northern Italy was more appropriate than Rome for combating the Germans on the Rhine and Danube. Rome was a long way away from them, and was easily cut off from the sea. For all practical purposes, therefore, the capital moved out of the city. The walls of Rome were greatly strengthened by Aurelian (270–5),[4] but its role as political and miliary capital of the empire was over. 'The old empire . . . of Rome and Italy as queen of the provinces was dead or dying.'[5] It was not at Rome, for example, but at Mediolanum, that Maximian felt it necessary to rule;[6] while his senior colleague Diocletian only visited Rome upon a single occasion, namely his twentieth anniversary (*vicennalia*).[7] The ancient city, as capital of the empire, was already an anachronism.

And in 410 it was sacked, by Alaric I the Visigoth. The event appalled St Augustine. And it caused great distress to St Jerome, far away in Palestine.

> I was so stupefied and dismayed that day and night that I could think of nothing but the welfare of the Roman community. It seemed to me that I was sharing the captivity of the saints, and I could not open my lips until I received some more definite news. All the while, full of anxiety, I wavered between hope and despair,

Map 1 Italy and Sicily

torturing myself with the misfortunes of others. But when I heard that the bright light of all the world was quenched, or rather that the Roman empire had lost its head and that the whole universe had perished in one city, then indeed 'I became dumb and humbled myself and kept silence from good words.'[8]

The British or Irish theologian, or 'heretic' Pelagius was equally disturbed.

> It happened only recently, and you heard it yourself. Rome, the mistress of the world, shivered, crushed with fear, at the sound of the blaring trumpets and the howling of the Goths. . . . Everyone was mingled together and shaken with fear; every household had its grief, and an all-pervading terror gripped us. Slave and noble were one. The same spectre of death stalked before us all.[9]

Yet in spite of the disaster – and, indeed, even after the final demise of the western empire in 476 – Rome remained highly privileged, and it was also still the spiritual and cultural and traditional centre of the world.

> It remained the centre of western society, and its refugees were particularly vocal and influential. Above all, Rome was the symbol of a whole civilization. It was as if an army had been allowed to sack Westminster Abbey or the Louvre. . . . Rome symbolized the security of a whole civilized way of life. To an educated man, the history of the world culminated quite naturally in the Roman empire, just as, to a nineteenth century man, the history of civilization culminated in the supremacy of Europe.[10]

In addition, Rome even now remained the home of the senate. But the character of that body had changed. It decided nothing – it was the emperors who decided everything; nor were they necessarily keen to be near the senators. These were largely rich landowners, who were, it is true, extremely influential: though often they did not bother to come to the meetings of the senate at all, but stayed on their enormous estates. The tradition of their opposing the emperor still existed – and some emperors were afraid of it – but it had greatly diminished.

So if the rulers no longer ruled from Rome, where were they? 'Where Caesar is, there Rome is', as we have seen; and Caesar was in a good many different places. Mediolanum has already been mentioned: the new concept of imperial defence had also made Aquileia and Verona more important. It was right that Mediolanum (like Verona) should become a *colonia Gallieniana*,[11] because Gallienus (253–68) was based there, making it his capital, as we saw. In 268 Aureolus was proclaimed emperor in the city[12] (though he did not last). Aurelian (270–5) fortified Mediolanum at the same time as he built the walls of Rome; traces of his construction are still visible.[13] Mediolanum was rising as a great political centre, largely because of pressure from the Germans, but also for the other reasons that have been stated. Maximian, it may be repeated, reigned there; and he abdicated there (305; for a time); Valentinian II (375–92) moved his court to the

3

city. Ambrose was bishop of Mediolanum, and it was there that he won his great victory for the Church.[14]

But Mediolanum was not the only imperial centre in north Italy. Aquileia and Verona have been mentioned, and Gallienus, when he established his residence at Mediolanum, had his military headquarters at Ticinum (Ticino), which, moreover, replaced Mediolanum as a mint under Aurelian (274). In 402 the emperor Honorius decided to establish himself at Ravenna, where there was landward protection from the marshes, and easy maritime facilities in case escape to the east became necessary.

The later story of the monk Fulgentius is also illuminating.

> One day in the year 500 the African monk Fulgentius, later bishop of the small town of Ruspe, fulfilled a life's ambition in visiting Rome. . . .
>
> Rome, centre alike of law and the tradition of human authority and of Christian orthodoxy and primacy, had beckoned to him. He had read in the pagan poets their eulogies of this city, elevated to the status of a goddess, to be revered and justly revered throughout the world. But what he saw amazed him. 'How wonderful', he is said to have exclaimed, 'must be the heavenly Jerusalem, if this earthly city can shine so greatly!'[15]

> For Rome was the centre, *the* city, the lawgiver, the fact that had dominated and made the world men knew. From Iraq to Wales, from the Baltic to the Sudan, she had fashioned and left all in her image. On the countryside her language had left the place-names men used; in the towns men lived by her organization, her law, her peace. 'What was once a world, you have but one city', a poet of the previous century, Rutilius Namatianus, had declared.[16]

> The good monk, from the small white towns on the edge of the desert . . . could yet know that he was at home. All this was the work of time. Rome was now in the thirteenth century of her foundation, and in the eleventh of her domination, a matter to move men's minds in awe.[17]

For one thing, Rome was the headquarters of the Pope, who now became increasingly important. And, as we have seen, it was still the meeting-place of the senate.

Another very important centre in the west was Augusta Trevirorum (Trier) on the River Mosella (Moselle). Not only was it the capital of the diocese (group of provinces) of Gaul, and residence of the Prefect, containing one of the best universities of the west (attended by St Jerome), but it was the capital of Constantius I Chlorus (305–6), who contracted for the construction of his fleet there, and it remained the capital of his son Constantine I the Great until 312; then he moved to a fifty-room villa-palace on the Mosella, five miles out of the city. Subsequently, Augusta Trevirorum still figured as an imperial town for at least another century.[18] Valentinian I (364–75) made the place his headquarters for operations against the Germans, and his son Gratian (c. 380) lived there.

During the same period Arelate (Constantina, Arles) also became more important;[19] Constantine had lived in that city as well, in addition to other places. One of them was Naissus (Niš), where he had probably been born. He often visited the town later, and erected splendid buildings within its precincts. It was probably the earliest permanent military camp in Moesia, possessing great strategic significance.

In 314–15, however, Constantine had moved his headquarters to Sirmium (Sremska Mitrovica),[20] which was a road junction and the most important strategic centre of the Danube region, containing arms factories, a fleet station and an imperial mint. It had been, for a time, the residence of Marcus Aurelius (161–80) and Maximinus I Thrax (235–8) and others. Claudius Gothicus (268–70) mopped up the Goths from his base at the imperial palace at Sirmium, which was also where he died. Possibly Aurelian (370–5) came from the place, and it profited from the encouragement of grape-growing by Probus (276–82), who had been born there.[21] Maximian was a peasant's son from Sirmium, and his senior colleague Diocletian spent much time at the place, promulgating numerous laws. Galerius resided for a long time at Sirmium; it was his 'favourite city'.[22] Constantine, too, moved his administration from Augusta Trevirorum and Mediolanum to Sirmium, and he had seriously thought of giving his name to the last-named town, if his first war against Licinius[23] had proved decisive (which it did not). It was from there, perhaps, that Licinius promulgated the Edict of Milan, published at Nicomedia.[24]

But subsequently Constantine, who transferred his headquarters from one place to another – including Thessalonica (Salonica), which was strong and had served as a capital[25] – moved from Sirmium to Serdica (Sofia) (317/18). He liked the Balkans, because the region was pivotal for the army; he enlarged the already existing palace at Serdica, and seriously considered the place as a possible imperial capital, declaring that it was his Rome.[26] But Serdica had disadvantages as well as advantages, and Constantine finally opted for somewhere else.

He did not fancy going out of Europe, because of the threat from the Germans. So the ancient and wealthy cities of Antioch and Alexandria did not attract him, despite their imperial connections, intellectual ferment, and loud noises regarding ecclesiastical affairs.[27] Nor did Nicomedia

Map 2 The western provinces

(Izmit), which had been the capital (and place of abdication) of Diocletian; and Galerius, too, had resided at Nicomedia. It had a great deal in its favour, including a good harbour, large fertile territories, and a position on the trunk road from the Danube. But it was too far away from the northern frontier, being in Asia Minor; and there were other things against it too.[28] Its position has been estimated as follows:

> The dawn of late antiquity even saw it [Nicomedia] become capital of the Roman empire, a role it was to maintain for a generation. Events of the fourth century, however . . . brought this moment of glory to an end, as the city resumed its old role as a major provincial centre. . . . The foundation of Constantinople, only sixty miles away, sealed the fate of Nicomedia forever,

6

though not immediately. . . . [Constantinople] created a far more powerful rival than Nicaea [Iznik] had ever been, and permanently deprived the city [of Nicomedia] of its ephemeral glory.[29]

To sum up, it had been clear long before the fifth century began that Rome, however great its prestige, could no longer effectively be the political or military capital of the empire. So the emperors, who made wherever they went their capitals for the time being, tried a good many other centres. But none of them proved really satisfactory until Constantine I the Great fastened upon Constantinople – which is the theme of the third chapter of this book. The second chapter, which will now follow, deals with the division of the empire which seemed to have become inevitable.

2

THE DIVIDED EMPIRE

The doctrine, then, that the empire was too large for a single man to govern was not new. It had a lot to do, as we have seen, with the fact that the northern (as well as the eastern) frontier was dangerous and liable to damaging explosions.

As I wrote on a previous occasion,

> it had long been felt that the empire was too large, and its frontiers too menacing, to be controlled by one man. In other words, the practical division of the empire into two parts had already taken place. Marcus Aurelius (161–80) had been conscious of this when he sent his junior colleague Lucius Verus to the east. Then Valerian (253–61) acted similarly, though in the opposite direction, himself moving to the east (with fatal results) while he left his son Gallienus to command the armies of the west. Subsequently the brothers Carinus and Numerian (283–4) operated a comparable division, which was regularised by Diocletian [284–305] when he introduced the quadripartite monarchy, himself with his subordinate Caesar Galerius remaining in the east, while Maximian (whose Caesar was Constantius I, the father of Constantine I the Great) remained in Italy. . . .
>
> [Thus Diocletian's actual achievement was] to regularise the division, with himself remaining in the east and his fellow-Augustus Maximian in the west. . . . This situation was partly the product of necessity, for Maximian could not have lower rank than the British usurper Carausius [c. 287–93], against whom he or his subordinates was fighting. . . . But the arrangement was developed into a system which was intended to be permanent. This Tetrarchy [i.e. with a Caesar attached to each Augustus] multiplied authority, but did not divide it; in spite of the regional subdivisions, the empire was still 'an undivided patrimony'. . . .
>
> Constantine I the Great reunited the empire, but when he died in 337 he left it divided between his three sons (and two others).

In 364 Valentinian I more or less formalised the position when he gave the east to his brother Valens. The empire was still, officially, united, and the emperors coined in each other's territory, but the division was nevertheless very real.

The institution of this division by Valentinian I has been described in the following terms:

It was in 364 that Valentinian I was hailed emperor by the army. Immediately afterwards, the soldiers demanded that he should appoint a colleague to share his power. For whenever there was only a single emperor, the troops felt that the risk of his death, and of consequent chaos, was too great, and indeed the death of the last monarch, Jovian [363–4], had resulted, like similar moments of transition throughout the past centuries, in a perilous emergency. Valentinian I, in his inaugural address to the troops, expressed agreement that a joint Emperor should be nominated. . . . He was thinking in particular of pressing external threats on many sectors of the frontier; and there were dangers of internal revolts as well. So he immediately raised his brother Valens to an equal share in the empire. . . .

Henceforward, the western realm consisted of the whole of Roman Europe except the Black Sea coast and its immediate hinterland. It also possessed North Africa as far as Tripolitania [Tripolitana] – the western part of modern Libya – inclusive. The remaining part of Libya fell to the eastern empire, which also comprised the European Black Sea fringe (extending down to the capital Constantinople) and Egypt, and the Asian territories that now belong to Turkey, Syria, Lebanon and Israel. . . .

[Valentinian's son Gratian probably] ceded to [his eastern partner] Theodosius I most of the former western possessions in the Balkan peninsula. Henceforth, the frontier between the western and eastern empires, while remaining unchanged in North Africa, ran in Europe from Singidunum [Belgrade] due south to the Adriatic, where Albania is today.[1]

The split was perpetuated in 395 when Theodosius I, who had finally become ruler of the entire empire, had the Roman world, on his death, divided between his two young sons, Arcadius, the elder, aged seventeen, in the east, and Honorius, aged ten, in the west. From that time onwards, until the official fall of the western empire in 476, there were separate western and eastern empires.

One cannot help wondering why Theodosius I left the empire, thus divided, to his two young sons. They were not only young, but sure to prove incompetent. He himself may not have deserved the title 'the Great', which the Christians called him because of his support for their cause, but he was no fool, and he had succeeded in reuniting the empire. Why, then, did he throw all this away, by dividing the Roman world, and dividing it between two such feeble boys? The answer, I think, lies in dynastic feeling. This was very strong among emperors, as Septimius Severus had shown, when on his death (211) he left the rulership to his two young sons, Caracalla and Geta; and Constantine I the Great, too, bequeathed the empire to his inadequate sons. There is every reason to suppose that Theodosius I felt the same. Despite all the dangers implicit in bequeathing the summit to Arcadius and Honorius, he had long favoured the idea of their succeeding him, and succeed him they did. It is true that dynastic feeling could, on occasion, save the Roman world: witness the decline of the empire in the west after the death of its dynastic inheritor Valentinian III (455). But it is also true that this same dynastic feeling, under Theodosius I, contributed to the final and fatal division which caused the downfall and destruction of the western empire.

It has been repeated here that the Roman empire had become too large and unmanageable, with perilous frontiers for administration by one man, at one centre, to be any longer practicable. For some time past, therefore, there had been a tendency for there to be two emperors simultaneously, one in the west and one in the east. By the beginning of the fifth century, the epoch with which the present book is concerned, this tendency had become stratified, so that Arcadius (395–408) was the emperor in the east, and his younger brother Honorius (395–423) in the west; and their administrations were quite separate.

3

CONSTANTINOPLE

And so Constantine I the Great fastened on Byzantium (Constantinople) as the new, restored city named after him – and destined to become the future imperial capital. This he surely knew, but it was a somewhat hazardous decision.

> Owing to the rush of population . . . the emperor [Constantine] soon had on his hands a housing problem which he disposed of with an efficiency we may envy. The forests of Belgrad, which still exist to the north of the town, supplied unlimited timber, and the island of Proconnesus [Marmara Adasa] no less unlimited marble. And, as the building unions of the day were unable to provide a sufficient number of architects and artificers, the emperor diluted them with apprentices from his own technical schools. The work was done at surprising speed. And judging from contemporary complaints of jerry-building, the capital was run up very much on the lines of a modern Empire Exhibition. If Rome wasn't built in a day, New Rome very nearly was. . . .
>
> One advantage that Constantine had was that he could lay the whole empire under contribution for ornaments, tombs, trophies, and statues of gods and heroes. These with a north-country thoroughness he 'conveyed' in cargo-loads from Rome, Athens, Alexandria, and all the cities of Europe and Asia. . . .
>
> Of the Great Palace . . . nothing remains . . . Gone are the university, the two theatres, the fifty-two porticoes, the four law-courts, the fourteen palaces, and the four thousand three hundred and eighty-eight family mansions, all built by Constantine. . . .

His 'obvious' decision was, in fact, quite a gamble. He himself did not pay the price for it, but his immediate successors had to do so, in the form of immensely expensive works of engineering and diversion of funds on a huge scale to make sure that the imperial capital was properly supplied and defended.

Great men place great burdens on their descendants. Once the

11

investment had been made in the fifty to eighty years after Constantine's death, it was too late to change course, i.e. to relocate the capital.[1]

This is what I said earlier about Constantinople, basing myself on the sixth-century historian Zosimus:

> Eventually he [Constantine] found a site which suited him . . . at the point where the road from Europe to the River Euphrates is crossed, in spectacular fashion, by the maritime passage of the Bosphorus linking the Aegean and Black Seas. Moreover, it was in this area that Constantine had won his final and historic victory over Licinius (324), at Chrysopolis (Scutari, Üsküdar). . . .
>
> The dating of the new Constantinople is a little uncertain, but it seems probable that it was inaugurated in 326 and that its dedication took place in 330. The whole initiative was given an impetus by Constantine's presence on the Danube. . . .
>
> The new city was fortunate to possess the magnificent harbour of the Golden Horn. It was also defensible both by land and by sea. . . . And it enjoyed ready accessibility, again by land and sea alike, to the vital industrial and cultural centres of Asia Minor and Syria. It was also accessible to the grain supplies of Egypt which were required in order to feed the large population which, it was hoped, this great new town would attract. . . . Nevertheless, by the time of [Constantine's] death the population is unlikely to have exceeded 50,000, and Constantinople did not become a great commercial centre very quickly.
>
> Constantine's apparent determination to make it a truly Christian place [is noteworthy]. It is likely that he did not announce initially that the new city he had brought into being was to become his sole capital, and that it should therefore be entitled the New or Second Rome, *altera Roma* (although the expanded city seems to have been called informally by that name as early as 324). However, this must have been his ultimate aim . . . and it was not very long before this intention came into effect. . . .
>
> [But] Constantine was, as usual, proceeding with circumspect caution. That is to say, Rome lost none of its privileges, and at first Constantinople did not share its traditional position . . . although the grandeur of the palaces in the new city, and its proposed dimensions, promised that this would not always be so.[2]

These were the comments of A.H.M. Jones:

Constantinople . . . was founded as an imperial residence, and grew to greatness as an administrative centre. . . . For a number of reasons we know much more about Rome than about Constantinople. . . .

Constantinople first received a *praefectus urbi* [prefect of the city] on 11 December 359. . . . The supply of food and drink was elaborately organised. . . . Next came the two essential luxuries of city life, the Baths and the Games. . . . Both Rome and Constantinople were centres of higher education. . . . At Constantinople the emperor in the fourth century appointed salaried professors on the recommendation of the senate. . . . The finances of Constantinople were doubtless as involved [as those of Rome], but we know little of them. . . .

Constantinople grew rapidly in the first century of its existence.[3]

H. St J.B. Moss wrote about the place as follows:

Even its relative obscurity . . . aided the founder's intentions. It would have been impossible, at Antioch or Alexandria, with their celebrated past and independent traditions, to realise that remarkable vision of a 'second Rome' founded in the Greek-speaking east, with . . . its sense of continuity with the purely Roman sentiments and ideals associated with the city of Romulus on the Tiber. . . .

It was [its] impregnability, unique among ancient and medieval capitals, which gave to the Byzantines a visible symbol of the eternal destiny of the empire, an ever-present assurance that their city was guarded by God and designed by Providence for the ultimate realisation of the Divine Purpose.[4]

This was what Steven Runciman said:

Few cities have enjoyed so magnificent a commercial site as Constantinople, placed on the sea-channel between North and South and the land-bridge between East and West. . . . It was hardly a matter for wonder that Constantinople was for centuries a synonym for riches, a city of whose treasure 'there was neither end nor measure'.

But the treasure had not been won all by accident. Care as well as circumstance was needed to enrich the city. Till Columbus and Vasco da Gama opened out a new era, the main trade of the world was from the Farther East to the Mediterranean. . . . In the early centuries AD the eastern trade was highly flourishing. . . . It was her position on the world trade-routes that gave Constantinople her great days of prosperity. . . .

Rome itself, with its old senatorial traditions, its unruly mob, and its vulnerability caused by the need to import all its food from overseas, was no longer a suitable administrative capital. After some hesitation he [Constantine] picked for its site the Greek city of Byzantium, on the extreme tip of Europe, where the narrow strait of the Bosphorus opens out into the Propontis [Sea of Marmara].

It was a superb site, on a peninsula that was roughly triangular, with curved sides, the convex side protected by the sea and the concave by the magnificent harbour of the Golden Horn. Its landward side was comparatively short and easy to fortify. It commanded the sea-route from the Black Sea to the Mediterranean, and the easiest land-route from Europe into Western Asia. It was well-placed for the two frontiers that were of most concern to the Empire, the Danube frontier beyond which lived the most restless of the barbarians, and the eastern frontier beyond which was the active, aggressive kingdom of Sassanid Persia. . . . This city was to be New Rome, but to most of the world it was known as Constantinople after its founder.[5]

And in the eighteenth century even Edward Gibbon, although far from enthusiastic about the Byzantine empire, had been obliged to write approvingly of the site of Constantinople.

Situated in the forty-fifth degree of latitude, the imperial city commanded from her seven hills, the opposite shores of Europe and Asia. The climate was healthy and temperate, the soil fertile, the harbour secure and capacious, and the approach on the side of the continent was of small extent and easy defence. The Bosphorus and Hellespont [Dardanelles] may be considered as the two gates of Constantinople, and the prince who possessed these important passages could always shut them against a naval enemy and open them to the fleets of commerce. . . . [Constantinople was] formed by nature for the centre and capital of a great monarchy.[6]

In fact, 'the focal role of Constantinople can hardly be exaggerated. . . . [It was] the spiritual, imperial, administrative and strategic centre of power,' and became a model for all the world – not least in western Europe. Admittedly the city was in perpetual danger, full of violence and nervous tension, and grew in a somewhat disorderly fashion – which the emperor Zeno (474–91) sought to control. And there was bitter opposition to its rise as ecclesiastical capital, not only at Rome but at Antioch[7] and Alexandria[8] as well. But already by the end of the fifth century the city of Constantinople, growing in size and wealth, had 4,388 private houses, and had to draw 175,200 tons of wheat yearly from Egypt. It was impregnable because of its walls, of which more will be said later (Chapter 11).[9] Moreover, the senators of Constantinople, unlike those of Rome, had very often started their careers as craftsmen, so that the senate of that city fulfilled a fairly constructive role.

> The empire [was] no longer of Rome but of Constantinople. . . . Constantinople was now clearly the ruling city, in which the emperor resided and where government was administered.
>
> Compared with the ancient Christian centres, on the other hand, Constantinople was a newcomer, lacking status. At the Council of Chalcedon [Kadiköy] in AD 451, therefore, the emperor Marcian took advantage of a dispute within the Church to humble the Patriarch of Alexandria, and so to secure the position of Constantinople as the leading Christian city of the empire. . . .
>
> All attempts to achieve unity in the Church passed through the court at Constantinople. . . . As the residence of the emperor [it] was not only the ruling city, the centre of government, but also the holy city, the centre of the Church. . . .
>
> And Constantinople rapidly became the administrative and

Figure 1 The walls of Constantinople, erected in the time of Theodosius II (412). (The Conway Library, Courtauld Institute of Art)

social centre to which gold was attracted by every device at her disposal.[10]

Once the empire was divided, then, it was not long before Constantine the Great's foundation Constantinople became recognised as the capital at least of its eastern half. The new foundation, or rather refoundation, had, as we saw, numerous advantages, which enabled it to survive as a city and the capital of the Byzantine empire for many hundreds of years: a survival imperfectly appreciated by westerners even today, when too little is said about Constantinople or the Byzantines in educational curricula, which prefer, as we have seen, to concern themselves with western states. It was in the fifth century, however, that this far greater permanence of the eastern empire, based in Constantinople, first became apparent.

4

THE FALL OF ROME[1]

'The emperor Honorius', said A. Ferrill,

has been asked by ancient and modern historians alike to take far
too much of the blame for Rome's fall. Partly that is because
Rome suffered its great humiliation in 407–410 under his rule,
and since he did not prevent it, he must undoubtedly be held
responsible for it. As citizens we apply this kind of standard to
our present leaders, and it is perhaps not unreasonable to do the
same for leaders in the past. On the other hand, if it is possible to
be right and still lose, Honorius may have done just that. He does
not deserve the criticism he uniformly gets for doing nothing,
since doing nothing was almost certainly, for him, an 'active' or
conscious strategy, not simply negligence, a strategy that might in
fact have worked if someone had not opened a gate to Rome for
Alaric's Visigoths in August 410. . . .
   Possibly, if the resources of Britain [Appendix 2] had been
united with the army of Italy in the crisis of 408–10, it might
have been possible to have defeated Alaric again. But . . . Honorius decided to pursue a strategy of exhaustion rather than to
bring Alaric to battle.[2]

As it was, Alaric descended upon Rome in 410, and sacked the city. Its
sack

caused a tremendous shock to Christians and pagans alike. . . .
The fall of Rome spelt the fall of the empire. It even meant the
end of the world. . . .
   To pagans, the explanation of the catastrophe was only too
obvious. The misfortunes of the empire had increased with the
growth of Christianity. . . . The Christians made several answers,
none of them very convincing. . . . To the Christian [said

17

Figure 2 Gold *solidus* of Honorius, western emperor 395–423. Mediolanum (Milan). The issue was made to mark the joint consulship of Honorius and Arcadius in 396. Honorius holds a sceptre and a *mappa* (a napkin used as a signal for starting the Games). (Photograph: Michael Grant)

Augustine], earthly disasters were indifferent; they were even to be welcomed as sent by God to discipline and purify the faithful.[3]

Nevertheless,

> The sack of Rome (410) does not represent the definite fall of the empire, often as the event and its date are mentioned in accounts of the period. It was a costly raid which damaged Roman prestige; but it was essentially only a raid.
>
> Alaric led his people, laden with their booty, to southern Italy. There he built a fleet with which he intended to cross to Africa [Appendix 2], a rich grain-land which he thought would serve as a home for the Visigoths. But the fleet was destroyed by a storm, and Alaric died soon after.[4]

All the same, the western empire now stood little chance of surviving. Alaric was succeeded by his brother-in-law Ataulf,[5] who was, at least initially, in favour of an understanding with the Romans, although the latter were not generally pro-German.

Ataulf once said that he had often dreamed of the establishment of a

18

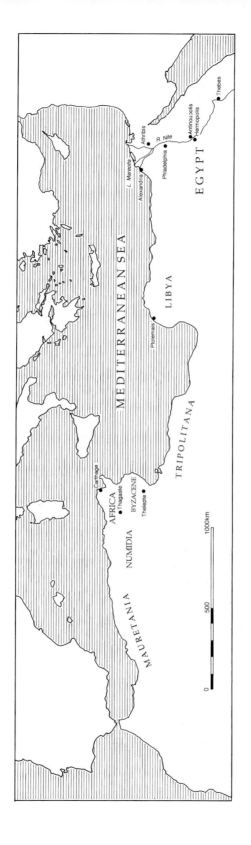

Map 3 North Africa

great Gothic kingdom, but had been forced to conclude that his people did not have the necessary qualities, so that the best thing for them to do was to give up the idea of 'Gothia', and support the Roman empire, 'Romania'. In 412 Ataulf took the Visigoths to Gaul in the service of Honorius. But he was refused the recognition which he had bargained for, and he led his people to Spain (Appendix 2), where he was murdered and succeeded by Wallia (415–18).

Thereafter, Attila the Hun was, with the possible exception of Gaiseric the Vandal (see below), the greatest of the opponents of Rome. This is a curious fact, since the Hunnish kingdom collapsed immediately after Attila's death, and before the western empire did. Attila's northern kingdom, however, was the first emergence of a barbarian empire *equal* to the empire or empires of the Romans. His first target had been the eastern Roman empire in 441, 443 and 447; on the last occasion the defences of Constantinople were further threatened by a disastrous earthquake. But he was somehow persuaded to tackle the west instead – probably the eastern emperor Theodosius II bought him off, with 700 lb. of gold. Then Attila tackled the west instead: as Jordanes remarked,[6] he realised that the western empire could be milked, and need no longer be feared. But his attack on Gaul, though severe, was miraculously thwarted by Aetius at the battle of the Catalaunian Plains (451). Yet this caused grave difficulties for Italy itself, since Attila then proceeded to invade that country. Christian tradition made great play with the Pope's role in sending him back home, northwards. But what really happened, in all probability, is that Attila was concerned about how to supply an army so far away from its, and his, base, with the result that Valentinian III succeeded in buying him off, though he himself fled to Rome.

Aetius, who had defeated Attila at the Catalaunian Plains, was a man of heroism and ability – 'the last of the Romans' according to the sixth-century historian Procopius[7] – who succeeded in neutralising the power of Galla Placidia (Chapter 8), although his quarrel with the east was unfortunate; because of it (it can be argued), he failed to save the western empire – or he might have postponed its downfall for several decades at least. His son was engaged to the daughter of the western emperor Valentinian III, but Aetius himself was murdered by the jealous Valentinian in 454. 'You have cut off your right hand with your left,' Valentinian was told.[8] And a year later the emperor himself was assassinated by Aetius's former retainers.

This was only twenty-one years before the final downfall of the west; and with these events its terminal phase may be said to have begun. Its penultimate crisis came about through the activities of a German king who was almost the equal of Attila, namely Gaiseric (Genseric) the Vandal.[9]

His sack of Rome in 455 was helped by the large number of Germans and other barbarians in the employment of the empire, many of whom, no doubt, were irregularly paid. And the western empire made a marked psychological error in its failure to assimilate or welcome these people. The Vandals (Appendix 2) were the only barbarian kingdom on Roman soil which took to the sea, and in 431, 441 and 467 Gaiseric heavily defeated attempts to overthrow him, sponsored by the eastern empire but assisted by the west. Africa had been conquered by the Vandals in 429 and was an easy prey, because the defensive system of the province was suited for no more than policing and the suppression of sporadic tribal revolts. With his fleet, Gaiseric controlled the western Mediterranean throughout his reign, and he died undefeated in 477: he never became western emperor, because it was understood that no German could do so; but he put Rome in the shade.

The final decades of the western empire saw a succession of emperors, some of whom had reigns of a year or even less (see List of Emperors), and many of whom were more or less nominal rulers, dependent on powerful German figures such as Ricimer or, later, Orestes. Western coinage, however, continued to the end, in gold mainly in the form of *solidi* and *tremisses*, with a much diminished silver coinage of *siliquae* and halves, and in bronze the small coins with a Victory type or the emperor's monogram on the reverse.[10]

One of these final rulers suffered the supreme damage and humiliation of a Vandal attack on Rome.[11] This was the greatest of the Vandals' exploits: their descent on Rome itself which, as has been said, took place in the year 455. It was a large-scale robbery and little else. Like other raids, it was designed to augment the material resources of the Vandal kings. The city was systematically looted of everything capable of being carried off by the robber expedition.

Then the western empire finally collapsed, and gave way to the German kingdom of Odoacer in 476.[12]

Those historians who regard the year 476 as the year of the fall of the empire have something of a point. Although Odoacer recognized the authority of the emperor in Constantinople, he was still only the commander of the German soldiers assigned to the defence of Italy. Africa had been lost to the Vandals, and Gaul and Spain were under the *de facto* control of the German kings there [see Appendix 2]. So when Italy came under the control of Odoacer, it may in fact be said that the former Roman type of government in the west had disappeared.[13]

21

Among the historical questions which men have posed through-out the ages none has attracted more attention over a longer period of time than the one which asks, Why did the Roman empire in the west collapse? It has remained a vital question because each age has seen in the tale of Rome's fall something significant and relevant to its own situation. The theme has proved especially attractive in our own time; the fate of Rome looms large in the cosmic speculation of Spengler [Oswald Spengler, 1880–1936] and Toynbee [Arnold Toynbee, 1889–1978], and has been intensively treated from countless points of view.

The first treatment of the decline of Rome as an historical problem had to wait until the Renaissance, when the humanists became aware of their own break with the medieval period and, therefore, of the break between the Middle Ages and classical antiquity. Whether they blamed internal failures, as did Petrarch [1304–74], or the barbarian attacks, as did Machiavelli [1469–1527], they were the first to show awareness of the problem. . . .

The usual categories of explanation – political, economic, social, or moral – prove none too helpful, for all played some role. There are, perhaps, four applicable categories: death by accident, natural causes, murder and suicide. . . . It is safe to guess that future histories will . . . bring to the problem of Rome's collapse new ideas, deriving in part from the experience of their own age, and, at the same time, seeking light for their own problems from the circumstances of Rome's fall.[14]

So how significant is that fall in 476? For the western empire had clearly been destined to fall for some time. But what, finally, caused it to happen?

Hundreds of reasons, it may be repeated, have been suggested for the collapse of the Roman west. Some indication of their variety can be obtained from reading Edward Gibbon's superb and never truly super-seded *History of the Decline and Fall of the Roman Empire* (1776–88). He lists at least two dozen supposed causes of that decline and fall – military, political, economic and psychological. When I wrote my book *The Fall of the Roman Empire* (1976, 1990), I listed its contents as follows:

I   The failure of the army
    1   THE GENERALS AGAINST THE STATE
    2   THE PEOPLE AGAINST THE ARMY

II   The gulfs between the classes
    3   THE POOR AGAINST THE STATE
    4   THE RICH AGAINST THE STATE
    5   THE MIDDLE CLASS AGAINST THE STATE

III   The credibility gap
    6   THE PEOPLE AGAINST THE BUREAUCRATS
    7   THE PEOPLE AGAINST THE EMPEROR

IV   The partnerships that failed
    8   ALLY AGAINST ALLY
    9   RACE AGAINST RACE

V   The groups that opted out
    10   DROP-OUTS AGAINST SOCIETY
    11   THE STATE AGAINST FREE BELIEF

VI   The undermining of effort
    12   COMPLACENCY AGAINST SELF-HELP
    13   THE OTHER WORLD AGAINST THIS WORLD[15]

All these causes for the downfall of the western Roman empire, possessing the connecting thread of disunity, are still valid; and the fall of Rome remains a most historic event.

To Rome we owe an incalculable debt for building a great civilisation which incorporated and preserved the Greco-Oriental culture which she herself inherited, and for providing a setting in which Christianity, her own heir, could come into being. For more than two thousand years the western world has been taught and inspired by Rome.

And yet, in the fifth century, and more particularly in 476, Rome fell.

> Roman civilization did not die a natural death. It was murdered. Yet people attacked by would-be murderers sometimes survive if they are strong enough to fight back. And the Romans could have survived, if they had possessed sufficient strength. But when the murderous blows were delivered, they could no longer muster the force to parry them. . . . By this time [the western empire] had become paralysed by its internal disunities.[16]

But I think that on further consideration I should blame the fall, though Averil Cameron, for one, does not agree, chiefly upon pressure from the Germans along the northern frontier, which the western empire proved unable to resist owing to its failure to provide itself with the financial backing which was needed in order to underpin such resistance.

These are the comments of R. Dochaerd and W.E. Kaegi, who stress the misery and poverty which resulted from the eclipse of Rome:

Poverty is for us the essential characteristic of the society of the early Middle Ages. It explains the forms and weaknesses of the authorities, their problems and their inefficiency resulting from lack of means. . . . If [poverty] takes from men the capacity to govern, at the same time it takes from those they govern the strength to grasp reality and to overthrow the intellectual and social structures which dominate their thoughts and behaviour.

The nature and causes of the fall of Rome have been controversial issues since the fifth century and doubtless will remain so. The experience of the Byzantines in the fifth and sixth centuries demonstrated how difficult it was to phrase the problem of Roman decline properly for rational consideration. Modern scholarship, in attempting to explain the decline of the Roman empire, has encountered the same challenge Zosimus [see Bibliography] did: the difficulty of explaining in one theory both the decay of the western Roman empire and the survival of the eastern Roman, or Byzantine, empire.[17]

And this is what Brook Adams had already noted about the west:

The 'monied class' [of the empire] wasted the state by working only to concentrate all wealth in their hands. . . . As the sustaining force [money] failed [see Chapter 5], the line of troops along the Danube and Rhine was drawn out until it broke, and the barbarians poured in unchecked.[18]

Rome was weary beyond the days of her strength. The expense of maintaining a luxurious court and an idle population sapped the provinces; the legions, permanently encamped on the frontiers, put down their roots and lost mobility and flexibility. A great tide of peoples was building up, clamouring for admission to the sweets of empire; and the emperors, strangers to their city, remained permanently on guard, moving to threatened points, shoring up the overloaded structure.

Drastic measures were taken; control of all aspects of their subjects' lives was rigorously enforced; prices, jobs and homes were all frozen to support stability. The emperors lost sight of the republican origins of their office and with lavish ceremony surrounded their persons with the mystique of divine kingship. . . . In 410 the Visigoths under Alaric [I] had sacked Rome itself, eliciting from St Augustine a great search for the meaning of human and divine government. . . . Ephemeral emperors, sponsored by the generals and ministers, rose and fell until the last, a boy, was placed on a meaningless throne by his father Orestes, who – such were the revolutions of the times – had once served as Attila's secretary. He did not last long. . . . The imperial insignia were returned to the east.[19]

The development of an elaborate bureaucracy in the late Roman empire was administratively inevitable. As Christian Lucas has noted, 'the growth of the interference of the imperial bureaucracy in local concerns proceeded alongside the decline of spontaneous municipal government'.

Again, unwise currency manipulations in the third century had led to inflation and to spirals of rising prices which could only be kept in check by an elaborate and steadily increasing system of state controls.

Finally, fourth-century legislation tended to regulate to the smallest detail the activities of every citizen.[20]

The bureaucracy expressed itself by very severe taxation (see Chapter 5):

The land-tax . . . reached more than one-third of a farmer's gross produce. It was inflexible and thoroughly ill-distributed. . . . Nothing shows more clearly the ineluctable victory of the two unseen enemies of the Roman empire – time and distance. Tax assessments were conscientious; but in so huge a society they could never be either complete or frequent enough. Hence, the only way to alleviate one's burden was to evade it, leaving the less fortunate to pay up.

The emperors recognized this. Occasionally they would ease the burden of taxation by spectacular gestures – privileges, remissions, the cancelling of bad debts. But these were like spouts of steam from a safety-valve; though impressive, they did nothing to redistribute the burden itself. Hence, in the western provinces of the empire, the wealth the emperor could tap shrank steadily into the hands of the great landowners, leaving the small man to have his property ground fine by the constant demands of the tax-collector. Not for nothing in the Christian hymn 'Dies Irae' is the coming of the Last Judgment thought of in terms of the arrival of a late Roman revenue official.[21]

Salvian (c. 400 to after 470; see Bibliography) had already had a lot to say about the damaging effects of western taxation:

Taxation, however harsh and brutal, would still be less severe and brutal if all shared equally in the common lot. But the situation is made more shameful and disastrous by the fact that all do not

25

bear the burden together. The tributes due from the rich are extorted from the poor, and the weaker bear the burdens of the stronger. The only reason why they do not bear the whole burden is that the exactions are greater than their resources. . . .

As the poor are the first to receive the burden, they are the last to obtain relief. For whenever, as happened lately, the ruling powers have thought best to take measures to help the bankrupt cities to lessen their taxes in some measure, at once we see the rich alone dividing with one another the remedy granted to all alike. Who then remembers the poor . . . What more can I say? Only that the poor . . . are outside the number when the remedies are being distributed.

Under such circumstances can we think ourselves undeserving of God's severe punishment when we ourselves continually so punish the poor? . . .

Who can find words to describe the enormity of our present situation? Now when the Roman commonwealth, already extinct or at least drawing its last breath in that one corner where it still seems to retain some life, is dying, strangled by the cords of taxation as if by the hands of brigands, still a great number of wealthy men are found, the burden of whose taxes is borne by the poor; that is, very many rich men are found whose taxes are murdering the poor. Very many, I said: I am afraid I might more truly say all. . . .

The rich have thus become wealthier by the decrease of the burdens that they bore easily: while the poor are dying of the increase in taxes that they already found too great for endurance.[22]

This, then, according to Salvian – and he was probably right – was one of the principal reasons why Rome finally fell in 476. The importance of this particular event and year has been regarded as arguable.

Looking back, Byzantine historians of the sixth century canonized this year 476 as the epoch-making final moment of the long decline and fall. . . . There has [now] been a tendency to minimize the importance of the date, because, after all, it was only one more in a long series of disintegrations, and a somewhat unspectacular happening at that. Nevertheless, the expulsion of the emperor in 476 did signify that the last important territory of the west, and indeed its metropolitan territory, had become, for good or evil, just another German kingdom.

The western empire was no more. That long-drawn-out withdrawal from the vast imperial spaces, which reached its end in

476, 'will ever be remembered', as Gibbon [Edward Gibbon, 1737–94] declared, 'and is still felt by the nations of the earth'.[23]

So the western Roman empire ceased to exist in 476, amid general apathy in the west, although subsequent ages have never ceased to magnify the event. Its relevance, I have written, extending to numerous western countries,

> has never seemed more visible than today. Britain thinks of its own vanished empire. The United States of America think of their current leadership, and of how it might be in danger of coming to an end. The Soviet Union [I wrote this in 1976] seems to be showing at this very moment how smaller peoples break away from empires. France is the country where, in ancient times, this first happened. Germany spans the east–west border, and is very conscious of its ancient role as the destroyer of the western Roman empire. Italy is the country where that empire ruled and fell.[24]

> In the eighteenth century the debate on the fall of the [western] empire was resumed, and it has gone on ever since.
> Rationalists like Gibbon saw religion as a primary cause of its decline. . . . Other historians, according to the temper of their time, have emphasized the empire's military decline, its political or social weaknesses, or its economic decay. . . . The simple but rather unfashionable view that the barbarians played a considerable part in the decline and fall of the empire may have some truth in it [see above]. External pressures and internal weaknesses of course interacted. The enfeeblement of the empire no doubt encouraged the barbarians to win easy spoils. . . .
> The western empire bore much more than its fair share of the burden and was much less favourably placed to make a recovery when its first line of defence was broken. . . .
> [The enemies] all realised that Constantinople was too tough a nut to crack. . . . In the east not only were legitimate emperors rarely challenged but when an emperor had already designated his successor an election was held in a constitutional manner, and its result accepted. The record of the west is by no means so good. . . . The incompetence of a feeble emperor was more glaringly revealed because he had greater difficulties to face. . . . The basic economic weakness of the [western] empire was that too few producers supported too many idle mouths. . . . The most depressing feature of the later [western] empire is the apparent absence of public spirit.[25]

One thing that was quite certain was that the weakness of the western emperors meant the rise of the importance of the popes: under Leo I the Great (440–61), the primacy of Rome was finally established, though this involved tension with Constantinople.[26]

And yet the Germans who came next did not act badly.

> Owing to the progressive depopulation of the countryside, there would be ample accommodation for new occupiers. The new-comers restored prosperity to Italy; for now that the traditional external sources of the supply of grain were in alien hands, the Italian harvest became once again a prime factor in the life of the country; so much so that, stimulated by this necessity, Italy, which had for centuries imported corn as a tribute, was soon able to export it at a profit.
>
> Odoacer deliberately maintained, even enhanced, the established authorities of Rome. The senate he regarded as a partner. . . . Most significant of all, Odoacer, [although] an Arian, showed every deference to the Pope.[27]

Indeed, E.A. Freeman felt able to write equally optimistically about Rome, even before its collapse, with the implication that its collapse could not be total.

> No frontier was safe against foreign enemies. Yet the wonderful thing is how often the empire came together again. What strikes us at every step in the tangled history of these times is the wonderful look which the Roman name and the Roman power still kept when it was thus attacked on every side from without and torn in pieces in every quarter from within.[28]

Others, however, will hold that the situation at Rome, when the western empire, in spite of this talent for survival, had finally collapsed, and the prospects for its future, were bleak. Certainly, if we may turn to a later date, Justinian I's recovery of Rome did not last (Appendix 3), and its fall in 476 could not be forgotten.

The fall of Rome, which has been the subject of this chapter – and of innumerable books, including one by myself – has, as we saw, excited the feelings and imagination of all successive ages.[29] And yet perhaps it remains true that AD 476, when the last western emperor was overthrown, is not quite the landmark that it has always seemed, largely because of all the factors, already in existence, which made this fall both inevitable and foreseeable (even if it was not always foreseen). In other words, once the empire was divided, the west, the weaker partner, was bound to fall. Yet its actual fall, for all its inevitability, cannot fail to be of concern to us, because it brought into being not only the power of the popes but the whole history of the Middle Ages, to which, as indeed to the previous antique period, we owe such a lot. Indeed, it is not too much to say that the fall of Rome in 476 has coloured our entire history.

5

FINANCE AND THE ARMIES

One reason, it would seem from the foregoing comments, why the western empire fell was because of the crushing burden of taxation, deemed necessary to maintain the frontier against the Germans.

Successive emperors, I have pointed out, each tried to turn the screw a little tighter. . . . Valentinian III openly admitted the savagery of his own system, and even remitted arrears of taxation, at least for the rich. When Majorian [457–61] came to the throne shortly afterwards . . . and Sidonius [Apollinaris] welcomed his accession with a congratulatory address, he managed to insert a reference to the tax burden which oppressed his native Gaul [Appendix 2]. And the new emperor himself issued a legal pronouncement deploring these severities with a frankness that left nothing to the imagination. . . . The hardship [resulting from continued inflation] was colossal. . . . There was also a terrifying amount of corruption involved in applying all these compulsions. . . .

When critics of the system pointed out that by far the worst sufferers were the rustic poor, what they said was no more than the truth. . . . It was incumbent upon city councillors [*curiales*, see below and n. 3], and their sons when their turn came, to induce their fellow-citizens to disgorge the many taxes, demanded by the State, as well as the required levies in kind: foodstuffs, clothing and the like. . . . To Salvian [see previous chapter], the councillors' behaviour towards the poor seemed horribly brutal: he saw them as rapacious persecutors of widows, orphans and monks. . . . Yet [this view] was too one-sided all the same, since the situation of the councillors, also, was appallingly difficult. . . . The Code of Theodosius II contains no less than 192 edicts threatening and browbeating them with every sort of menace. . . .

[Whatever its faults], that was the culture which had held the ancient world together, so that the obliteration of its middle-class

30

nucleus meant that this world could not remain in existence any longer.[1]

And the rich withdrew into their estates, which were economically self-sufficient and fortified. These men, apart from not contributing what they should, allowed refugees from the tax system (and brigandage) to become their labourers.

Anyway, the western government was bankrupt.

> In the east, the greater importance of trade, and the proliferation of small but viable cities in the hinterland of the Mediterranean, ensured a more balanced, even a more egalitarian, society. The local landowners of a Greek city might be very rich and very conservative, but while Gaul and Italy fell into the hands of half a dozen great clans, ten families at least competed for influence round Antioch alone. The gains of a Greek civic magnate remained limited to his locality, and the city itself remained the fray of his energies.
>
> The Greek idea of *energeia*, of a rivalry of great houses in showing good for their community, was remarkably resilient. . . . Such an evenly balanced gentry was never overshadowed and cowed by over-mighty landowners. They provided an unfailing reservoir of well-educated and conscientious civil servants for the administration in Constantinople. And throughout the late Roman period they decorated their towns with statues, inscriptions and churches whose richness is only beginning to be discovered by archaeologists in Turkey [see Chapter 11].
>
> Furthermore, the peasants of Asia Minor, Syria and Egypt were very different from the excluded serfs of the western provinces. They could get a good enough price for their corn in the towns to pay both their rent and their taxes. . . . In the middle of the fifth century, the difference in atmosphere between the two parts of the empire was largely due to the different role of the small man. . . . The parting of the ways between western Europe and the eastern Mediterranean, which is the most important immediate legacy of the late antique world, goes back to such humble, concrete contrasts.[2]

There were more ancient and richer cities (in the east) than there were in the west, and there was a large and substantial middle-class besides the much criticised *curiales*.[3]

Furthermore, the rural population in the east, for all their woes, were stronger and larger, and were able to survive. So, despite much poverty, the eastern empire was richer, and in a position to last out during this

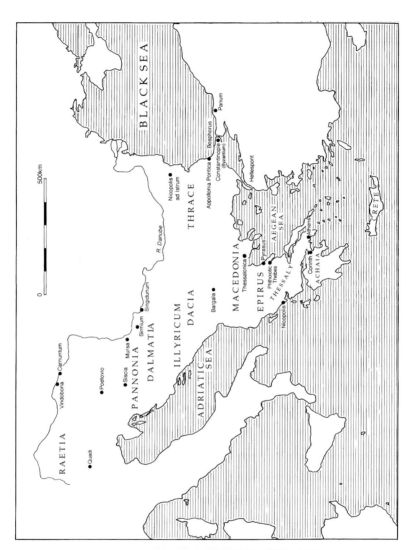

Map 4 Eastern Europe

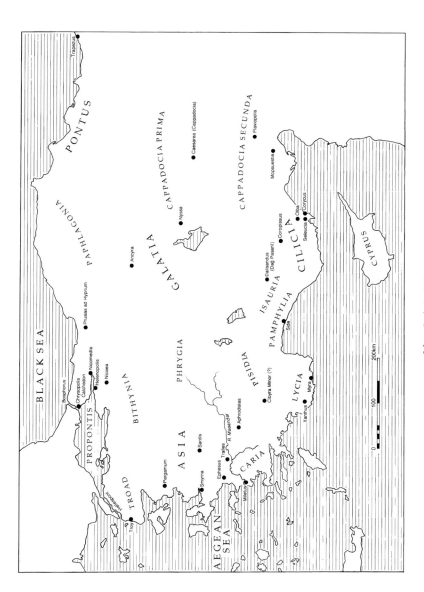

Map 5 Asia Minor

difficult century. Furthermore, the eastern emperor Anastasius I *filled* the eastern treasury (unlike his predecessor Zeno who had emptied it). Life in the eastern empire may not have been agreeable, but it was tolerable and liveable: and the Byzantine state was the result. There was no need to generalise, and talk of the apocalyptic extinction of the human race.

See also Chapter 6 for more on the differences between west and east. Here it is the financial field that has been discussed.

The armies, in which, incidentally, desertion and vagabondism were rife, were the guardians of the western empire's survival. But their guardianship was ineffective. For in this empire, faced with terrible wars on every front, there was a

> general failure of its armies to perform the tasks that were required of them. . . . Faced with recalcitrant public opinion, and an almost total failure of understanding between the army and the people, Rome had allowed its armies to become fatally weakened. . . . The terrific attacks on the frontiers were nothing new. But they were, certainly, becoming more and more frequent – mainly because of the weakness within, which invited external encroachments. . . .
>
> The weakness of the late Roman army was largely due to the eventual failure of the imperial authorities to enforce regular conscription. . . . Regimentation became the order of the day – and that included compulsion to remain in one's father's profession, so that there was a rapidly increasing tendency to force the sons of soldiers or ex-soldiers to become soldiers in their turn. . . . By the fifth century [this doctrine] had become obligatory, as in civilian jobs. . . .
>
> If the Romans *had* been able to maintain an army, they might well have saved themselves from destruction. Their failure to raise the troops any longer was one of the principal causes of their downfall.[4]

The officers were also to a large extent responsible for the series of usurpations of the imperial throne that ruined the west. Moreover, to make matters worse, the army itself, and the ranks of its generals, consisted, by this time (when not of Huns), largely of Germans, whose loyalty, as *foederati*, could not be relied upon, although they were very necessary because available manpower, from other sources, was so scarce: and those responsible for the constant changes of emperor were largely German Masters of Soldiers, such as Ricimer and Orestes. Besides, a great deal of money was needed to keep the western army (by now very sizeable) in existence. The coinage of the time shows clearly the supreme priority of defence needs.

All this was perceptible by AD 400.

> The fifth century is about to begin, in the very first decade of which the balance clearly changes. Now it is the barbarians who enjoy the final say. . . .
>
> In any military sense the empire was no longer a sovereign state. And the sack of its ancient capital by Alaric [410] – a high imperial official and even a born Roman, so far as the word has meaning – had no quality of invasion about it at all. He and his men *were* the Roman army, and had been for decades.[5]

Once again, the east escaped the fatal hazards that encompassed the west. Beyond the frontiers, Constantinople achieved a measure of peace with the one threatening power, that of the Persians, in marked contrast to the German menace that constantly threatened the western empire. As for the Germans, the eastern capital was protected by a wall, and the Long Wall of Thrace, both of which proved more impregnable than anything to be found in the west. Gainas, it is true, gained power in the eastern city in 400, but it got him out (Chapter 6). True, too, the eastern Roman army, and its command, largely consisted of Germans, but the eastern emperors Leo I and Zeno succeeded in replacing most of them by natives of Asia Minor, Isaurians, who in turn were got rid of by Anastasius I (491–518).

But in any case the eastern population was much better equipped to deal with the military crisis than the west. Certainly, a high level of taxation was once again needed to maintain the eastern army, but the eastern people were well enough off to pay it without, for the most part, excessive hardship, and they did not suffer so much from unpatriotic rich who added to the miseries of the westerners. As so often, we tend to underestimate the role of the very varied countries of Asia Minor in maintaining the eastern army at a high and not too oppressive level of efficiency.

As previously, I am anticipating here the discussion of the differences between west and east in the next chapter. I am doing so because of the special need to consider here the condition of the armies, as well as of finance.

When Synesius [c. 370–413] demanded *a nation in array*, it is understandable that this is what he felt was necessary, and the eastern empire was more easily able to afford it than the west.

As was asserted at the beginning of this chapter, it is possible to make a strong case for ascribing the fall of the western empire to financial inadequacies. True, historians with Marxist leanings like to follow Salvian and over-emphasise the misery of the poor. There *was* appalling poverty – especially in the west: this was not new (there had always been famines), but owing to the weakness of the western government the situation had become worse. The despotic intentions of that government were no use; and most of the western emperors had no real or sensible idea of finance or money. For that matter, most of the eastern emperors were equally incompetent; it was very fortunate for Constantinople that Anastasius I understood something about it, or at least had an adviser, John of Cappadocia, who did. The whole story of the empire could be rewritten from a financial point of view. And most of all does that apply to the fifth century, and to west and east alike.

In this difficult situation, the role of the army had become distinctly equivocal. It was greatly needed to safeguard both the western and the eastern frontiers, the former being by far the more perilous at the time. Yet its existence, at the high totals of soldiery required, raised many, and indeed for the west, insuperable problems. First of all, the army cost a very great deal of money: far more than the wesern empire could afford. Second, the necessary funds were raised – if and when this became possible – by brutal and forceful means which did not endear the army to the population. Third, the soldiers were now mostly Germans; which raised problems when they were supposed to fight against other Germans, and did not raise enthusiasm among the peoples of the empire whom they were expected to defend, and indeed *had* to defend, unless everything collapsed (as, in the west, it did).

6

EAST AND WEST

[Valentinian I's] son Gratian [the western emperor] failed to come to the help of [the eastern emperor] Valens, when the latter was about to fight the fatal battle of Adrianople (Hadrianopolis, Edirne) against the Visigoths (378). Where the blame for this failure of cooperation lay is not quite clear, though Gratian's principal German general was suspected of sabotage. . . . And then in 383 . . . when the usurper Magnus Maximus rose against Gratian in Gaul, the preoccupations of the eastern emperor Theodosius I [379–95] with his own frontier problems meant that he, too, did not send help in time to save his colleague's life. . . .

When, after [Theodosius's] death in 395, [the empire] was divided into two parts once again, between his two sons Arcadius and Honorius . . . relations between the two empires began to become really bad. . . . At a moment when the civilized world could only survive if west and east co-operated, the split between their two governments [represented, most authoritatively, by Stilicho, d. 468, in the west, see below and n. 9, and Rufinus, d. 395, in the east] became almost total. . . . The hostility between the two empires . . . was exacerbated by savage ecclesiastical disputes. . . . Irreparable harm had been done – particularly in the more vulnerable west. . . . When Marcian (450–7) was proclaimed the eastern emperor, the west showed an initial reluctance to recognise him. . . .

As a result of the tension and mutual ill-will, the frontiers had been gravely undermined, and the enemies of the Roman world were strengthened in every quarter.[1]

Furthermore, east and west were differently administered: the sons and grandsons of Theodosius I did not inherit his ability, and the actual direction of affairs came into the hands of generals and ministers such as Stilicho and Rufinus, in the two empires. A significant difference between east and west appeared at once. In the west, the men who guided the administration at its highest level, down to the end of Roman rule there, were almost all generals. In the east, civil officials were in charge, while military figures had less influence.[2] The western aristocrats also formed a deplorable unit which the east lacked: they took care of their own selves and neglected everybody else's interests, including the emperor's; whereas the career bureaucrats of the east had only themselves and the state to serve,[3] and that made them more useful.

This was yet another of the reasons why the eastern empire, unlike the western, survived. The differences between the two regions can be summed up in the following terms:

The eastern empire, thanks partly to its geographical position, was much less subject to external pressures, particularly those of the barbarian peoples, than was the western empire which attracted and absorbed most of the barbarian invasions. The eastern empire, also, enjoyed relatively stable and purposeful administration, either by effective emperors or, in less fortunate reigns, by praetorian prefects or others near the throne. . . . Attempted usurpation in the provinces was rare in the eastern empire.

The great strength of the Roman empire, added Haywood, is shown by the long and stubborn fight for survival which it waged against odds often greater than those which had prevailed in the west. In the long run the Byzantine government did prove itself capable of governing, in spite of periods of weakness and of shameful corruption. The techniques of production and distribution were maintained. The high intellectual tradition of the Greco-Roman civilization was largely directed into religious channels, but its secular form was not allowed either to die out or to degenerate. . . .

It must be remembered that during this time the east had suffered no comparable damage. The Huns had caused it considerable damage, but it had lost no important territory, was economically fairly sound, and had restored the citizen army of other days. . . .

Norman Baynes asserts that the reason why the eastern, or Byzantine, empire was able to protect its integrity at this time and go on, while the west gradually slipped into the hands of the Germans, was the superior wealth of the east. . . .

Once the empire had gotten into the unfortunate position of acting as two practically separate halves, the west was the weaker partner.[4]

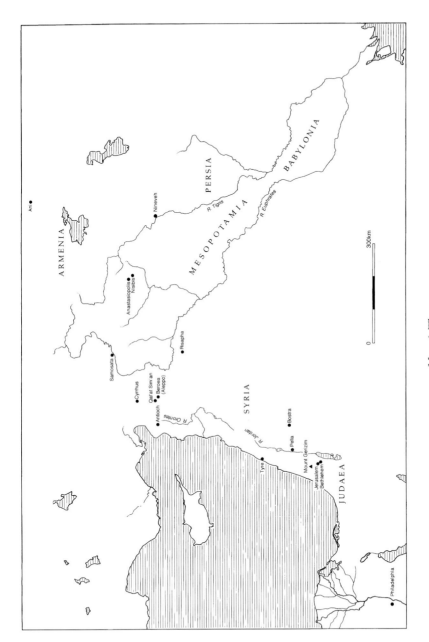

Map 6 The east

Ani •

ARMENIA

PERSIA

Nineveh •

R. Tigris

MESOPOTAMIA

R. Euphrates

BABYLONIA

Anastasiopolis •
Nisibis •

Samosata •

Risapha •

Cyrrhus •
Qal'at Sim'an •
Beroea •
(Aleppo)

Antioch •
R. Orontes

SYRIA

Bostra •

R. Jordan

Tyre •
Pella •
Mount Gerizim •
Jerusalem •
Bethlehem •

JUDAEA

Philadelphia •

0   300km

The eastern empire was for a time under grave threat from the Germans, notably under Arcadius, when Gainas actually occupied Constantinople for six months (400–1).[5] And, after all, the disastrous memory of the battle of Adrianople (378), when Valens had been killed, was quite fresh. Moreover, from 396 until 401 the Alans ruled over the east Balkans, and before that, in 395, trans-Caucasian Huns had poured through the Caspian Gates as far as Syria. But Gainas, although helped by his relation Tribigild, was miraculously dislodged from the capital by Fravitta, with the help of the Patriarch of Constantinople, and fled north, where he was killed, while the Germans inside Constantinople itself became powerless. Later, it is true, there were renewed threats, under Leo I (457–74) and then from the Vandals in the time of Zeno (474–91), but a peace that lasted for nearly sixty years followed. What, exactly, had saved the eastern empire from the fate meted out to the west? It has been suggested that when the northern tribes made incursions into the eastern empire, their eyes were always fixed on the west, towards which the eastern government helped to impel them. The fortifications that made Constantinople impregnable (Chapter 11) and sealed off Thrace were also a great help. As for the west, on the other hand, it was hemmed in by an arc of powerful German tribes, from the Black to the North Sea, and, as we have seen, there was a new frequency and simultaneity of barbarian attacks.[6]

For one reason or another, then, the eastern empire – lacking deep internal barriers, civilian-run, and better at keeping peace – survived, and the western empire did not. Above all else, the west was more vulnerable to external attack owing to its geographical location, which was far inferior to that of Constantinople.[7] Glanville Downey summed up the whole situation in the following terms:

> The structure of the government differed significantly in the east and west [see above and n. 2]. In the west, the land-owning aristocrats, some of them fantastically wealthy, contributed much less money than they should have to the cost of the army and the government. The eastern empire, in contrast, possessed a civil service composed largely of middle-class professionals, and while graft unavoidably existed, the eastern government received in taxes a higher proportion of the national income than the western government could enjoy.[8]

The government of the east was consequently much better able to defend itself. It had therefore survived the third-century horrors more effectively.

The particular advantage of the east, and its strained relations with the west, has been further enlarged upon:

It was now [in 395] that the relations between the two empires began to become really bad, so bad that this must be regarded as a major factor in the debilitation of the weaker partner, the west. The worsening of relations was directly due to a western leader, one of the most able men of the age. This was Stilicho. . . . It became his determined ambition to reunite the whole empire – with himself as its real controller. This would necessarily involve the suppression of Rufinus [Stilicho's personal enemy, whom Theodosius I had chosen to be the guardian of his older boy Arcadius, the eastern emperor of the future. Stilicho's plan would necessarily involve the suppression of Rufinus]. . . .

At a moment when the civilised world could only survive if

Figure 3 Wing of ivory diptych, *c.* 400. The man represented, Stilicho, was commander-in-chief and regent to the western emperor Honorius, the juvenile younger son of Theodosius I, from 395 to 408. (Archivi Alinari/ Anderson)

41

west and east cooperated, the split between their governments had become almost total. One of the worst results of this serious misunderstanding between Rufinus and Stilicho was that it enabled Alaric to penetrate into Greece. Claudian declared that Rufinus had treacherously withdrawn his troops, but in all probability it was Stilicho's deliberate plan that Alaric should be diverted against the eastern empire in order to keep him out of the west. Next, Rufinus fell from power and was assassinated. . . .

Stilicho, after the east had invited him to intervene against Alaric in Greece, mysteriously let him escape from his clutches in 397 and depart. Noting his unhelpfulness, Eutropius [eunuch, successor of Rufinus, likewise attacked by Claudian; see Bibliography], on behalf of the eastern government, not only declared Stilicho a public enemy, but felt it necessary to appease the Visigoths by appointing him Master of Soldiers in the Balkans – a step which caused understandable consternation [in certain quarters]. . . . And so [Claudian] proceeded to assail Constantinople as the sink of all the vices. . . .

In 401 . . . Alaric crossed the border from the eastern to the western empire. . . . Stilicho . . . defeated him in two successive years, but twice let him go when he could have finished him off.[9]

Before that, in the year 400, the Visigoth Gainas, and his relative Tribigild,[10] revolted against the east Roman regime, in the army of which they were serving as officers, having presumably some idea of seizing the eastern empire for themselves. They evidently intended not to cut themselves off from east Roman life or overthrow the eastern government, but to establish a powerful position *inside* the eastern empire. In this respect, however, they differed from the main bulk of the rebels with them, who no doubt wanted to destroy that empire altogether; and that is why these rebels marched so extensively (and pointlessly) round eastern Europe and Asia Minor.

However, Gainas, as we saw, was thwarted at Constantinople by another German, Fravitta – backed by the Patriarch – and left the city for the north, towards the Danube. North of that river, however, he was captured by the Huns, and was put to death.

As for the west, however, an invasion of 406 was particularly damaging; at the end of the year Stilicho failed to stop the Vandals, Alans and Suevi (Quadi) from crossing the Rhine, and they were never rolled back. Numerous cities were destroyed by them and depopulated, and too many of the western emperor's subjects joined the enemy. As for Alaric's sack of Rome in 410 – which, as we have seen, was little more than a raid, bent on large-scale robbery – reference has already been made (in Chapter 4) to the horror it caused, notably to Jerome and Augustine.[11]

Meanwhile, most other Germans were less interested in invasion than in sharing in the material benefits and prosperity of the Roman empire, a hope that had been encouraged by their receipt of land, with an invitation to become cultivators, from Constantine I the Great and Theodosius I.[12] The Visigoth monarch Ataulf, for example, was far more interested in fusion than in fission.[13] But the Romans, most of them, remained irrevocably anti-German: Christian Romans were especially shocked by the Germans' Arian and barbarian ways, and the upper classes, as a whole, hated them.[14] Nevertheless, by 425 there were five Germanic kingdoms in the west, and the northern frontier was totally unsound.[15] And, everywhere, the army was increasingly Gothic. So it was only a question of time before Rome finally fell, as it did in 476.

At first sight, however, it would seem that the external threat was more severe in the east than in the west, because beyond the eastern frontier there was a single, powerful co-ordinated state, that of Sassanian Persia, in contrast to the diverse, separate tribes of the Germans beyond the western boundaries.[16] And indeed Ammianus Marcellinus was very much afraid that Roman civil wars would facilitate and encourage Persian invasion.[17] The principal Sassanian rulers of the age were Yazdagird I (339–c. 421), Vahahran (Bahram) V Gur (c. 421–38/9), Firuz (or Peruz) (459–88/9), and Kavad I (488/9–531). Nevertheless, in actual fact, contrary to what might have been expected, the existence of a single state to the east encouraged rather than discouraged friendly relations. Early on, the eastern emperor Arcadius reached a close personal understanding with Yazdagird I, whom he actually appointed as the guardian of his son Theodosius II – although Yazdagird later executed a Christian bishop (419–20). Yazdagird was not liked by the Iranian conservatives, but he was popular in Mesopotamia.

In 421 Vahahran V, far from conciliatory to the eastern Roman regime, raised its siege of Nisibis (Nüsaybin), brought a two-pronged east Roman offensive to an end, and invaded the Roman empire. But in 422, so as to deal with an emergency in Thrace, Theodosius II, despite victories – celebrated by Aelia Eudoxia (Chapter 8) in a poem – made peace with the Persians. And the peace lasted, partly because of the troubles regarding the succession among the Iranian feudal lords, and partly because of the very damaging threats to Persia from the Kushans (who were nomads) and the Hephthalites ('White Huns', for they were related to the Huns). The Persian monarch Firuz, after seven years of famine, was killed with his whole army in a rash and disastrous campaign against the Hephthalites, and Kavad I, severely threatened by internal unrest, only maintained his position with their aid (they had placed him on the throne, and penetrated deeply into his kingdom).

So, for most of the period, Persian relations with the Roman empire remained relatively static and stable; the Persian danger was elsewhere. Certainly the Latin writer Claudian (see Bibliography) was exaggerating when he wrote, 'Persia, at our foot, with humble air, spreads costly ornaments and jewels rare.' Such chauvinism would hardly have appealed to the Church in Persia, which became Monophysite (Chapter 9), that is to say opposed to the imperial churches of the Romans. Yet at any rate the zones of dispute were allowed to stay as they were, and peace treaties remained relatively durable. This was a much happier position than the west enjoyed with regard to the Germans.

The reason why the Romans and the Persians did not war with one another as forcefully as they might have done was because they had learned from experience that one could not destroy the other and because each of them had other enemies – both external and internal – who were constantly threatening them both; indeed, Constantinople often wanted a strong Persia, for help against the nomads. Thus the remarkable peace of one hundred and fifty years. Nevertheless, in 502 Kavad I attacked Anastasius I, who built a fortress against him at Dara near Nisibis (Nüsaybin); but then peace was resumed.

The coinage illustrates the determined, or at least outward, efforts of the eastern and western emperors to collaborate, in spite of everything that was driving them apart.

> The beginning of the reign of Valentinian III was marked on *solidus* coinage at Rome in 425 by a reverse inscribed VICTORIA AVGGG., [depicting] two emperors standing facing, each holding long cross and globe. Theodosius [II] is shown as taller than Valentinian who is crowned from heaven. Aquileia also in 425 struck *solidi* for Theodosius with reverse SALVS REIPVBLICAE: Theodosius seated enthroned and Valentinian a smaller figure standing, each holding the insignia of their joint consulship in that year. . . . A similar coinage was struck for Valentinian [III] by Theodosius [II] at Constantinople. . . .
> Rome and Ravenna [were] the main mints for the coinage of this reign. . . . In the last years of Valentinian [III] *solidi* were struck at Ravenna and Rome also for the eastern emperor, Marcian.[18]

Nevertheless, as was perhaps inevitable, the eastern empire (which would very soon be known as the Byzantine empire), as we well know, survived, and the west did not. The victorious eastern empire was a fusion of the Hellenistic and Roman traditions: it was much safer than the west, we may conclude, partly because of its more favourable geographical and therefore military location, but also because of its less hazardous social

Figure 4 Gold *solidus* of Valentinian III (Placidus Valentinianus), emperor of the west 425–55. Rome. He is shown draped and cuirassed, wearing a pearl diadem. (Photograph: Michael Grant)

and economic structure. And so, a century or so later, it was to become the greatest power, and greatest trading power, in Christendom. Moreover, it was Christendom that it stood for. Furthermore, it preserved and maintained an equilibrium which had never been maintained elsewhere, by the guidance of bureaucrats who may have been tiresome, but were never, or not usually, as fatally repressive as their western counterparts. With their help, Constantinople kept alive the whole machinery and concept of empire, which had fallen into desuetude and disrepute in the west.

In fairness to the eastern regime, it must be pointed out that it was difficult for it to spare sufficient troops for the western Mediterranean, which is partly why it never committed its full resources to the area. Yet Constantinople itself was strong enough (see Chapters 3, 11), and it was that very strength, to a large extent, which diverted barbarian attacks to the west, and thus, as Gibbon pointed out, helped to bring about its downfall. Besides, Constantinople was too much preoccupied with its own survival to help a great deal in the west.

So when the penultimate western emperor, Julius Nepos (474–5), went to his eastern colleague Zeno for help, he did not get any, except for kind words.[19] In this age of weak western rulers, however, Julius Nepos was reasonably strong. He had been a successful general in Dalmatia, but he found it necessary to cater to Rome's now almost exclusively barbarian army by appointing a generalissimo acceptable to the barbarian troops. Eventually, in 475, the choice fell on Orestes, a man who, like Aetius, had spent time at the court of the Huns, as Attila's secretary. Although he was Roman by birth, the long association of Orestes with non-Romans made him acceptable to the largely non-Roman army. Before the year was out, however, he rebelled against Nepos, and the emperor fled to the east (Dalmatia), while the general elevated his own son, Romulus (475–6), to the western throne.

The emperor at Constantinople still recognised Nepos, but for the next year Orestes ruled in Italy under the banner of his young son, who took the title Augustus but was generally called Augustulus (or 'little Augustus') because of his age.

In the end not even Orestes was able to control the Germanic troops who officially served the Roman emperor in the west. They wanted a settlement in Italy, just as the Visigoths and others had been settled in Gaul. Whether their demands involved a third of the land or merely of the tax revenues remains uncertain, but it was a large concession in either case. Orestes refused, and in a meeting the Germans elected one of their own officers, Odoacer, as king. The new ruler deposed and executed Orestes and sent Romulus Augustulus off to retirement in Campania on a public pension. The Roman empire in the west was finished. Rome had joined the company of Nineveh and other fallen empires.

Odoacer ruled in Italy as king (*rex*), and the Roman senate returned the imperial regalia to Constantinople, sending a delegation to the eastern emperor Zeno (474–91) which declared that there was no longer any need for an emperor in the west. Zeno did not, officially, acquiesce. Indeed, he requested the Roman senate to take back Julius Nepos. But Odoacer ignored these instructions, and Nepos died four years later (480).[20]

> The prudent Zeno soon deserted the hopeless cause of his abdicated colleague [Nepos]. His [Zeno's] vanity was gratified

Figure 5 Gold *solidus* of Romulus 'Augustulus', last western emperor, 475–6. Mediolanum (Milan). (British Museum)

by the title of sole emperor, and by the statues erected to his honour in the several quarters of Rome. He entertained a friendly, though ambiguous, correspondence with ... Odoacer, and he gratefully accepted the imperial ensigns, the sacred ornaments of the throne and palace, which the barbarian was not unwilling to remove from the sight of the people.[21]

Long ago, remarked Mortimer Chambers, summing up this whole controversy with a timely warning,

> Montesquieu (1689–1755) pointed to a fact that must be kept before us at all times. When we speak of the fall of Rome, we must remember that this term can be applied only to the western empire. The eastern, Byzantine empire certainly did not fall in 476 and in fact continued for nearly another thousand years until the capture of Constantinople in 1453. Therefore any explanation of the fall must show why the eastern empire avoided the fate of the western one. This dilemma has raised difficulties for more than one of the sometimes extravagant suggestions put forward in modern times.

> And so, when Rome fell in 476, Zeno continued to reign in the east (474–91). But Zeno, while careful about the emperors in the west, had succeeded in alienating the Pope, who was now the strongest power in Rome, and indeed had been so for some time, when the last western emperors had shown themselves to be so weak and ineffective.
>
> The breach with the popes became more complete with Zeno's publication of his *Henotikon* (481/2), the edict designed (in vain) to reconcile east and west.[22]

The *Henotikon* was ostensibly addressed to the Egyptians, urging a return to the fold. It implied that the decisions taken at the Council of Chalcedon (431), which annoyed so many people (Chapter 9), might have been an error. This was an open door for the repudiation of the *Tome* of Pope Leo I, which had stressed the two Natures of Christ, and, it was complained in Egypt, had excessively aggrandised Rome. Besides, even Pope Leo I's successor at Rome itself, Pope Simplicius, remarked that the *Tome*'s authors, Acacius and Peter Mongus, had been going too far, acting as though they possessed an authority that belonged to the Pope alone as head of his see. He therefore excommunicated both of them, and thus perpetuated open schism between the papacy and most of the east, which had accepted the *Tome* at the Council of Chalcedon.[23]

This was a complicated affair, but in any case, for one reason or another, the east and west split up – and the east survived while the west did not. Geza Alföldy was another who summed up the situation, as follows, covering a satisfactorily wide field:

> In the empire of the east circumstances were better: there was not such a thorough alienation of society from the State as had occurred in the west. There was a close relationship between the emperor of the east and the landowning upper strata, particularly the senate at Constantinople. The Church of the east was very much bound up with the state and supported it energetically.
>
> In general the cities of the east still possesssed a fairly sound economic potential. Thus even the curial order in the various cities of the east was not only less weak, but also supported the state more than in the west. Moreover, the compulsory inheritance of urban occupations did not apply in the east, by and large.
>
> Above all, the empire of the east was much better protected against the barbarians than the western empire. Thus it was spared collapse.[24]

So the eastern empire survived but the western empire did not. But this chapter has been concerned, among other things, with one difficult and awkward question. When the western Roman empire fell, could the eastern empire have done more to save it? You can take one view or the other. Either the decline of the western empire had gone altogether too far, and nothing on earth could have propped it up, or, you may conclude, alternatively, that if Constantinople, which was increasingly at odds with Rome, Mediolanum and Ravenna (both politically and spiritually), had intervened more decisively and effectively, on a variety of occasions, the western empire might have been saved, or at least its collapse might have been postponed. Personally, I adhere somewhat to the former conclusion. It seems to me that, once the division of the empire had taken place, the west was bound to succumb before the east did.

7

THE EASTERN EMPERORS

Curiously enough, although the eastern empire survived these horrors – overcoming even the hazard of excessive taxation – its emperors during this period, like those of the west, are mostly not very exciting, although they, or their advisers, succeeded in keeping their state in existence. They are Arcadius (395–408), Theodosius II (408–50), Marcian (450–7), Leo I (457–74), Zeno (474–91), and Anastasius I (491–518).

The permanent division of the empire into east (which survived) and west (which did not) dates from the time of Arcadius in the east and Honorius in the west (395).[1]

> Arcadius and Honorius . . . became the founders of two sub-empires in the east and west respectively. Though, in strict law, Arcadius and Honorius remained joint rulers of an undivided realm, in actual practice they became independent of each other, so that the history of the eastern and western divisions hencefor-ward ran on separate lines.[2]

In contrast to his western counterpart Arcadius – although mocked at the time for the lack of military skill and interest, and, nowadays, for the persistence of VICTORIA on his coins – successfully got rid of the German Gainas (a 'miracle' made possible, as we have seen, by another German Fravitta, helped by the Patriarch). And the successor of Arcadius, Theodosius II, at least under guardianship (his ministers were Rufinus and Eutropius [395–9], both attacked by Claudian, and Anthemius, from 408), was not so bad as he has sometimes been painted, considering that, in his last years, the empire was threatened by three powerful enemies, who were successfully fought off. Theodosius II seems to have been well educated and humane, though untalented and lazy and something of a bigot. But it can be argued that his policies did some-thing to distance the eastern empire from the western decline. Then,

49

Figure 6 Probably Arcadius, eastern emperor 395–408. National Archaeological Museum, Istanbul. (Archivi Alinari/Anderson)

Figure 7 Gold *solidus* of the eastern emperor Theodosius II, 408–50, attributed to the emperor's eastward journey in 443 after securing peace with the Persians. (Photograph: Michael Grant)

Theodosius II, responding to Placidia's appeal to help her four-year-old son Valentinian III to ascend the western throne [425], struck a hard bargain: he would help, and would remove a usurper who had intervened [Johannes, 423–5], on the condition that a large strip of central Europe, bordering the middle Danube west of Singidunum (Belgrade), must be transferred to his territory. . . .

This 'cooperation' was celebrated by the last coinage of Constantinople ever to show one of the emperors in the company of his western colleague. Theodosius II and his successors also assisted the west against the German invaders of north Africa – Gaiseric and his Vandals – on at least three occasions.

But . . . it seemed better not to pour too many troops down the drain. . . . The last cooperative enterprise in which the two Roman empires both had a share was the legal code of Theodosius II, published in 438.[3]

Theodosius II was succeeded in 450 by Marcian.

Since the death of the younger Theodosius [II], the domestic repose of Constantinople had never been interrupted by war or faction. Pulcheria [Chapter 8] had bestowed her hand, and the sceptre of the east, on the modest virtue of Marcian. He gratefully reverenced her august rank and virgin chastity; and, after her death, he gave his people the example of the religious worship that was due to the memory of the imperial saint. Attentive to the prosperity of his own dominions Marcian seemed to behold with indifference the misfortunes of Rome. And the obstinate refusal of a brave and active prince to draw his sword against the Vandals was ascribed to a secret promise which had formerly been exacted from him when he was a captive in the power of Genseric [Gaiseric].[4]

Marcian was a retired military officer of no distinction . . . who had been 'domestic' [personal assistant] to Aspar [German general 424–71], and one of his first acts was to appoint one of Aspar's sons, Ardaburius, *magister militum per Orientem* [Master of Soldiers in the East]. There can be little doubt that Aspar arranged Marcian's election by the senate and the army, probably with the co-operation of Pulcheria Augusta [Chapter 8], who consented to marry the new emperor and thus confer upon him the hereditary prestige of the Theodosian House, which was sorely needed at this moment of dynastic exhaustion.

The new emperor . . . refused to pay Attila his subsidy.[5] This rash gesture of defiance, which might have involved the European provinces of the empire in even deeper ruin, turned out luckily, for Attila was too busy with his western schemes to retaliate at once, and died before he had time to take his revenge. Or, it might be argued, Marcian had deliberately turned him against the west instead of against himself.[6]

But our sources for the reign of Marcian are poor. He was, however, clearly both pious and courageous. And it was beginning to be clear that the troubles of the eastern empire were less perilous than those of the west.

As for the next eastern emperor, Leo I (457–74), he had little formal education; but, as Gibbon indicates, there were points in his favour.

This emperor, the first of the name of Leo, has been distinguished by the title of the Great from a succession of princes who gradually fixed in the opinion of the Greeks a very humble standard of heroic, or at least of royal, perfection. Yet the temperate firmness with which Leo resisted the oppression of his benefactor [the German general Aspar, d. 471] showed that he

Figure 8 Gold *solidus* of the eastern emperor Leo I (457–74). Thessalonica (Salonica): a mint as well as an important regional capital, formerly an imperial residence. Leo is described, like other eastern emperors, as PERPET(*uus*), rather than as the more common P(*ius*) F(*elix*). (Photograph: Michael Grant)

was conscious of his duty and of his prerogative. . . . It was impossible that the reconciliation of the emperor and the patrician [a title accorded to Masters of Soldiers] could be sincere, or, at least, that it could be solid and permanent.[7]

Leo I had sound common sense and a mind of his own. Consider, too, what A.H.M. Jones has added:

The eastern emperor Leo I acted decisively by replacing his German troops, whose loyalty he doubted, by people from Isauria (bordering on Pisidia and Pamphylia), who had previously been known for their brigandage in that area. This brought them to order, and made them civilised subjects of the eastern emperor, like many other peoples of this highly diversified and heavily populated peninsula.[8]

Although the eastern ruler Leo I may not deserve the title of 'the Great', he was distinguished by remarkable talents: his mind was enlightened, he was active and wise and knew how to attain his ends. His piety is said to have been sincere, but his conduct

towards Aspar [who helped him to come to the throne] has left
an indelible stain upon his memory. Although himself illiterate, he
appreciated literature and science, and when reproached by one of
his courtiers for having given a pension to a philosopher he is
reported to have replied: 'Would to God I had to pay no other
people but scholars!'[9]

Nevertheless, he refused to recognise the last competent emperor the
west ever produced: namely Majorian (457–61). And his help to the west,
by (partially) backing Julius Nepos, is questionable (Chapter 5). So while
there are points in his favour, there are others against him. In addition to
those just quoted,

> It is often stated that Leo freed the eastern empire from the
> menace of German domination. This would seem to be an over-
> statement of his achievement. He finally succeeded after fourteen
> years in ridding himself of his patron, Aspar, and ensuring that
> the throne should pass to his favourite, Zeno, and his grandson
> Leo. But he left to his successors the problem of dealing with the
> Gothic federates in Thrace and Macedonia.
>
> Financially his reign was ruinous. On the great Vandal expedi-
> tion of 468, which proved such a disastrous failure [see Appendix
> 2], he spent all the accumulated reserves in the treasuries of the
> praetorian prefects, the *largitiones* [largesses], and the *res privata*
> [personal estate of the emperor], amounting to 65,000 lb. gold
> and 700,000 lb. silver. It is not surprising that after this he was
> driven to the ruthless confiscations of which Malchus [*c.* 500]
> accuses him.
>
> Leo I was soon followed by his son-in-law Zeno (474–91).
> Zeno's position was extremely precarious. Save as son-in-law of
> the late emperor he enjoyed no domestic prestige, and even here
> he had rivals. His mother-in-law Verina [Chapter 8] detested
> him. . . . By the senatorial aristocracy Zeno was hated and
> despised as an upstart, and as an Isaurian he was unpopular
> with the mass of the people and of the army. Nor was he the
> man to win the respect of the army by his personal qualities; he
> was not physically an impressive figure, and he was no hero. . . .
> Finally, the treasury was extremely low.
>
> Zeno's reign was as a result punctuated by a series of revolts,
> and it was only by adroit and unscrupulous diplomacy that he
> managed to survive for seventeen years.[10]

J.B. Bury had already tried to dissect the strange personal qualities of
Zeno, and the acute difficulties that he had to face.

Figure 9 Bronze coin of Zeno, eastern emperor (474–91). Rome. Zeno is described as 'Always the Augustus', SEMPER AVG(*ustus*). (Photograph: Michael Grant)

Historians of the time vent their feelings by describing him [Zeno] as physically horrible and morally abominable, and he was said to be a coward. . . . If the Emperor was able to cope with foreign foes by negotiation or arms, his position amid a hostile court and people was highly precarious. . . .

A modern historian who was perhaps the first to say a good word for Zeno observes that 'the great work of his reign was the formation of an army of native troops to serve as a counterpoise to the barbarian mercenaries' – and goes on to remark that the man who successfully resisted the schemes and forces of the great Theodoric (Theoderic) [Ostrogothic king of Italy, 493–526] cannot have been wholly contemptible. And even from the pages of a hostile contemporary writer we can see that he was not so bad as he was painted. He is said to have been in some respects superior to Leo, less relentless and less greedy. He was not popular, for his ecclesiastical policy of conciliation did not find general favour, and he was an Isaurian. But he was inclined to be mild; he desired to abstain from employing capital punishment.

[Yet] in fiscal administration Zeno was less successful than his predecessors. . . . We are told that he wasted all that Leo left in the treasury by donatives to his friends and inaccuracy in checking his accounts.[11]

Unfortunately, too, Zeno's decree the *Henotikon* (481–2), though aiming to end the discord between emperor and pope, actually caused anger at Rome, even if it reconciled moderate Monophysites.[12]

> The Emperor Zeno died in 491. The day after his death he was replaced by Anastasius [I], appointed by the widowed Augusta Ariadne, who married him within a month [Chapter 8].
>
> The choice was popular at first, but before long Anastasius's ecclesiastical policies stirred up the wrath of [part of the] population of Constantinople. Some vociferous monks (called 'The Sleepless' because of their perpetual chanting) were fanatical on the subject. The new emperor was inclined towards opinions that were popular in Alexandria and Syria, but at least initially he considered it his duty to support the *Henotikon*.[13]

Jones has this to say about Anastasius I:

> Anastasius was a man of somewhat puritanical piety. . . . [But his] great title to fame is the financial rehabilitation of the empire. . . . Anastasius seems to have achieved his results mainly by careful measures to prevent peculation and cut out waste. . . . It is a measure of Anastasius's financial achievement that, despite . . . substantial fiscal concessions, and despite three major wars, he left, after a reign of twenty-seven years, a reserve in the treasury of 320,000 lb. gold.[14]

Figure 10 Bronze coin of Anastasius I, eastern (Byzantine) emperor 491–518, an example of the new, larger, bronze issues of which the introduction in 498 traditionally marks the end of the Roman coinage and the beginning of the Byzantine series, with its use of Greek lettering. The reverse depicts the seated figure of Constantinopolis, with her foot on a prow, accompanied by the letter M, the Greek numeral 40, which shows this to be a piece of 40 *nummi*. (British Museum)

Here is a further, more personal comment about Anastasius I:

> Anastasius had one blue eye and one black one. . . . He was
> intelligent and highly cultivated, given neither to those outbursts
> of cruelty nor to those sudden fits of ungovernable rage that had
> characterised so many of his predecessors.
>
> His chief defect was an almost pathological parsimoniousness –
> a failing which, combined as it was with a strong puritanical
> streak, made Constantinople a duller place to live in than its
> inhabitants could ever remember.[15]

However, Bury thought that Anastasius deserved more credit than he
received:

> Personally, Anastasius was generous and open-handed. . . . His
> parsimonious resourcefulness, stigmatised by his successor Justin
> [I], was entirely in the interests of the state. And the general tenor of
> his policy was to finance the empire by economy in expenditure, and
> not to increase, but rather to reduce, the public burdens. This
> feature of his administration corresponded to his character. Though
> resolute and energetic, he was distinguished . . . by his mild-
> ness. . . .
>
> If he had not held heretical opinions, historians would have little
> but praise for the emperor Anastasius. . . . [But] partly through his
> religious policy and partly through his public economy Anastasius
> failed to secure the goodwill of various classes of his subjects.[16]

The eastern empire had shared in many of the western horrors, and
survived them, while its people overcame all the hazards. Moreover,

> A long period of comparative tranquillity followed [after Theo-
> dosius I], during which east Roman emperors found leisure to
> continue the work of internal reorganization. . . .
>
> But the separation of the eastern empire from Italy inevitably
> caused it to lose its Roman character. The Byzantine monarchy,
> which grew insensibly out of the east Roman empire, was a
> Hellenistic kingdom, with a Christian Church and a Roman law-
> book. . . .
>
> From the middle of the third century the Roman empire ran a
> course which led to its disappearance in the west and to its
> transformation into a Greek kingdom in the east.[17]

The eastern empire's reaction after the fall of the west remains a little
mysterious. Zeno, it would appear, officially assumed control over the

Figure 11 Wing of ivory diptych: the Barberini Ivory. Paris (Louvre). The mounted emperor is likely to be Anastasius I or Justinian I. (Musée du Louvre, Paris. Agence Photographique de la réunion des musées nationaux – Chuzeville)

whole empire; and Odoacer ostensibly recognised this. However, Zeno later encouraged Theoderic to destroy him. Were Odoacer and Theoderic kings? Their coins say they were, but this remains a slightly misty area.[18] So does the assumption of 'cultural continuity'. What can be said, however, is that, although Odoacer's army consisted mainly of Danubian Germans, the Italian aristocracy retained its position, with no great damage done. There were also, it is true, *comites Gothorum*; yet civil posts were reserved for Romans,[19] and Latin literature suppressed Gothic. It may be concluded that the western world continued on its way, 'with different blood in its veins'.[20]

This chapter has tried to show why the eastern empire, unlike the western empire, survived, although its emperors during the initial period – covering the fifth century – were not outstandingly distinguished. But they did at least have fairly long reigns, unlike their western colleagues (after Valentinian III). Moreover, they were not deluged with usurpers, although at times (for example under Zeno) it became necessary to deal with them.

We must end, then, as we began: although the eastern emperors of the fifth century who guided their empire into Byzantine times, even if not wholly inefficient, were not outstandingly great, nevertheless they reigned for quite substantial periods; and somehow or other the eastern empire, unlike its western counterpart, survived for hundreds of years. C.W.C. Oman summed up the reasons for this in the following terms, which are not unfavourable to the eastern emperors; whom he singles out for quite distinctive achievements.

> Both east and west were equally exposed to the barbarian in the fifth century, and the difference of their fate came from the character of their rulers, not from the diversity of their political conditions. In the west, after the extinction of the house of Theodosius (455 AD), the emperors were ephemeral puppets, made and unmade by the generals of their armies, who were invariably Germans. The two *magistri militum* [Masters of Soldiers], Ricimer and Gundovald – one Suabian [Suebian], the other Burgundian by birth – deposed or slew no less than five of their nominal masters in seventeen years.
>
> In the east, on the other hand, it was the emperors who destroyed one after another the ambitious generals who, by arms or intrigue, threatened their throne. . . . They were greatly helped by the fact that the German element in their armies had never reached the pitch of power to which it had attained in the west; the suppression of Gainas forty years before [Chapter 6] had saved them from that danger.[21]

This, it must be repeated, is to estimate the eastern rulers fairly highly. But perhaps they deserved it, for at least their empire survived.

8

EMPRESSES

In my book *The Severans* I wrote:

> One of the outstanding aspects of the period, and one that is of
> particular interest today, is the universal prominence of powerful
> women. We are used to hearing about Messalina and Agrippina
> the younger in the first century AD, because we have a great
> historian (Tacitus) who writes about them.
>
> But we hear much less about the cunning and ambitious
> Severan women, Julia Domna and her sister Julia Maesa, and
> the latter's daughters Julia Soaemias and Julia Mamaea, because
> there is no first-class historian who writes about these startling
> 'Syrian princesses', as Gibbon calls them. Yet, certainly, these
> women for a time were in supreme control of the huge Roman
> empire.[1]

And exactly the same is true of the fifth century AD, in which – while
there were also other well-known Christian ladies – Galla Placidia, Honoria, Pulcheria, Aelia Eudoxia (or Eudocia) and Ariadne were outstanding,
and outstandingly powerful, personalities.

Aelia Galla Placidia, born in 388/90, was the daughter of the emperor
Theodosius I, and the half-sister of Arcadius and Honorius. In her child-
hood she was greatly dependent upon Serena, the wife of Stilicho (d. 408).
In 408–9 she fell into the hands of the Visigoths. And at the beginning of
414 she was obliged to marry their king Ataulf, whom she appears to have
influenced in favour of approaching the western empire as an equal, with
the result that a treaty was agreed upon at the beginning of 416.

But in 417, against her will, but at the wish of her brother Honorius,
she married Constantius III from Naissus (Niş), consul in 414, 417 and
420 (Augustus in 421; probably died in the same year). Raised to the rank
of Augusta, but widowed, and at odds with Honorius, Placidia fled at the
beginning of 423 to Constantinople, with her children Honoria and
Valentinian (III). Returning to Ravenna after the death of Honorius later

Figure 12 Gold *solidus* of Galla Placidia, Ravenna. On the obverse, Placidia has the Christian chi-rho on her shoulder. (British Museum)

in the same year, she managed, two years later, to secure the western throne for Valentinian.[2] She was described as 'the most pious, everlasting mother of the emperor', and, granted the title of Augusta again by the eastern ruler Theodosius II, became virtual ruler of the western empire.

This woman sought and obtained the support of the Church; but her interest in good legislation also won her the adherence of some of the senators. However, she managed to remain independent of them, and got on badly with some of them: the Master of Soldiers Felix (d. 430?), Boniface (d. 432), and especially Aetius (d. 454)[3] – though the details of the ensuing intrigues are hard to reconstruct. After the marriage of Valentinian III to Aelia Eudoxia (see below) in 437, Placidia moved somewhat into the background, concentrating on works of piety – such as the building and decoration of churches at Ravenna,[4] which she made into a worthy western capital. Yet she also continued her involvement in high imperial politics until her death in November 450.

Placidia was wealthy and worked hard, and encouraged good relations with the Germans, which would have helped the western empire; but she was too quarrelsome (and therefore inadequate) to save it or even to delay the demise of that empire.

The daughter of Placidia and Constantius III, and thus sister of Valentinian III, was Justa Grata Honoria Augusta. Valentinian coined for her, with the inscription BONO REIPVBLICAE.[5] This lady deserves credit for the last great western Roman victory, over Attila the Hun at the Catalaunian Plains (see Châlons-sur-Marne) (451).[6]

> The most spectacular event of this part of the century was the great battle with Attila's Huns in 451. This has been called one of the decisive battles of the world.
>
> It was brought on, curiously enough, by the fact that Honoria, one of the imperial princesses, feeling that her great political abilities had little scope, managed to convey a request to Attila that he would help her to have more influence in the Roman government [and to cancel her compulsory betrothal to the rich senator Flavius Bassus Herculanus]. He chose to interpret the

message as a preliminary proposal of marriage and accepted it as such. He then marched west to claim his bride and her dowry, which he asserted was Gaul. . . .

The Huns suffered great losses in the battle, but were allowed to withdraw.[7]

Subsequently Attila turned on Italy, mysteriously left it, and died. And much of what had happened was due to Honoria.

Pulcheria, the daughter of Arcadius, was born at Constantinople in 399. Appointed Augusta in 414, she acted as regent for her brother Theodosius II (who was only fourteen when he came to the imperial throne), and her court was one of extreme piety, chastity and Mariology (Chapter 9). Despite the insults of the anti-Marian Nestorius, she was loudly applauded at the Council of Chalcedon (431), which she helped to control. In *c.* 440 she quarrelled with her sister-in-law, the empress Aelia Eudoxia. When Theodosius II died in 450, she helped Marcian to succeed him, and placed the crown upon his head (see Chapter 7, n. 5). She also agreed to become his nominal wife, the 'virgin empress', thus formally preserving the Theodosian dynasty. She built three Churches of Mary the Mother of God (*Theotokos*) in Constantinople. In 453 she died, leaving all her possessions to the poor.

Pulcheria's power, tactfully asserted because she was never seen to overstep her position, met, on the whole, with the consent and satisfaction of the people, impressed by her philanthropy. Although forceful and domineering, she admired holy men, and was virtually an imperial saint herself, earning much praise from the Church – and indeed from others, for, according to Sozomen (d. *c.* 450; see Bibliography), she 'took control of the government, reaching excellent decisions and carrying them out with written instructions'.[8] She also claimed to be the master of imperial Victory.

Aelia Eudoxia (or Eudocia) (II), daughter of a pagan philosopher, Leontius, was the wife of the eastern emperor Theodosius II (she must be

Figure 13 Gold *solidus* of Pulcheria, Constantinople. The reverse, with the familiar inscriptions SALVS REIPVBLICAE ('The Health of the State'), shows the winged Salus, seated on a cuirass and inscribing chi-rho upon a shield. (British Museum)

Figure 14 Gold *solidus* of Aelia Eudoxia [II; Athenais], Constantinople, depicted here draped and diademed, with the hand of God reaching down to touch her head. On the reverse appears SALVS REIPVBLICAE, and the winged figure of Salus. (British Museum)

distinguished from the woman of the same or similar name who was that emperor's mother, and the wife of Arcadius). Aelia Eudoxia was introduced to Theodosius by his sister Pulcheria (after having been victorious, it was said, in a beauty-contest), and changed her name – from the pagan Athenais – when she was baptised a Christian by the Patriarch of Constantinople; but she fell out with the Grand Chamberlain (*praepositus sacri cubiculi*) Eutropius. Nevertheless, she married Theodosius II in 421. In the next year, she gave birth to a daughter (Licinia Eudoxia) who married the western emperor Valentinian III in 437. However, she got involved in too many quarrels; and in 438 she went on a pilgrimage to Jerusalem, from which she returned in the following year. In 443, however, she left the capital a second time, in some disgrace, and spent the rest of her life in Jerusalem, where she devoted herself to piety and charity, and constructed magnificent churches – as well as rebuilding the fortifications of the city, where she died in 460. For a time she showed leanings towards Monophysitism, but died a Catholic. She was a poet: her Greek poems included a panegyric on the east Roman victory over the Persians in 422, and a number of religious works.[9]

The imperious Eudoxia has been hailed, or dispraised, as the first of a long line of worldly, beautiful, luxurious Byzantine empresses. She was not afraid of changing her mind, when her superstitious piety seemed to require this.

> She was very beautiful, being rather tall, with a wonderful figure, and curly blond hair that framed the features in a golden aureole and enhanced the brilliancy of her fair complexion. Her lovely eyes were intelligent and full of life, and she kept them modestly lowered. She had a pure Greek nose, and she carried herself with grace and dignity. Furthermore, she could express herself well. . . .
>
> Athenais-Eudoxia had indeed a strange career . . . she was born in Athens a pagan; through a love-match she became empress of Byzantium; and she died in exile at Jerusalem near the tomb of Christ, a devoted and impassioned Christian mystic.
>
> And it is just because of these contrasts in her romantic and

melancholic life that she is of such interest to the historian. . . . Combining in herself the dying traditions of pagan culture with the precepts of victorious Christianity, and having, withal, suffi- cient intelligence and education to understand the evolution in process around her, she presents a curious and significant exam- ple of the way in which the most contradictory ideas and the most violent contrasts could, in that century, exist side by side in a simple personality.[10]

We next come to a period when the eastern empresses, although they still wanted to be powerful, did not achieve quite the success for which they had hoped. One such personage was Aelia Verina, the wife of Leo I. She conspired against Zeno, supporting the usurpers who rose against him, Basiliscus (476–7) – who was her brother – and Leontius (484–8), an officer in Syria, who joined the revolt of Illus. But in both cases Verina failed; and she died in exile (from which she had temporarily been released by Illus, in *c.* 484).[11]

Ariadne, in whose name, like that of Verina, coins were issued, was the daughter of Leo I and Verina, and married Zeno before his succession to the throne. She tried to have Illus murdered. Her importance is shown by what happened after Zeno's death in 491 (which she was accused, by some, of causing; she certainly did not like Zeno). Once he was dead, she summoned the ministers and senate to decide on his successor, but on the proposal of Urbicius, the Grand Chamberlain, the choice was referred to herself. She selected Anastasius I, and married him.

In Daphne [the auditorium, *kathisma*, at Constantinople] were played many of the dramas of Byzantine history. Here in Daphne you might have found a scene of some agitation in AD 491. . . .

Figure 15 Gold *solidus* of the eastern empress Aelia Verina, the wife of Leo I (457–74). Her coins show the well-worn theme of Victory. (British Museum)

Figure 16 Gold *tremissis* of the eastern empress Ariadne. (British Museum)

The political situation was delicate. The Emperor Zeno had just been formally entombed while in an epileptic fit and the sentry reported that he was clamouring to be let out. The city having got news of this was pouring into the Hippodrome shouting 'give the Romans back their emperor.'

On the advice of the chief Eunuch the empress Ariadne went into the *kathisma* and pacified the populace by promising that an emperor should be immediately appointed. An elderly courtier Anastasius was chosen, and the obsequies of Zeno were solemnly performed at his tomb. . . . The next day was the coronation of Anastasius in the Hippodrome, which went off very well.[12]

Figure 17 Statuette of an empress. (Cabinet des Médailles, Bibliothèque Nationale de France)

Nevertheless, it is reported that Ariadne and Anastasius later quarrelled, when Anastasius refused to meet Ariadne's wishes by appointing Anthemius, son of an emperor of the west, to the Praetorian Prefecture of the east.

Although, as far as I can see, we are rarely told any such thing, this was an epoch when the leading men, on the whole, were second-rate or worse, and women ruled the roost. These women were certainly impressive. Not only did they fulfil a vital role in ecclesiastical and monastic movements, but, as in the third century, with which, as I said, I have dealt in another book, this was a time when they were supreme personages; and they remained a powerful factor in Byzantine history.

Diehl has this to say about the eastern empresses in general:

> One is too ready to assume that the Byzantine empresses were perpetual recluses. . . . [But] under few governments have women had a better position, or played a more important part, or had a greater influence upon politics and government, than under the Byzantine empire. This is, as has been justly remarked, 'one of the most striking characteristics of Greek history in the Middle Ages'. . . . In almost every century of [Byzantine] history, one meets with women who either have reigned themselves or, more frequently, have with sovereign power disposed of the crown and made emperors. And these princesses lacked neither the outward and visible signs of authority, nor the substance of it.[13]

Holy women, not empresses, also played a considerable part.[14] (The role of women in the ancient world has lately received a good deal of attention.)

9

RELIGION

It has already been mentioned that the fifth century was a deeply religious age, and the fact is underscored by the incessant series of Church Councils. Christianity replaced paganism; it was a long struggle,[1] but the outcome was clear. Something ought to be said, however, about the paganism that had been the doctrine of the past, and still had not died.

> Paganism was not so much a religion as a loosely-built amalgam of cults, myths and philosophical beliefs of varying origins and even more varying levels of culture. . . . Its main strength lay in the fact that it incorporated everywhere ancient cults, hallowed by tradition and fortified by local loyalty . . .
>
> Of the beliefs of the ordinary pagan we know little. He no doubt believed in all the gods, and in the various contingencies of life might make prayers and vows and offerings to the appropriate deity.[2]

Paganism was still pretty strong in Rome, especially in the senatorial class, among which there was throughout the fifth and sixth centuries a large circle of pagan 'Hellenes'.[3] And after Theodosius I had put an end to any official *modus vivendi* with the pagans,[4] paganism still managed to survive, since both Honorius and Arcadius felt obliged to promulgate laws against such beliefs.[5] They were attacked at Rome – although Theodosius II, who applauded such measures, was premature in believing paganism was at an end, for it still pervaded higher education.

Athens remained the principal base of the pagan tradition. This was the place of study, for example, of the pagan, Neoplatonist philosopher Proclus (416/17–85), who had been born in Lycia (see Bibliography). Still hoping for a toleration of paganism, he did what he could to systematise and popularise the somewhat shapeless beliefs of the pagans,[6] which were eclipsed by the more direct and dynamic and attractive doctrines of Christianity, with its insistence on the afterlife.

Yet the eastern emperor Zeno was seriously, for a time, contested by the rebel Illus of Leontini (Carlentini) in Sicily, who possessed prominent pagan links.[7] He was defeated (d. 488), and the pagans continued to be attacked, along with the Jews,[8] although the Latin Church criticised the Greek Church for neglecting the evangelisation of non-Christians, whom the east never regarded as a serious political force. But the strength of the pagans lay in their interpretation of the fall of Rome, which the pagan writer Zosimus (see Bibliography), for example, ascribed to the abandonment of the traditional pagan rites, despite the senate's self-proclaimed role as 'guardian of tradition'. And indeed, by the sixth century, paganism had truly disappeared.[9]

This gradual collapse of paganism is an interesting phenomenon:

> In 416 Theodosius II banished all pagans from the civil or military service of the empire, and in a rescript a few years later a sovereign could state: 'We believe that the pagans are no more.' [see above]. The wish [as stated already] must here have been father to the thought; for in the sixth century there were still thousands within the empire . . . dragooned into Christianity. . . . All too often the fear of these new adherents towards the Christian God was taught by the precepts of man, and their hearts remained far removed: retaining that allegiance to the older faith. . . .
>
> The ruin of paganism, in the age of Theodosius [II], is perhaps the only example of the total extirpation of any ancient and popular superstition, and may therefore deserve to be considered as a singular event in the history of the human mind. The Christians, more especially the clergy, had impatiently supported the prudent delays of Constantine [I] and the equal toleration of the elder Valentinian [I]. Nor could they deem their conquest perfect or secure as long as their adversaries were permitted to exist. . . .
>
> [Through the influence of later Christians] specious principles of religious jurisprudence were established, from whence they deduced a direct and rigorous conclusion against the subjects of the empire who still adhered to the ceremonies of their ancestors. . . . The zeal of the emperors was excited to vindicate their own honour and that of the Deity.[10]

What a historic event, of permanent significance, was the establishment and virtual universality of the Christian faith, in a Roman ambience! And the state and the Church very much stood together in this deeply religious age.[11] In the words of Haywood:

> The civilization of the eastern, or Byzantine, empire continued to advance during the fifth and sixth centuries. It was, first and

foremost, a Christian empire, and had been so since the dedication of Constantinople in 330. Whatever one may think about the union of church and state, such a partnership has often proved itself capable of producing a very sound social fabric, not only in great, highly civilized states such as Byzantium, but also in certain far simpler civilizations (that of the Zuni Indians, for instance) which the anthropologists have taught us to appreciate as well-organized and successful societies.[12]

The *Pax Romana*, the peace which Rome gave to the ancient world, facilitated the spread of Christianity, and made possible the translation into reality of the idea of a universal religion.

When the political unity of the Roman world was destroyed, a new spiritual unity, represented by the Church, took its place and served as a binding force for the Middle Ages. In its triumph the Church did not reject the past, but built upon Roman foundations and within the frame furnished by the Roman empire. From Rome the Church inherited its institutions, its organisation, its administrative system, and its Law.[13]

But there were disputes among Christians which, in our largely irreligious age, can only seem misguided and, indeed, ridiculous.[14] Arnaldo Momigliano, following Gibbon, concluded that 'the prosperity of the Church was both a consequence and a cause of the decline of the state'.[15] Consequence, perhaps, but scarcely cause, because, in fact, the arguments and disputes on the subject were far more acute in the eastern empire, which did not collapse, than in the west, which did. Towards the end of the fifth century Constantinople began to emerge as the second centre of the Church, after Rome: it had already been called the New Rome, partly for that reason. And in certain other eastern centres, too, notably Antioch, the churches were filled. Yet, as stated, there was bitter turbulence in the Church, ever since the previous century. For one thing, the prelates were keenly jealous of the importance of their sees.

But above all, there were debates turning on the unity of the Godhead and manhood in one person. This Christological controversy remained the most important intellectual problem for both learned and illiterate individuals. The leading eastern intellectuals of the fifth century devoted most of their efforts to an examination of the Nature of Christ.[16]

Arcadius reaffirmed all the prohibitions implied by Pope Leo I's call for unity: 'truth, which is simple and one, does not admit of variety'. But unfortunately that is not how things were.

From the earliest times there had been periodic divisions of opinion among Christians. And these conflicts had been resolved by the expulsion of such minority groups as refused to conform to the general consensus of the Church. Many of these groups had died out, but a substantial number survived as dissident sects or heresies, which often in their turn split into smaller groups. . . .

[From the time of Constantine I the Great onwards] the imperial government normally, if not very persistently, penalised dissidents in various degrees, but heresies and schisms nonetheless continued to proliferate. . . .

In general the Latin-speaking half of the empire [although this was the half that collapsed] was less troubled by heresies than the east . . . the eastern provinces on the other hand pullulated with queer eccentric sects, many of them of very ancient origin. . . .

[Yet] we need not believe all the fantastic doctrines and grotesque practices which Catholic writers attributed to the sectarians. . . . But there certainly were some very curious communities on the lunatic fringe of Christianity.

For one thing,

From 381 to 457 the duel between Constantinople and Alexandria for ecclesiastical supremacy was fought out with increasing bitterness. At the Council of Chalcedon (451) the struggle was decided in favour of Constantinople. But the definition of Orthodox faith formulated by the Fathers only gave birth to fresh disputes. . . .

In a theological age nationalism found its expression in heresy – in the belief in the presence of but one Nature in the incarnate Christ, in opposition to the two Natures asserted by the Chalcedon confession of faith. . . . Zeno and Anastasius . . . capitulated before the east, and broke off communion with the west.[17]

The number of sects, altogether, has been variously assessed at 56, 60, 87 and 128.[18]

What *is* Christianity? Which of its Protean forms is the real one? . . . These divisions . . . must cause the conscientious historian great searching of heart. . . . They began almost as soon as Christianity was born, and as early as the end of the second century they had increased and multiplied. Hippolytus [*c.* 176–*c.* 236; Roman presbyter] 'refutes' thirty or forty. . . .

It is not unlikely, indeed, that many of these so-called heresies . . . represent an important aspect of Christian belief. . . . [But they] are often expressed in language hard to comprehend, and are the product of forms of thought long since dead. . . . By the end of the third century . . . the number of disputed doctrines was still great.[19]

There was a violent dispute about the Nature of Jesus Christ – whether it was wholly and only divine (Monophysitism) or both human and divine (Dyophysitism). (In a close relationship to this basic question was that of Mary as the Mother of God [*Theotokos*], which was officially agreed upon at the Council of Ephesus [431].) The result of this dispute was that the various provinces of the eastern empire came into disagreement with one another. Alexandria was Monophysite; Antioch was Dyophysite; Constantinople had to reconcile the various divergent beliefs.

After the Council of Chalcedon (Kadiköy) had been held in 451, the disagreement became intensified. Syria and Egypt, by the prompting of Aramaic and Coptic monks from the interiors of those countries, fought for Monophysitism, while Constantinople, closer to Hellenistic traditions, adopted, cautiously, a more Dyophysitic approach. There were various efforts to reconcile the two points of view, but they only resulted in more serious disagreements. (And one incidental effect of these arguments was that the ecclesiastical liturgies in the various parts of the eastern empire became more and more different.)

On the other hand, the existence of these disputes increased the strength and potency of the eastern emperors themselves and their courts. For, whichever faction gained the upper hand, the Church stood in need of imperial support.[20]

In general, it has been said, the west stressed the divinity of Jesus, and the east the singleness of the supreme deity.[21] But other destructive conflicts too, not lessened by superstition, remained. It was in the fifth century, in order to combat these tendencies, that heresy became a crime against the state. St Augustine fell in with this punitive view.

> The Christian State . . . must punish crimes, *treason, murder and sacrilege.* Were not, he asked, the emperors right in inflicting death on those who sacrificed to idols, or in banishing those who would not submit to law? How then could it be wrong for the Church to destroy those who were guilty of the treason of heresy, or to call in emperors to help her, by fire and sword, to crush her enemies? 'Compel them to come in' were the words of Christ; and this involved surely, in the last resort, the use of compulsion not merely moral but physical.
>
> Thus early had the Church, having ceased to be persecuted, learnt to persecute others. And thus quickly had Augustine, but lately a heretic himself, learnt to maltreat heretics. That he, like the Inquisition later, persuaded himself that he persecuted them

because he loved them – he dwells on his love for them with endless repetition – only makes matters worse.[22]

Yet people's minds and hearts could not be compelled in such a way. Pope Leo I had failed to do so when he issued his *Tome* (n. 23 below), and the eastern emperor Zeno found the same when, in a brave attempt at compromise, he issued in 481/2 his decree the *Henotikon* (adopting the work of two patricians, Acacius and Peter Mongus). This was meant to be conciliatory, but, far from putting an end to controversies, it exacerbated them, so that its two authors, as we have seen, were excommunicated by the Pope, and Constantine's dream of Christian unity was now truly at an end.

One of the few 'heresies' which still rings a bell today was Arianism, from which Unitarianism is descended. Most eastern Christians supported it, most westerners were against it. The fundamental belief of Arianism is that the Son of the God was a creature. This is what I wrote on the subject:

> The earliest of the important 'heretics' of the Christian empire was Arius, probably a Tripolitanian by birth, who . . . became a religious leader at Alexandria. Like Unitarians in recent times, he was accused of stressing the humanity of Jesus at the expense of his divinity.
>
> Among Alexandrian Christians brought up in the classical tradition, such opinions already had a long and complex past. These philosophically minded men could not tolerate the *duality* of God the Father and God the Son, for it seemed to them that only one God was possible. Their views culminated in Arius, [*c.* 260–336], who concluded that Jesus could not be God, since, being the Son, he derived his being from the Father, and was therefore both younger and inferior.[23]

The aim of Arius was to protect the uniqueness and transcendence of God. But it is easy to see why straightforward Christians deplored his doctrines, as diminishing the role of Jesus as less than the Father. Hence the proscription of the Arian sect in 325 and 381 and 388, and the banishment of all its office-holders. Yet the emperor Constantius II (337–61) had upheld Arianism as a philosophically acceptable statement of the relations between the Father and Son, and Valens, too (364–78), had supported the doctrine. All the same, it was savagely put down by others, amid attacks from Basil, Athanasius, Gregory of Nazianzus, Gregory of Nyssa (brother of Basil), Nestorius and Ambrose.[24] Nevertheless – or perhaps partly because of the strong east Roman view to the contrary – Arianism was enthusiastically backed by the Germans,[25] whose religious views the Huns, too, enlisted against the empire. And so, as Jerome had observed (360), the whole world groaned in astonishment to find itself Arian. But this was scarcely true, since both the western and eastern Roman regimes turned sharply against the 'heresy'.

The Manichaeans[26] sound rather reasonable, with their belief in God and the Devil: it is difficult nowadays to explain how an all-powerful and all-good God has been responsible for the horrors of the twentieth century. They also fostered an impressive social and economic movement, but action against them was continued by Pope Leo I the Great (440–61).

Pelagius, the other leading 'heretic', was British or Irish. He came to Rome as a monk in *c.* 400, and his works are the earliest extant British literature. He encountered and provoked much opposition. If Britain (Appendix 2), in the darkest days of imperial decline, won a precarious independence not only against barbarian invasions, but against the corruption and tyranny of an effete and incompetent regime, the fact is only partly intelligible as a triumph of Pelagian ideology. Nowhere else at that time could be found the human idealism, or the self-reliance, or the devotion to the basic ideas of freedom and justice, which Pelagius propagated.[27]

In his *Dialogue against the Pelagians*, Jerome attacked him and his followers, since they seemed to depreciate Jesus – and Pelagius was banished in 417/18. But John Wesley believed that he was not a 'heretic' at all.[28]

Montanism, Novationism and Donatism were all, in part, movements of protest against what was felt to be an abandonment of the standard of individual holiness required if the Church was itself to remain holy.

> The Donatist sect was named after Donatus (313). . . . [The protest in his favour, at Carthage] stood for a . . . deeply rooted disharmony. For the Donatists completely spurned traditional, classical, urban culture, and rejected the sovereignty of Constantine's official Church. The Donatists were aided by tough bands of *circumcelliones*, singing 'praise be to God'. But the strife they caused was virtually ended in 411 and 429, though the Vandal Genseric [Gaiseric] saved them from complete extinction.[29]

More dangerous, for a long time, to imperial unity, especially in Alexandria and among the Egyptian masses and in Syria, were the Monophysites, protagonists of a doctrine of a single divine Nature that accentuated the divinity of Jesus at the cost of his humanity. They were attacked by the government and denounced at the Council of Chalcedon (451), but the emperor Zeno (474–91) rather favoured their views,[30] and Anastasius I (491–518) was a pious Monophysite. The products of the controversies thus caused are virtually unreadable today. Nevertheless, they were extremely vigorous at the time.

> The Council of Chalcedon (451) . . . declared that in Christ there existed two Natures in one person, these Natures being 'united unconfusedly, unchangeably, indivisibly and inseparably'. Clergy, monks and laity in Egypt and Palestine reacted violently to what they considered the denial of the supreme significance of Christ's divine Nature. From their insistence on the ascendancy of the divine element in the Saviour they were called Monophysites, or adherents of the 'one Nature' doctrine. . . .
>
> Affecting as it did fundamentals of belief in the work of the Saviour, the Monophysite controversy stirred the passions of people of all classes. Eventually the theological question became a political problem as well . . . Monophysitism became the national religion, and whenever the government in Constantinople attempted to instal a Chalcedonian Patriarch in Alexandria, he had to be escorted to the city by imperial troops and his residence had to be guarded by soldiers to protect him from bodily harm. . . . Clashes . . . often ended in bloodshed. Here was grave trouble for the future.[31]

Nestorius – bishop of Constantinople (428) – had a lot to say about the Nature of Christ, the 'juxtaposition or conjunction' of the two Jesuses (two persons, one human and one divine, instead of one). He attacked Cyril of the rival See of Alexandria (d. 444), who, however, after the Nestorian 'heresy' had been denounced at the First Council of Ephesus in 431, brought him down.[32] Nestorius also made the rash political mistake of attacking the empress Pulcheria and her Mariology (Chapter 8). Proclus, on the other hand (see Bibliography), delivered a famous *Panegyric on the Virgin*, whose position as *Theotokos* (Mother of God) was formally accepted by the same Council – before the meetings at which the court worshipped at a church named after Mary.

The emperor Arcadius (395–408) also found it necessary to attack Montanism, the prophetic movement that had emerged in Phrygia (Asia Minor) in the second century AD and had subsequently gained great strength, and indeed became an organised Church with a hierarchy of its own. 'It was not', said E.R. Dodds, 'until the reign of Justinian [I; 527–65] that the last Montanists locked themselves into their churches and burned themselves to death rather than fall into the hands of their fellow-Christians.'[33]

Another very divisive element, and one which was extremely influential – encouraging ideals of asceticism – was provided by the monks, who again were far stronger and more numerous in the eastern than in the western empire, although the east and not the west survived. Their intention was, by retirement, to shun the distractions and temptations of the world.

> The monks and nuns of ancient times are in some ways less comparable to modern monks and nuns than to modern drop-outs, supporters of gurus; or others – not necessarily with any religious motivation – who abandon the conventional world and sometimes leave their houses for the streets or mountains or deserts. For the numerous monastic recluses of the Roman empire, too, often shook the dust of the social, financial and political system off their feet as completely as if they had never belonged to it at all.
>
> And so, as the final political and military reckoning rapidly approached, this substantial number of men and women was no longer available to contribute either to the actual defence of the empire or to the revenue needed to pay for the defenders.[34]

St Basil of Caesarea (330–79),[35] who wrote a *Rule for Monks*, gave monasticism its definitive form, though, since we do not possess this work, we have to rely on Jerome, instead, for pictures of its reverse side – monkish avarice, vanity and hoarding. Monasticism particularly flourished in the east – encouraged by the growing fashion for pilgrimage – but had also come to the west. Yet, having been born in Egypt, it remained a fundamentally eastern phenomenon, so that it can hardly be blamed, exclusively, for the fall of the western empire. But it does remain true that both sections of the Roman world lost a good many people to the monastic movement, and it seems necessary to conclude that the west was less able than the east to cope with this loss: in this sense Alexander Pope was right to say: 'the monks finished what the Goths began'. The best spokesman for the monks was Evagrius (*c.* 536–*c.* 600).

But it was above all the austerity of the holy men that exercised a popular appeal:

> After all it was the holy eremite dwelling in the lonely cavern or on the precipitous cliff who awoke the wondering awe and passionate enthusiasm of the common folk.
>
> Pilgrims came from west and east to catch a sight of the Stylite saint [Simeon the Stylite] who had spent long years upon his pillar until he could stand no longer and could only rest upon the framework which surrounded him [see below, Chapter 11]. . . .
>
> There is no reason to suppose any direct connection with earlier forms of pagan asceticism. . . .

Once more the Church sought to turn this popular devotion to its own purpose.[36]

The most articulate of all the ascetic holy men of the fifth century was Jerome, whose career, in this capacity, we are able to follow:

Like most provincials of talent he was attracted to Rome and there studied rhetoric under Donatus, returning to Aquileia in 370. In that town he established his first society of ascetics, which lasted for just three years.

Then some event – referred to by him variously as 'a sudden storm' and 'a monstrous rending asunder' – broke up the fellowship, and Jerome with a few of his closer associates went eastwards to Antioch. The adjacent desert . . . was already full of hermits and Jerome soon joined their company, living in a bare cell, submitting himself to vigorous penances, and giving all his days to study and devotional exercise. . . .

This went on for five years, and then [after three years in Rome] the second period of Jerome's life begins. . . . Taking Paula and Eustochium with him he went once more to the east and settled down in Judaea at Bethlehem, where he remained for the last thirty-four years of his existence. At Bethlehem he built a monastery and a convent, a church . . . and a hospice to lodge the pilgrims who came from all parts of the world to that holy ground.[37]

And we even have the opportunity of hearing what Jerome himself, in his gloomier moments, thought of this life:

Oh, how often, when I was living in the desert, in that lonely waste, scorched by the burning sun, which affords to hermits a savage dwelling-place, how often did I fancy myself surrounded by the pleasures of Rome!

I used to sit alone; for I was filled with bitterness. My unkempt limbs were covered in shapeless sackcloth; my skin through long neglect had become as rough and black as an Ethiopian's. Tears and groans were every day my portion; and if sleep ever overcame my resistance and fell upon my eyes, I bruised my restless bones against the naked earth. . . . My face was pale with fasting: but though my limbs were cold as ice, my mind was burning with desire, and the fires of lust kept bubbling up before me when my flesh was as good as dead.[38]

10

LITERATURE

Byzantine literature as a whole is not a great literature; although there were a good many poets, notably in Egypt.

> Few would study all these Byzantine writings for pleasure unless they were already interested in the culture of the east Roman empire. . . . It is not on purely aesthetic or literary standards that it must be judged. . . . Here there is no break with the ancient world as there is in western Europe.[1]

So the literature of the period is mostly, as literature, second-rate and unoriginal: the educated public of both empires, who were quite numerous, expressed themselves through architecture and, to some extent, visual art, rather than through writings. The only exceptions were provided by the Latin writers Augustine and Jerome (see previous chapter, and Bibliography, below, with some details). A great deal has been written about them both, but on Augustine it is legitimate to add here that it is noteworthy, even perhaps astonishing, that the western Roman empire produced this outstanding thinker and writer at a time when the empire in question was failing, when literature, both Latin and Greek, was at a somewhat low ebb, and when Greek, even if poorly represented in literature, had gained strength as the language of the western world. Since Cicero and Caesar there had been no first-class Latin literature – until Augustine.

That he came from Africa is not so remarkable, since north Africa, and especially Carthage, was the great remaining home of Latin culture (see Appendix 2) after the establishment of Christianity, which, far from diminishing its importance, increased it.

> Augustine developed his ideas with an independence that disquieted even his admirers. He has left his distinctive mark on most aspects of western Christianity. Augustine's major works are landmarks in the abandonment of classical ideas.

His early optimism was soon overshadowed by a radical doctrine of grace. . . . The authority of the Catholic Church . . .
enabled his restless intellect to work creatively. . . . In his *Retractationes* Augustine criticized his super-abundant output of 93
works in the light of a Catholic orthodoxy to which he believed
he had progressively conformed – less consistently, perhaps, than
he realised.[2]

Augustine was inferior to the Greek writers Clement (b. *c.* 150) and
Origen (185/6–254/5), both of Alexandria, in learning, but exercised a
stronger appeal because he seemed 'a human being like ourselves'. He was
the master of St Thomas Aquinas and Calvin. It is the *Confessions* that have
won human hearts. And the *City of God* has been described as the first
great philosophy of history.

St Augustine . . . though a far subtler thinker [than Jerome],
infinitely more influential in shaping subsequent theology, and a
more amiable personality, and though himself thoroughly
grounded in the classics and a consummate rhetorician, marks a
special break with the classical tradition. . . . He was perhaps
particularly suited to serve as [the culmination] of the new world
and as introduction to the new era brought on by the stunning
blow of the fall of Rome. . . . It is no accident that millions who
could barely recognize the names of Augustine's fellow doctors
have read with eagerness his *Confessions* and his *City of God.*[3]

Although he was not perhaps so profound a scholar [as Jerome],
he possessed in a supreme degree some qualities of genius that
Jerome lacked. His character is a medley of contradictions. . . . He
studied, more deeply perhaps than any other writer, the mysteries
of the human soul and the laws that should govern conduct; but
while in one place he insists on freedom of judgment, in another
he demands implicit obedience to authority. . . .
   Taken all in all Augustine is a marvellous genius and one of the
most fascinating of Latin writers. . . . Augustine is perhaps the
greatest mind revealed to us in Latin literature. And not only did
he emerge triumphant from all his difficulties, but he succeeded
in imprinting his mark more deeply than any other writer upon
the life of the Middle Ages. . . . In the history of Christianity
Augustine holds a place second to St Paul. Strong as his influence
was in his own age, it grew even stronger as time went on, and it
persists today. . . . If one wishes to trace the development of
European civilisation and European morals, from this author
and from that he will derive a certain amount of information;

but until he has made a serious study of Augustine's writings he has scarcely begun his task; Augustine is the foundation-stone.[4]

St Jerome, too, further details of whom are (like those of Augustine) given in the Bibliography, was likewise an extraordinary man and writer. We have already encountered his ascetic life and his violent reaction to the sack of Rome by Alaric (Chapters 9, 4). But there was much more to him than that. M. Hadas has said that he was

> the doctor who comes nearest being the professional scholar and writer (though he was a tremendous force besides), and was sainted for his services as such. . . .
>
> Despite Jerome's rejection of Ciceronianism in favour of Christianity . . . his writing is fully in the tradition of Rome. . . . Jerome even possessed the pride of literary craftsmanship and the assurance of literary immortality characteristic of the Classical writers. . . . His ecclesiastical preoccupations do not, indeed, affect what seems to be Jerome's natural, and very high, place in the history of Latin literature.

His most important work, in all probability, was his translation of the Bible.

> The Bible stood complete in its new and scholarly Latin version. Jerome had added the Old Testament to the New. It had been a mountainous labour. In antiquity an accurate text of any work was hard to come by. . . . Jerome himself suffered from faulty transmission. . . . Jerome had spent fifteen years in checking his sources. . . . Jerome's great book, known as the Vulgate . . . is marked by vigour, aptness of expression and a flair amounting to genius for catching the meaning rather than the letter of the original.[5]

> St Jerome was brought up in the Latin culture and had little knowledge of Greek. He studied in Rome. . . . He moved to the east and began then to improve his slight bookish knowledge of Greek. . . . The authors were not the old Greek Classics, but the great theological writers.[6]

Jerome reinforces the somewhat paradoxical point made above in connection with Augustine. It is interesting that at the time when the western empire collapsed, and when Greek was making such strides as the language of the Roman world, Jerome's remarkable Latinity prevailed. Moreover, he did not write only to please, but to assert the Christian way. '[Yet] his controversial works [adds A. Souter] are characterized by the foulest abuse. His reputation is due to the study of scripture in the west rather than to saintliness of character.[7]

Perhaps the man is best illustrated by his *Letters*, which have been carefully edited and translated. They are an essential source . . . They include fierce invective and fervently extol virginity among women.

It may be repeated, however, that in general – apart from Augustine and Jerome – the literature of the period is mostly not very good. Let us face it: we are dealing with an epoch in which, if we once again leave out those two men, people did not express themselves chiefly through literature, which is not therefore outstanding. Nor did the intense current preoccupation with theology help, although, towards the end of the fourth century, it had produced some remarkable literary results.

It must not be forgotten, however, that Constantinople and the other centres of the eastern empire (notably Alexandria, Antioch, Athens and Thessalonica) were the principal places where Classical, especially Classical Greek, literature was preserved, and where the writings of later times also survived. Moreover, in the philosophical school of Alexandria, the Patriarch cherished his power and independence. The east was always more deeply penetrated by Christianity than the west.

One reason for the weakness of literature during the fifth century, with the two exceptions (Augustine and Jerome) mentioned, was the strong religious inclinations of the period, which do not make for great writing. Indeed, apart from these two men (who wrote, as we have said, in Latin), there were no very remarkable authors in the west, and in the east there were no impressive Greek writers at all. That is one reason why this chapter is so exceptionally short: there were writers, but most of them are not worth dealing with here; they will be found duly listed in the Bibliography. And it is partly because of the second-rate character of so many of the writers – despite the excellence of certain other arts, as will be seen – that the fifth century has been so gravely neglected. The Classics departments at schools and universities do not care for a period in which good Latin literature was restricted to two men (both Christian), and there was no good Greek literature whatever.

So this has been a very inadequate survey. As stated above, more detailed information will be given in the Bibliography.

11

ARCHITECTURE

Although there were Jerome and Augustine in the west, there is, as we have seen, startlingly little good literature in the eastern empire during the fifth century. This might, at first sight, seem to be a delusion, based on the subsequent relative unpopularity of the Greek language, as against Latin, in the west (which we inherited), but on further investigation it turns out to be true. Such scholarship as there was, as we have seen, was devoted to theology, but even in that field the Cappadocian Fathers, for example, were dead.

There was no lack of artistic ability, but it was largely diverted to architecture, and religious architecture at that, rather than to literature.[1] We are in an age in which that was how people expressed themselves, and that may be one of the reasons why the fifth century has not attracted so much interest as other epochs. And yet, in fact, it was in the fifth century that one major branch of architecture, church building, began.

Church building was very remarkable indeed, in the east as well as the west, although it is difficult for us to appreciate what was done in the east because the buildings there are still often inaccessible or difficult to get to. It does emerge, however, that the churches constructed during this period, in the eastern and western worlds alike, are without any equals at any period, even though mighty individual churches, such as Santa Sophia at Constantinople, were erected afterwards (Appendix 3). In other words, the fifth century, so often neglected or deprecated except for a few choice sites, was outstanding for its architecture over a huge area, covering both west and east alike. If we do not appreciate what was done in the field during the period, we are giving ourselves a very inadequate picture of ancient development. For architecture was the spirit of the age: and some of it was first-class.

It is in its art, expressed chiefly in architecture, that the fifth century chiefly excelled. Byzantine art is functional, being mainly religious: it is one very effective means of delineating the relations between God, the emperor and humankind. In other words, the principal art of the eastern, as well as the western, empire was religious: art successfully compromised with faith. And this art was particularly expressed by the creation of churches, mostly following, in some form or other, the basilica pattern.

H.P. L'Orange stresses the close relation between the Church (and its architecture) and the imperial state.

> While previously the Christian basilica was thought to be derived from the antique market-basilica, modern scholars emphasize the differences between the market and the Christian normal-basilica. The market-basilica, which is dedicated to secular and everyday life, stretches along the side of the market as a sort of architectural addition to it, a kind of market under a roof. In the Christian basilica, on the other hand, which is dedicated to the Christian cult, the entire architecture is axially directed towards the centre of the cult in the rear, toward the altar, glorified under its central baldachin, the *ciborium*: precisely in the same way in which the imperial *palatium sacrum* was oriented axially towards its cult centre, the enthroned emperor under the *ciborium*.
>
> Indeed it is just these fixed architectural elements of the

Figure 18 The Church of Santa Sabina on the Aventine Hill at Rome, built between 422 and 430, and incorporating the remains of more ancient constructions, is typical, in plan and proportions, of a new standard type of basilica. (Archivi Alinari/Anderson)

Figure 19 The Church of San Giovanni e Paolo, Rome, originally of early fifth-century date although much altered subsequently, had a huge five-arched façade, such as disappeared from the city after 430. (Archivi Alinari/Anderson)

imperial *palatium sacrum* – first the open *atrium* in front of the palace, then the vast covered assembly hall before the holy of holies, and further, a number of glorifying architectural forms such as the glorification gable and the *ciborium* – which recur in more or less remodeled form in the Christian normal-basilica of Constantine [I the Great].

The sacral architectural forms, which framed and glorified the appearance of the god-emperor before the people, are taken over and sublimated in the Christian normal-basilica, which framed and glorified the presence of the celestial king in the sacraments – the altar of the land. . . .

The whole decoration of the church interior . . . follows the ascending line towards the apse. . . . Again, as we found in the imperial *palatium sacrum*, this applies also to the figurative decoration. The emperor, in other words . . . is the centre in a land of superhuman symmetry, he is the apex of the hierarchy of the state, he is God on earth.[2]

In any case, the basilica pattern became fully established. But it also displayed local and rural styles and differentiation. That is very true of the fifth century AD; and this we may concede without discussing whether the art of that century should be regarded as late Roman or early Byzantine.[3] Owing to the functional, religious character of the art of this period, mentioned elsewhere, by far its most important artistic creations are churches, some small, others vast buildings for masses of the population, incorporating, often, *martyria*, places where the faithful celebrated a martyr's feast-day.

Such edifices in the west are fairly well known. For example, there are the basilicas of Santa Maria Maggiore and Santo Stefano Romano (468–82) at Rome, preceded by one of the largest and oldest circular churches, Santa Sabina (422–31), and by the remodelled San Pietro in Vincoli (*c.* 450). And there was also the restoration of St John Lateran by Pope Leo I (440–61), now disappeared – and its baptistery, too, was reconstructed at about the same time.[4] In addition, we can see the 'Mausoleum of Galla Placidia' at Ravenna[5] (*c.* 425–440), roofed with a domical vault – perhaps the earliest cruciform building. Whether she was buried there or not, she

Figure 20 Mausoleum of Galla Placidia. Ravenna, *c.* 425–440. It is a cross-shaped, barrel-vaulted construction, whose decoration includes important mosaics of St Lawrence and starred Heaven and four pairs of apostles, on a blue ground. (Archivi Alinari/Anderson)

was, as we have seen, the first to adorn the city of Ravenna splendidly. And what has been said about the ornamentation of the mausoleum named after her has a bearing also on its construction (as of the construction of other buildings at Ravenna and elsewhere).

> There is nothing that could not have come from Rome [however, see nn. 8, 9]. But how much of the ornament that appears here . . . actually emanated from the east at a much earlier date is another matter, which art historians are still debating.[6]

> These brick buildings, whose outer surfaces are occasionally enlivened by blank arcades, renounce all attempt at external embellishment. The impact of the interior is thus all the more intense, for here the structure and decoration work together to create a sanctuary such as the ancient world had never known. Marble incrustations and mosaics dissolve the walls, banish all restrictiveness by the splendour of their colour and transport the worshippers, as they scan these pictures, into a heavenly world [cf. below] . . .

Figure 21 The Church of S. Giovanni Evangelista, Ravenna, built by Galla Placidia between 424 and 434. Later reconstructions make many aspects of the fifth-century church conjectural. (The Conway Library, Courtauld Institute of Art)

The intensification of the architecture by this means is seen at its most incomparable in the little church known as the Mauso-leum of Galla Placidia. . . . This simple edifice is the most perfect example of a building in which the entire artistic effect is reserved for the interior.[7]

In Ravenna, too, there was the Baptistery of Neon, or of the Orthodox (San Giovanni in Fonte).

The bottom parts, now deep in the ground – and with them the octagonal plan and the marble revetment – date from about 400. . . . This first building was not vaulted. Not until fifty years later, under Bishop Neon, were the dome and the top part of the outer walls built. . . . Likewise, the interior received its decoration partly about 400, partly about 450.

The Baptistery of the Orthodox [is] a domed octagon. . . .

There is a rich, draped throne below a baldaquin, a vacant throne, for it symbolizes the preparation for the Second Coming of Christ (*Hetoimasia*). . . .

In the mid-fifth century Ravenna was in full communication with Constantinople [but see n. 5], and this contact is reflected in the elegance and courtly bearing of the Apostles, as well perhaps as in the blend of two apparently conflicting stylistic canons [Italian and Constantinopolitan].[8]

[At] the Baptistery of the Orthodox . . . there are elaborate architectural compositions . . . with the Apostles above them, and at the centre of the dome, the Baptism.

The architectural compositions are important, for they show the influence of the architecture-scapes of Hellenistic or Pompeian art. But the candelabra motifs probably owe their origin to the inspiration of Sassanian models, though the influence no doubt came by way of Syria.[9]

Much of the Ravennan technique is reminiscent of Mediolanum (Milan), and at Mediolanum, too, there were five huge early churches. San Stefano at Verona, of similar inspiration, dates from *c.* 450. The Roman Rhineland, too, always maintained strong architectural links with Mediolanum.

As for the new city of Constantinople, which had, as some have suggested, a marked effect on Ravenna, building operations there began at its refoundation by Constantine I the Great (306–37).

Figure 22 The Baptistery of the Orthodox. Ravenna, *c.* 400 and 450. (The
Photographic Collection, The Warburg Institute)

Although it was not yet a major architectural centre, Constantine
built important churches there . . . but scarcely a trace of these
buildings has survived.

About his cathedral at Constantinople, the church known as

Santa Sophia – the Holy Wisdom with which Jesus was identified – our knowledge is particularly deficient, because the edifice was burnt down in 404 and totally rebuilt, on a massive scale, in the sixth century by Justinian, whose magnificent construction survives today [Appendix 3]. . . . But the first church, completed in 360, had been started by Constantine and was endowed in his will. Probably this architect designed it as a basilica with double aisles and galleries.[10]

The architecture of Constantinople owed its vaulting techniques to Asia Minor. But there were also close links with Mediolanum (Milan). The general tendency was conservative. Much disruption, however, was caused by disastrous earthquakes in 408 and 447 (when Attila was near the city). Nevertheless, the brilliant, soapy marble of Proconnesus was easily accessible.[11] The remains of the Church of St Euphemia at Constantinople have been found, and St Mary Chalcopratia (one of three churches of Mary established by Pulcheria), and a basilica in the second court of the Saray (Turkish palace), of the fifth century. But most of this ecclesiastical building has disappeared, and is known only from descriptions.

The only major surviving church of the period – or at least its outline has survived – is St John Studios, founded by the Patriarch Studios (consul 454) in 463. It was inhabited by three groups of 'Sleepless' monks. In spite of its

Figure 23 The Church of St John Studios, Constantinople. (Photograph: Richard Stoneman)

poor condition today, it is quite easy to see what the building was like. It had a short nave punctuated by twelve-foot-high columns elevated on pedestals and joined to one another by parapets, and crowned on three sides by galleries beneath an entablature. The aisles had substantial windows, and the apse was of polygonal shape. The church was approached through a colonnaded narthex. The columns of the nave were of expensive green marble, and those of the galleries were veined with grey, and possessed graceful Ionic capitals.

The classical tradition had been maintained in Constantinian and post-Constantinian days, and pervades the elaborate decoration, although this also has original features, based to a large extent on contrasts between design and background, that is to say between light and shade. As has been said, the classical tradition, which Constantine had consciously maintained, remains paramount. And indeed it pervaded the entire architecture of Constantinople during the fifth century, although it was inevitable that this imperial capital would evolve new features all of its own in the design and technique of ecclesiastical buildings. The Studios church can be seen to illustrate all these tendencies.[12]

Figure 24 The Church of St Demetrius, Thessalonica (Salonica). The building is large – more than 180 feet long. (The Conway Library, Courtauld Institute of Art)

At Thessalonica (Salonica), too, one of the richest centres of eastern architecture, stands the basilica of the famous miracle-worker St Demetrius:

> St Demetrius is a large, five-aisled transept basilica provided with a gallery. . . . But what precisely were they coming to worship in the fifth century? . . . It seems that originally St Demetrius belonged to Sirmium, but moved to Thessalonica about 442. The cult of the saint may have migrated at the same time. However that may be, there arose a legend that St Demetrius had been martyred at Thessalonica, in the heating plant of the public bath that was next to the hippodrome. . . . The architect went to considerable trouble to locate the church over the spot where St Demetrius was believed to have suffered martyrdom.[13]

Originally of the later fifth century (probably not earlier), the church is an impressive blend of Hellenic and oriental elements. It is a basilica with cross-transepts, such as became fashionable in this century: the most elaborate and costly of its kind, influential in northern and eastern Greece, and still one of the most imposing churches of the entire Aegean region, as well as one of

Figure 25 The Church of the Acheiropoietos, Thessalonica (Salonica). *c.* 470. (Bildarchiv, Foto Marburg)

the largest, being twice the length of the basilica at Neos Anchialos (see below),[14] or the Acheiropoietos Church in Thessalonica itself.

Although smaller, however, than the Church of Saint Demetrius, the Acheiropoietos Church, of about 470, is not entirely dissimilar, since it too is fundamentally a basilica of the customary type. But remains that can be detected on the façade indicate that the narthex, at its entrance point, was adorned with two towers, which added impressiveness to the building. The windows within the aisles and galleries of the church itself also demand attention, because they are separated by piers which consist of two half-columns, one of which faces inwards and the other outwards – an architectural feature which is peculiar to Greece and the coastal region of Asia Minor.

The entire design of the Acheiropoietos, however, depends on the nave, as was proper in a building which performed the liturgical programmes of Constantinople, in which – as was not normally the case in the west – the nave (together with the chancel) was reserved for the priests, while the congregation was concentrated in the aisles (and the galleries).[15]

Elsewhere in the Balkans there were four early churches at Neos Anchialos (Pyrasos) in Thessaly,[16] and there was a good deal of ecclesiastical building at Corinth, showing both Aegean and Italian influences. By the end of the fifth century church construction in Greece was at its peak, outshining other provinces; and indeed the whole area was still making something of a recovery.

In Asia Minor, too – that vast and varied territory which, as we have seen, is too little studied – there were a good many fifth-century churches, although the region is still imperfectly known or, at least, described. Reference may be made, however, to the Church of St John at Ephesus (Selçuk: c. 450?) – cruciform in plan, inspired by the Church of the Holy Apostles at Constantinople; there was also, at Ephesus, an earlier Church of the Virgin Mary (c. 400). Probably the capitals and columns of the Church of the Holy Wisdom at Trapezus (Trabzon, Trebizond) date from the fifth century, and it seems to have been at about the same period that the temple of Augustus at Angora (Ankara) in Galatia was made into an apsed Christian church.

But it is in the southern part of Asia Minor – still regarded, as we have seen, as part of a single amorphous mass today – that a special architecture truly came into being, notably in Cilicia and Isauria,[17] from which the eastern emperors Leo I and Zeno came. The churches of this area raise particular problems. The Cilician and Isaurian basilicas – for the basilica formula remained dominant, while adapting itself to martyrial needs – include transepts, ambulatories, narthexes and other developments and expansions of the original plan: and the remarkable characteristic of Cilician–Isaurian church planning, it has been said, is the passage behind the apse.

Figure 26 The Church of the Holy Mary, Ephesus (Selçuk). It established a standard architectural plan for Asia Minor, closer in some respects to the Greek mainland than to Constantinople. (The Conway Library, Courtauld Institute of Art. Reproduced courtesy of Geoffrey House)

When, and where, were basilicas first given domes? We do not know for certain, although we do know that before the year 500 this sort of construction had already come into existence in Isauria – which is very likely to have derived its inspiration from Constantinople itself. Isauria was a distant, rugged and semi-barbarous region, but it should be remembered that Zeno himself came from the area, and that a good number of his fellow tribesmen were influential in his entourage. It remains, therefore, probable that the local links of the emperor and members of his court fulfilled a significant and active role in the construction of three Isaurian churches of remarkable distinction and originality. In other words, Isauria came into the forefront of eastern imperial architectural life, although the impetus, as has been said, had originated at Constantinople.[18] Others, however, have doubted the Constantinopolitan influence.

In any case, the enormous Basilica of St Thecla (the alleged disciple of Paul whose last retreat was believed to have been in a cave there, at Meryemlik or Meriamlik (Ayatekla) outside Seleucia (Silifke)), is a conspicuous example. It seems to have been built, or completed, by workmen sent out by the eastern emperor Zeno, who was especially interested in St Thecla, and constructed her sanctuary to commemorate his victory over one of his rivals.[19]

The date of the Meryemlik is known from contemporary reports, and is confirmed by the style of the capitals. The building lies in ruins, but its plan is clear. Preceded by a huge, semi-circular forecourt and an outer narthex, the short nave was flanked by barrel-vaulted aisles and galleries. . . . [According to one theory] the church at Meryemlik would have been the first example of a 'domed basilica'. But present opinion inclines towards a different reconstruction; the first bay was covered by an ordinary timber roof, the second bay by a pyramidal timber construction. The question still awaits a final solution. . . . It is of course possible that all these buildings, beginning with Meryemlik, simply trans-posed into timber construction a model that was entirely vaulted . . . a 'domed basilica'. . . . Indeed, it has been suggested that the plan for Meryemlik was designed in Constantinople.[20]

Important in the church at Meryemlik is the square bay west of the chancel formed by four massive piers which break up the rhythm of the colonnade and divide the nave into two.

The church is ill-preserved. But as it is known that the side aisles and shallow forechoir were all barrel-vaulted, it was long assumed that the western nave was similarly roofed, with the square bay at the east end crowned by a stone dome. West of the church, but of one build with it, was a very deep apsidal court.[21]

The churches at Alahan (Apadnas?), of the same region and period, offer an obvious comparison with their counterparts at Meryemlik.

The building complex at Alahan is now the most famous of the early Christian monuments of Isauria. This is, in a way, surprising, since in antiquity it can in no way have rivalled the marble splendour of the exactly contemporary buildings of the much more renowned pilgrimage shrine of St Thecla at Meryemlik. The buildings of Alahan are, of course, much better preserved than those at Meryemlik. But the popularity of Alahan probably owes as much to the wildly romantic nature of its setting as to its unquestionable claims to architectural significance.[22]

The monastery of Alahan is constructed upon a ledge on the southern flank of the Taurus mountains. The East Church is so well preserved that one can deduce its general design and elevation, except for details of the tower, which rested upon four pillars at the eastern extremity of the nave. There was no lack of wood or stone in Isauria, so that either material could be

Figure 27 The East Church of Alahan (Koca Kalesi), over the Göksu gorge in western Cilicia, Asia Minor. Fifth (or possibly sixth?) century. It was timber-roofed, with a pyramidal roof over the tower-like final bay of the nave. (The Conway Library, Courtauld Institute of Art)

selected for the construction of the roof. At Alahan, the aisles, and western end of the nave, had wooden roofs, and it is considered that the rest of the building was the same. But what is really important is that during the last years of the fifth century there were architects skilful and knowledgeable enough to convert the old-fashioned basilica into something rather different, by equipping it with a tower over a square bay. Clearly the architect of the East Church at Alahan knew all about this type of construction.[23]

> Throughout, the building was timber-roofed: truss roofs over the aisles, galleries, the first bay of the nave, and the fore-choir: perhaps a pyramidal roof over the tower-like final bay of the nave, although a dome has also been suggested.[24] Rising at the eastern end of a long rock terrace, half-way up the steep cliff, the church is preceded farther west by a sculptured gate and two buildings in ruins, one a basilica, the other a baptistery, and all belonging to a monastery, a suggestion supported by its size . . . as well as by its clear volumetric design, its excellent masonry, and the fine workmanship of its capitals. But both the date of its construction and its chronological relation to the other buildings on the terrace remain in doubt.[25]

> Alahan [lies] uphill, along an extremely rough dirty road. The ascent is well worth the effort, for the monastery at Alahan is the most interesting example of Byzantine architecture in Cilicia. The monastery was founded in the middle of the fifth century, and the oldest buildings date from that period. Its site is spectacular, perched on a platform looking out over the Göksu gorge and its surrounding mountains.[26]

Once again, the agency of Zeno has been suggested, since he was closely associated with two monks of the place named Tarasis, which was much the same as his own original name (Taracodissa).

There is also a third fifth-century group of churches in south-eastern Asia Minor, at Dalisandus (?) (Dağ Pazari), a steep site above a swift-flowing stream, on the northern flank of the Taurus (Toros) mountains. The best preserved of these churches at Dağ Pazari (the Standing Church) was a square bay with four pillars, as at Meryemlik. There were barrel vaults, it would appear, above the aisles – perhaps later. And an old photograph indicates that the eastern bay of the nave originally lay beneath a tower, of which only a fragment is still extant.[27] Churches at Olba Diocaesarea (Ura-Uzuncaburç) in Cilicia Campestris (Plain) were likewise built out of temples (see Ankara [Angora] above).[28] And there is a fifth-century Church of the Virgin Mary (formerly a temple) at Cennet Cehennem (the Corycian Cave), five miles west of Corycus, at the bottom of the chasm, 70 metres

Figure 28 This church at Dağ Pazari (?Dalisandus) is one of the great fifth-century churches in mountainous inland south-eastern Asia Minor. The stump of masonry on the left-hand side of the entrance is all that remains of a tower which formerly crowned the end of the nave. (The Conway Library, Courtauld Institute of Art)

down; and there are a dozen early Byzantine churches at Corycus itself (Korigos, Kiz Kalesi).[29]

The basilica at Side (Selimiye) in Pamphylia was erected on the site of temples of Athena and Apollo, and, in the same place, there is another church of the fifth or sixth century. At Myra (Demre) in Lycia, the Church of St Nicholas is a little complicated, because new portions were added to an original fifth-century church in the eleventh century. There was also a fifth-century church at Miletus (Balat) in Ionia.

Syria, too, was full of church buildings, of monumental styles and filigree delicacy, and music. Much of the architecture is by no means easy to see today, although rural Syria, on the whole, is better known than the towns (even if it is a mistake to think that western architecture was largely derived from the countryside of Syria). At Antioch itself, for example, few early churches have been found. But outside the city there are a good many; some of them are listed by Krautheimer.[30]

One notable example is Qal'at Sim'an. It is not far from Antioch, although there is a modern frontier, almost impassable, in between, so that Qal'at Sim'an is more easily approached from Aleppo (the ancient Beroea).[31]

Figure 29 The church at Qal'at Sim'an in north-western Syria. Late fifth century. (Photograph: Richard Stoneman)

Qal'at Sim'an was a very large monastic establishment, and we can still see its baptistery, church and guest-rooms. The church itself was a cross-shaped *martyrium* based on a central octagon, containing the pillar on which the saint had stood for so long. The roof was of timber. What is most important and peculiar is that the arms of the cross were framed by four basilicas, each open at one end to the central octagon. Rich mould-ings outside – and particularly on the windows and doors – contributed to a powerful articulation, and the whole exterior was far more impressive than the exteriors of western churches.

So the four flanking basilicas at Qal'at Sim'an, each equipped with aisles, led into the central *martyrium*. This *martyrium*, it would seem, was originally timber-domed. It contained the pillar on the top of which St Simeon Stylites had so famously spent the last four decades of his life.[32]

This building was so magnificent and ambitious – the most grandiose example of the new phase of ecclesiastical buildings – that, although ordin-ary parish or monastic churches could not hope to model themselves on it, it established in its region a tradition of monumentality combined with many classical features, but also in many respects novel, which (although later studied by Muslim architects) remained unique and unparalleled in the Roman and Christian architecture of the fifth century and bespoke the provision of eastern imperial funds. It is still uncertain whether there was a single dome or more than one. What is sure, however, is that this complicated design envisaged the housing of large numbers of pilgrims

Figure 30 Gold plaque from Syria, of the sixth century, part of a reliquary casket. St Simeon Stylites is shown as having outfaced the Devil, who appears in the shape of a huge snake. (Musée du Louvre, Paris. Agence Photographique de la réunion des musées nationaux – Hervé Lewandowski)

(often drop-outs) who flocked to the site.[33] The immense reputation of St Simeon made Qal'at Sim'an a major centre of the pilgrimage which was so fashionable in the fifth century, being encouraged (as far as the west was concerned) by Pope Leo I the Great (440–61).

Mention should, in addition, be made of a church at Kasr (Qasr) Ibn Wardan in the Syrian desert, though its fifth-century date is not certain.

There were also large, multiple pilgrimage churches at Gerasa (Jerash), including the Church of the Prophets, Apostles and Martyrs (465) – built in the shape of a cross on square, with the four arms subdivided into nave and aisles by thirty columns – and St George, with an interesting circular plan.

The churches of Gerasa are extraordinarily impressive – through their size, through their number, and through their tendency to group several structures within one precinct. . . . The principle of grouping . . . may well be due to the impact of the building complexes which had grown on Golgotha [Jerusalem] since Constantine's time.[34]

The cathedral at Bostra (Bosra) likewise had an interesting circular plan. There is also an important fifth-century church on Mount Gerizim. This was the emperor Zeno's Church of the Mother of God. It is octagonal, but on the eastern side an apse extends out of the side of the octagon, while the other sides each contain small door-porches; between them are chapels. The octagon itself carries four pillars, above which an ambulatory runs right round the building. Above the ambulatory was a pyramid (or, some would say, dome) made of wood. The church was, in essence, a centralised *martyrium*, although it was endowed with novel, clever features, as one might expect in a foundation in which the emperor himself appears to have played a leading part.[35]

So these inland countries of the near east reveal striking and distinctive architectural styles. In Egypt, too, there was a cathedral at Hermupolis (Deir-el-Abiad, 'The White Monastery', near Sohag, *c.* 430–40), with a three-lobed sanctuary transept and aisles, combining the influences of Constantinople and Italy in what has been considered a novel church type.

To this day the structure is extraordinarily impressive. Enclosed by huge walls, slightly sloping and built of beautifully cut large stone blocks, it has the grandeur of an Egyptian temple or, for that matter, of a Roman fortress.
Within the tall rectangle of the enclosure, the church is preceded by a narthex [porch] and flanked by a long hall on the south side. . . . Inside the church, colonnades rise from high pedestals and were surmounted by a second, lower order. . . . Profiles and capitals are crude but clearly reveal their classical ancestry, and the scanty remnants of the pavement are composed of splendid white marble and red granite plaques. The chancel is laid out along grandiose lines. . . . The lay-out then, is clear, despite the thorough remodellings the structure has undergone. . . . The trefoil [three-lobed] plan itself . . . may well date from about 400 when the great abbot Shenoudi [Schenoudi, Sinouthius] founded the monastery.[36]

The large Abu Mina Church in the Mareotis (Maryut) desert of Egypt (a long-aisled basilica combined with a cross) was financed by Arcadius and

Figure 31 The Deir-el-Abiad, 'White Monastery', near Sohag in southern Egypt. *c.* 440.

Theodosius II. It was near Alexandria, and of course Alexandria played a
leading role in east Roman and Byzantine ecclesiastical arthitecture.[37]

There were also palaces, or large houses, built for the emperors – imperial
residences – at all the capitals where they lived or stayed,[38] and the
establishment of Constantinople as a great city involved the building of
important roadways and fora.[39]

The building of walls was also significant. It can, perhaps, hardly be
described as art: rather as an important aspect of military defence –
although, as we shall see, aesthetic considerations were not forgotten.
But, however wall-building is defined, it was a very notable element in
fifth-century achievement. Pride of place must be given to the walls of
Constantinople itself (Chapter 3), of which the reconstruction was ordered
by Theodosius II and carried out by his Praetorian Prefect Anthemius
(413).[40] Anthemius demolished the earlier walls of Constantine I the
Great in order to construct his new version – extending 1,520 metres
west of the Constantinian walls, and very nearly doubling the size of the
city, which had already greatly exceeded the size of the old Byzantium.

> Better than anything else, the building of the new land walls of
> Constantinople attests to her position as an architectural centre of
> the first rank in the decades at the turn of the fifth century.
>   Four and a half miles long, the main wall rises to 30 ft.; it is 16
> ft. thick and preceded by an advanced wall and a 60 ft.-wide
> moat. Ninety-six towers, square or polygonal in plan, project from
> the main wall, and six major gates gave access to the city. . . .
>   The whole is remarkably well preserved. It gives a splendid idea
> of the working organization – the main wall was apparently
> completed in little more than a year – and of fifth-century military
> engineering, and of the building techniques of Constantinople at
> the time. While Roman fortifications as a rule had been limited to
> a towered main wall and a moat, the insertion of an advanced wall
> creates, perhaps for the first time in military history, a double
> enceinte. . . . The walls of Constantinople are one of the great
> sights of the late antique world.[41]

They are not only in themselves impressive, they are perfectly
expressive of all that the city stood for. . . .
   As we drive along the walls from the Golden Gate on the
Marmara [Propontis] to the Wooden Gate on the Golden Horn,
we can grasp, as we never could from books, the might and
majesty of a bulwark that protected the culture centre of civilization from tidal waves of barbarism for ten centuries.
   These long lines of walls and towers rising tier above tier from

sea to sea – their alternate courses of grey stone and red brick shattered here and there by earthquakes and siege engines, overgrown here and there with ivy and trees, and green under the aquamarine blue of a Constantinople sky – these walls [are] still grim and warlike in their ruin, their long history written on them in inscriptions and hurried repairs in the face of the enemy. . . .

On the Marmara the walls are flanked by a great medieval fortress, the original Strongylon or Kuklobion (the Round Fort), dating from Zeno (486). . . .

The Inner, or Great, Wall was the main defence. It is thirty to forty feet high, and thirteen to fifteen feet thick. It carried a battlemented parapet five feet high, and was ascended by flights of steps running up stone ramps.

[The wall's] ninety-six towers are about sixty feet high and of all shapes, from square to octagonal. They are, in structure, separated from the wall, as required by the principles of fortification. Each tower has two floors: the lower a store-house or arsenal, the upper a guard-room. On the roof were the military engines.

Between this Great Wall and the outer wall is an inner terrace (*peribolos*), sixty feet wide. The outer wall is from three to six feet thick, and about thirty feet high. The lower part forms a retaining wall for the inner terrace, the upper is an arcade, with a rampart over barrel vaults. Its towers rise about thirty feet above the terrace, and are alternately square or crescent; variations upon these forms being the result of hurried repairs. Beyond the outer wall, again, is the outer terrace, sixty feet high, and sheltered from the moat by a battlement six feet high. . . .

The moat is also sixty feet wide, and was probably at least thirty feet deep. . . .

The gates are alternately military and public; the former admitting only to the fortifications, the latter to the city highways. . . . Originally the Theodosian Walls continued along their own line across to the Golden Horn.

The next emperor to Arcadius, Theodosius [II, 408–50], was the builder of the walls. The city had by now reached its full growth, filling the present girdle of the sea and land-walls; though it was not to reach its full grandeur until Justinian [I]. The walls were building from [412–]413, under Anthemius, regent of Theodosius.

In 447 an earthquake threw most of them down, just when that tidal wave of barbarism, Attila and the Huns, was sweeping down on the city. It was one of the great crises in the history of civilization, and the city rose to the emergency. [We are told that] the walls were rebuilt in two months. . . . The citizens not only rebuilt the single wall of Anthemius, but added a second wall with 192 towers and a moat, which tremendous task was carried out by an interesting combination of socialism and the sporting spirit. The money was raised by a capital levy. The two great factions of the Greens and Blues, corresponding to our Radicals and Tories, started building in competition with one another from different ends, and proved their equal enthusiasm and efficiency by meeting almost exactly in the middle.[42]

Is it not as if life itself during the great, dangerous, all-encompassing metamorphosis leading from Antiquity to the Middle Ages, armours and encloses itself in these massive blocks and unbreakable rigid systems in the spheres of state and religion? Thus Rome and Constantinople, and behind the *limes* the whole Roman empire, at this period literally armoured and enclosed themselves within the hard shell of the most powerful fortifications of antiquity. Is it not as if life itself, both of the spirit and of the body, sacrificed liberty and mobility to security and permanence? Who knows if the seed could have survived without this firm shell?[43]

Great importance, too, as has recently been realised, should be attached to the Long Walls of Thrace, which may well have been erected before AD 469, although they are usually ascribed to Anastasius I (491–518).

The monument known as either the Long Walls of Thrace or the Anastasian Wall lies 65 km [nearly 41 miles] west of Istanbul and runs from the coast of the Black Sea. . . .
   Originally the wall was 45 km [28 miles] long. But less than half of that length survives above ground. . . . In front of the wall was an outer work and a deep ditch and associated with it are a system of forts mostly obscured in deep woodland. As it survives, it is the most monumental linear fortification dating from antiquity in continental Europe, comparable only with Hadrian's Wall [in Britain: AD 122–6] in its complexity and preservation. Yet compared with the Roman Wall in Britain almost nothing is recorded of the structure of the Long Walls, and there has never been a detailed survey or excavation.
   It is clear, however, that until the death of Marcian [457] there was a very real concern [at the eastern court] for the security of the Danubian provinces and Thrace, and that this was reflected in an active building programme. . . . The frontier no longer lay on the Danube bank . . . the Long Walls were symbols that 'the last frontier' was within two days' march of Constantinople itself . . .
   The verdict of Procopius [historian, sixth century] on the Long

Walls was that they were a failure, and that they were doomed to fail. But even a superficial review of the history of the Long Walls in antiquity reveals that the system succeeded in repelling the majority of its attackers during the later fifth and sixth centuries. . . . Gibbon was right to describe the Long Walls as 'the last frontier', but they were not defences of last resort – for that, the empire had to rely on the fortifications of Constantinople.[44]

Thessalonica (Salonica) also received new fortifications at this time.[45] There were also important walls, of the same period, at Corinth, the Isthmian Walls. Later, these were estimated as continuing for 3,750 m with 130 small towers, 19 large ones, and three castles, but it is uncertain how far this is applicable to the fifth century. Procopius refers to a garrison of 2,000 men for a defensive wall at Thermopylae, of which the reconstruction has been assigned to the first years of the fifth century. There was also a mud-brick wall at Nicopolis ad Istrum (ad Haemum), in the Thracian Chersonese, and there was also a wall at Nicopolis in Epirus (Paleopreveza). It has been suggested that at many other places, too, there were walls erected in the early part of this epoch.[46]

12

THE HUMAN AND
DIVINE FORM

Architecture was not the only interesting art during the exuberant and vital fifth century. Let us consider, for example, portraiture. Here, as in other respects, things are not what they were. A more hieratic, less realistic portrait was now in fashion, with emphasis on the emperor's relationship with the Almighty.

This tendency, although now accentuated, was nothing new. It had already shown itself in the previous century, under Constantine I the Great (306–37).

Constantine's enormous marble head, seven times life-size, now to be seen in the courtyard of the Conservatori Museum in Rome . . . was part of a statue of which the fabulous dimensions alone were deeply impressive. And, furthermore, it has mobilized the remains of classicism to infuse a sinister, imposing touch of realism into its hieratic pattern, which is reinforced by surrealistically, transcendentally huge upward-gazing eyes, and formidably aloof, exaggerated, scarcely mortal-looking features. An effort is being made to show a man in close contact with God. . . .

In certain respects, the head looked back to the earlier empire. But much has changed. . . . The old plastic language . . . had largely been jettisoned. . . . Life had stiffened into impersonality; and people are no longer individuals. But they are not yet entirely abstractions. That final and total spiritualisation was the work of Constantine. From now on the magnified faces of emperors stare immobile, with eyes surrealistically enlarged, into a distant world we cannot see – just as Constantius II [337–61] moved not a feature when he proceeded through Rome.

These heads, built up with a minimum of detail into a system of concentric arches including the arching brows that stress the steady gaze, are cult objects like the colossal statues of Persian monarchs, and Christian icons of the future. . . . The unapproachable gravity of this hypnotic gaze into unending space [was the principal feature of] the 'divine face', the 'sacred countenance', in which the artist of the Christian epoch saw a mirror reflecting the eternal order. . . . This new artistic style had reached its decisive stage under Constantine.[1]

Yet, thereafter, Byzantine stone sculpture was rare, because of Christian distrust of the graven image. Moreover, particularly in respect of this fifth century AD, the subject has been imperfectly studied, partly because so much of the eastern material is undiscovered, or at least unreported. There is, however, a certain amount of stone statuary at Istanbul (Constantinople). For example, one of the best portraits to have come down to us is a bust there attributed, without complete certainty, to Arcadius.[2] There is also a good head of an Augusta.[3] But portraits of imperial women are hard to identify. There are, in addition, some interesting heads of private citizens: a bust from Ephesus (Selçuk), considered to represent the minister Eutropius (under Arcadius and Theodosius II), is outstanding.[4]

Furthermore, there is an especially fruitful series of ivories (often of rather Hellenistic character):

> As a rule, it is very difficult to determine the place of manufacture, as the objects could be transported over long distances. Moreover, in many groups it was also easy for the artist to change his abode. For example, someone who carved ivory needed few tools in addition to the material, so he could travel without great expense from Alexandria or Constantinople to Trier [Augusta Trevirorum] if he saw possibilities of earning money there. . . .
>
> [A particularly valuable series consists of those known as the consular diptychs.] They are usually dated . . . they thus provide points of contact for classifying other ivories and further works of small-scale art. These are tablets connected by hinges (*diptychon*) on the insides of which the new consuls or other high officials announced to colleagues in office and dignitaries their accession to office (the original inscriptions are always lost). The outsides were decorated with various kinds of representation. Those which show the consul enthroned at the opening of the circus races, animal baiting or theatre performances which he gave at his accession are particularly impressive.
>
> The consular diptychs and related pieces were made in Constantinople and Rome and perhaps in other places.[5]

Important personages make their appearance on these diptychs, notably not only Stilicho but also Ariadne, the wife of Anastasius I (491–518). And so does the emperor Honorius (d. 423). The best representation of

Honorius, however, with his wife Maria, is provided by a pearl cameo.[6] Alaric I, too, is to be seen on a gem. These imperial or regal figures had become Roman consuls.

> The consulship was the only ancient Roman magistracy which survived with any importance into the late empire. To hold the office was a mark of distinction bestowed only on the noblest aristocrats and most distinguished imperial officials . . . it was hard to attain. . . .
>
> The most important function of the two annual consuls was the provision of Games seven times a year, and the colossal expense involved (Justinian once spent the equivalent of 288,000 *solidi*) was probably the reason for the decline of the office. An insufficient number of men could be found with the necessary means, and the last subject to be consul held office in 541. . . .
>
> Several representations of late Roman consuls survive, mainly on ivory diptychs. . . . The most important elements in their costume were the *trabea* or special toga, the sceptre and the *mappa* or napkin which was used as the traditional signal to start the Games. . . . Over a subsequent period of time the costume was absorbed into the imperial regalia.[7]

Ivories were also utilised to depict the emperors themselves. A famous example is the Barberini Ivory at the Louvre. This, wrote Michael Gough,

> is but one leaf of an imperial diptych, made originally of five panels, four of which survive. In the centre, beneath a victorious emperor mounted on his charge, is Earth bearing her tribute of fruit. The lowest panel depicts barbarians bearing tribute on the left, while to the right a band of elegant Indians bring gifts of ivory tusks and native animals.
>
> Anastasius [I] fought many successful Balkan campaigns and in 496 received an embassy from India, and both style and subject suggest a date towards the end of the fifth century.[8]

Jewellery was also greatly in evidence during this period.

> By the fourth and fifth centuries, an increasing emphasis had been placed on stones for their own sake, and less pains were taken over the working of the gold in which they were set. Here for the first time the very hardest stones were used: diamonds occasionally, though uncut; sapphires, and above all emeralds, from the newly discovered mines in the Red Sea Hills [Mts Claudianus,

Figure 32 A leaf from a 'consular' diptych in ivory. Victoria and Albert Museum, London. Here is the consul Probus (408), attended by personifications of Rome and Constantinople. (The Board of Trustees of the Victoria and Albert Museum)

Porphyrites], which were used in the natural hexagonal prisms in which these stones are found. . . .

The chief centres of production were probably Alexandria and Antioch, and also Rome itself, whither many immigrant craftsmen from the Greek east had migrated.[9]

One of the most prominent arts of the period was that of the mosaic. This was an age in which the mosaic, having crept from the floors of churches up to their walls and apses, continued to come into its own. The art of the mosaic, it has been said, was now attaining, or had attained,

> its zenith. The technical process alone demanded a maximum of concentration and precision: the wall was first painted over, and afterwards the host of tiny, even minute, lozenges had to be fastened into place. . . . These lustrous fields of mosaic are composed chiefly of myriads of tiny gold and enamel chips, which evoke an atmosphere of mystery and magic.[10]

> Floor-mosaics had long been known to the Roman world. . . . But the stone cube is heavy. Attempts to use it for wall-mosaics were unsuccessful. Then it was discovered, probably first in Alexandria with its vast glass-factories, that glass cubes were far more suitable for fixing on walls. They were lighter in weight and they were more luminous.
>
> The glass could be dyed, or coated with gold or silver dust. It could be cut rough or smooth. It could be set at an angle best fitted to catch the light. Patterns and pictorial scenes in mosaics could now be placed on the walls, and by careful lighting they seemed not to enclose but to enlarge the space that they surrounded.[11]

There were remarkable mosaics of this period at Rome, where the mosaics on the tribune of Santa Pudenziana have been dated to 401–17. Old Testament scenes were not uncommon, but those at Santa Maria Maggiore in Rome – which lay especial stress on the Virgin (see Chapter 9 on Mariology) – happen to be the most ancient that have come down to us. They had a specific and deliberate aim, to stress the triumph of orthodox, imperial religion – including the role of the Mother of God – at the First Council of Ephesus in 431. The papacy of Sixtus III only began in the year following the Council, and the Virgin of the Annunciation, in this mosaic, is not merely the 'handmaiden of the Lord' but the Queen of Heaven, accompanied by numerous angels. Very often the attributes of the Virgin are taken from imperial prototypes, she herself assuming the role of Augusta; and, by the same token, the Infant is clothed in purple and attended by a throng of courtiers. The fact that there is a continuous narrative, frequently rendered in two registers, seems to indicate that the mosaic may be derived from an illustrated roll (*rotulus*), such as was later to become incorporated in the pages of a book (*codex*). There is a good deal of Hellenistic tradition here. But the influence of later Constantinople is apparent in the emphasis on the holy and transcendental, rather than the physical, aspect of Jesus and his saints, despite the effects of Roman imperialism.[12]

The mosaic decoration of the 'Mausoleum of Placidia' at Ravenna is also very distinguished, and in harmony, for the first time, with the architecture. Doves – approaching a small spring or drinking from a basin – appear four times on the walls beneath the dome of the mosaic-lined building.

> This motif already had a long tradition. . . . This is one of the bucolic themes; gentle country motifs were contrasted with the life of the town.
>
> When it was transferred to a sacred Christian interior the idyll became a symbol. . . . The drinking of the doves became a symbol of believers drinking in the truth flowing out from God and containing the life of the spirit. . . . [And] once again the Good Shepherd motif was a classical Roman tradition which Christian art could adapt to its own purposes. . . . A youth surrounded by trusting lambs – the good, beloved Shepherd – is seated in a two-dimensional, ornamental landscape of rocks, softened by green plants. . . .
>
> The symbolism becomes specifically Christian with the tall cross on which Christ leans and at which his finger points. . . . [Christ's] character as a teacher and a miracle-working saviour is stressed more fervently in these works than his severe, judicial side. . . .
>
> Whether this small circular building was intended as a church or as a tomb it makes an utterly unified impression – architecture and mosaic blended together to form an almost super-worldly interior. . . . As almost no daylight enters the interior of the mausoleum, oil-lamps or candles had to be used and these brought out all kinds of reflections and light-effects.[13]

The blueness of the background reaches the summit of its effectiveness in the dome of the mausoleum, which contains a mosaic of a central cross with the animals that had figured in Ezekiel's vision at the four points of the cross. The transepts display two deer and a brook, illustrating a text from the Psalms: 'As the hart panteth after the water brooks, so panteth my soul after thee, O God' (Psalms 62.1). The two most famous mosaics in the mausoleum are in its main part, with the Good Shepherd in the west end and the martyrdom of St Laurence in the east end. Although the treatment is, naturally, religious, the way in which the Shepherd and his sheep are represented is not oblivious to the long Greek, Hellenistic tradition of the past. Who, and what, inspired this choice of subject by the mosaicist? It is hard to tell, but it has been suggested that some eastern cultural centre played a dominant part.[14]

There are also fine mosaics in the Baptistery of the Orthodox at Ravenna: where, indeed, mosaics are prominent (Chapter 11). Obviously, in a building that was a baptistery, baptism is prominent; as it was, indeed, in the whole of the Christian faith (see Chapter 9). 'Baptism – being accepted into the Church – was a particularly solemn act in the early days of Christianity and a special place was built and decorated for it, usually a round building: the baptistery.'[15]

The mosaics of Africa and Sicily continue to reflect the *dolce vita* of the great land-owners. Thessalonica, too, displays impressive mosaics. One is at the Church of St George.

It has been suggested that the buildings represented on the mosaic of St George's are less fantastic than might at first sight appear. Nevertheless, the ethereal lightness of the architectural framework of these mosaics has attracted attention, and, by way of contrast, emphasises the physical reality of the saints which also appear on them. Yet an atmosphere of spiritual unreality, and mysteriousness, remains dominant, and is further stressed by the liberal use of gold.[16]

Reference has been made to the saints: and a rich mosaic of saints standing against complex niches and gables covers the dome.[17] 'The plan obviously recalls more closely *martyria* . . . at Constantinople rather than . . . Antioch or Milan [Mediolanum]. But the closeness to the palace and the central plan make it equally plausible that it was to serve as a Palace Church.'[18] The mosaics on the floor of the Great Palace at Constantinople seem datable to the years 491–505, though some prefer 408–50.[19]

Asia Minor, too, had fine fifth-century mosaics. A mosaic representing a bear-hunt, from Xanthus (Kinik), is in the Antalya museum, and there are mosaics (as well as sculptures) of the fifth century in the Church of St Panteleimon at Aphrodisias (Ovacik). There are others at Mopsuestia (Misis).

> In the fifth-century church at Mopsuestia (Misis) in Cilicia Campestris [Flat Cilicia, its eastern part: the Plain], a square panel in the nave mosaic depicts a variety of creatures grouped round a little cabinet on four legs, labelled 'Noah's Ark'. There are no human figures, and the only occupant of the Ark is a bird, with another coming in through a side door. . . .
>
> An attempt, however inadequate, has been made to portray a

Figure 33 A floor mosaic in the fifth-century church at Mopsuestia (Misis) in Cilicia Campestris (the Plain, eastern Cilicia). Animals and birds surround a small cabinet representing the Ark, the remaining parts being filled with elaborate natural and geometrical decoration. (Reproduced courtesy of Leo Gough)

scene, and birds and beasts stand on a base line for the most part, and do not float about in the disembodied manner typical of what is probably slightly later work in the same genre.

Much more technically competent, however, is the ornamental background of squares filled with geometric ornament, of rectangular panels enclosing some item of church furnishing (e.g. a candle or a suspension lamp), with the rest of the composition occupied by a running acanthus scroll from which emerge, like gifts on a Christmas-tree, exotic flowers, free birds, birds in cages, goblets, and even animals like an antelope and a fine cat. . . .

This scroll has a plastic quality recalling the colouristic treatment of architectural sculpture characteristic of Syria and eastern Cilicia during the late Roman and early Christian periods.[20]

Another admirable mosaic survives in the hilly, western part of Cilicia (Rough Cilicia), at Corycus (Chapter 11). In the cathedral at this site, soundings have been made as far as the floor, and there a mosaic has been found with a piece of Isaiah's text (11. 6, 8): 'the wolf also shall dwell with the lamb, and the leopard shall lie down with the kid'. This is the Peaceful

Figure 34 A scene from the 'Peaceful Kingdom' of Isaiah at Elaeusa (Ayaş), less than two miles from Corycus, on the edge of Rough Cilicia. (Reproduced courtesy of Leo Gough)

Kingdom of Isaiah, which attracted this period; and the animals are found again on a mosaic at Elaeusa (Ayaş), between one and two miles from Corycus. It has been suggested that these symbols of a peaceful unity may have been motivated by the *Henotikon* of the eastern emperor Zeno, by which he attempted, without a great deal of success, to bring about more friendly relations between Orthodox and Monophysite.[21]

The influence of Syria is often perceptible: and Monophysitism was securely entrenched there. At Gerasa (Jerash, now in Jordan), in the remarkable mosaic in the Church of St John the Baptist, the River Jordan is the link and reconciliation between the men and women, and the buildings on the bank, and the water plants and birds in the river itself. The artist may or may not have wished to be realistic, but in any case it has been suggested that he was consciously nostalgic about the Hellenistic past.[22]

Figure 35 Painting in the funerary chapel of El Bagawat in the Kharga (Khargeh) Oasis in Egypt, named after the Book of Exodus. Here the Seven Wise Virgins are shown in single file, holding lamps. The style is naive. (Photograph: R. P. Pierre du Bourget, reproduced courtesy of Département des Antiquités Egyptiennes, Musée du Louvre, Paris)

Mosaics were of course derived from, and closely linked with, paintings. At Rome itself,

> during the fifth century, paintings continued to be executed in the Catacombs, though in a period when pilgrimages to the tombs of the first Christians were just starting, these paintings were made for the benefit of the living as much as the dead.
>
> Technique deteriorated considerably, and themes tended to be repeated interminably. Only a very few scenes hold the attention: for example, the sea-faring man in the Catacomb of St Pontianus, or Peter with a child in the Catacomb of St Gaudiosus in Naples [Neapolis]. . . .
>
> Composition adopted a more hieratic rhythm: standing figures are placed inside large rectangular frames, in scenes which sometimes cover considerable surfaces. . . . Outlines are apparently hastily sketched. A popular vein is to be detected . . . which had already been anticipated in the third century.[23]

As for paintings in the east, however, which were very important, we are much less well informed.

It is a pity . . . that very little of the early Christian paintings of
the east has survived. . . . The surviving artistic evidence is pri-
marily western, and the very rarity of eastern examples renders
any list of early Christian painting necessarily sketchy. . . . The
total lack of surviving work from the east . . . cannot be disre-
garded. . . . [Nevertheless,] though . . . the Roman catacombs
have provided most of the evidence . . . surviving Christian
edifices, in the east as well as the west, have made a particular
contribution which should not be ignored.[24]

It is at least possible to see, from paintings in east and west alike, the
varying and changing interpretations of Jesus from Good Shepherd to
young hero (like Alexander the Great) to Lord of the World.

Figure 36 Portrait head from Ephesus. It is often labelled 'Eutropius' – the
eastern minister (395–9) – but may be slightly later. (Kuntshistorisches
Museum, Vienna)

115

There are also significant illustrated manuscripts of the period, notably the Vergilius Vaticanus and the Quedlinburg Itala, mostly in Berlin.[25] The technique probably originated at Constantinople, not Antioch as has been suggested.[26]

Silver and gold work of the period is quite important.[27] And a word or two about the coinage, and especially the basic gold *solidus*, will also not be out of place.

> The scale of values in the ancient world was very different from our own. One gold *solidus* was enough to furnish bare subsistence for a year; four or five provided a soldier's annual ration, while six or seven bought a decent, if humble, standard of living. It was naturally more costly to live in a city than in the country, and all manufactured goods were very expensive. A modest suit of clothes, for example, is recorded to have cost one *solidus*. . . .
>
> Late Roman coins . . . bear the head of the reigning emperor or of a member of his family. On the reverse side, the victoriousness of the emperor is the abiding theme. . . . During the fifth century designs became stereotyped for long periods. . . . During the fourth and first half of the fifth centuries, a foremost feature of the design of both gold and silver coins was the wreath bearing imperial *vota*.[28]

And so most art, like architecture, served the emperor (and thus served religion). Textiles, however, served a purely private purpose: and there were evidently a lot of them, though few are still extant.[29]

> A tremendous quantity of textiles must have been produced all over the Roman empire in the early Christian period. They have survived almost exclusively in Egypt, where they were put into tombs and did not decay because of the dry climate.
>
> Garments, curtains and wall-painting with decorative and fig-ured decoration are particularly important for the sphere of art. The materials were linen and wool, and also valuable silk which in late antiquity and the early Christian periods had to be imported from Persia: only in 552 did it prove possible to get silk worms in the Byzantine empire and begin production there. . . .
>
> It is very difficult to date the textiles . . . [but they] are very important, first because they tell us something about the everyday life of the early Christians; second, because they attest the on-going existence of pagan designs well down into late antiquity; and third, because in part [also] they copy monumental cycles,

probably of wall paintings, with scenes from the Old Testament and New Testament.[30]

The taste for sarcophagi, already started in earlier years, also continued actively, and they displayed some very effective reliefs, reflecting, once again, the tastes of the time.

> Only in Rome have so many sarcophagi been preserved that we can say something about the technique of their manufacture. . . . The preparation was divided into several processes which were undertaken by sculptors trained in different ways. . . . In a great many examples we can see different states of finish in a sarcophagus: more progress has been made in one part than in another. The pieces were used nevertheless, probably because a sarcophagus was urgently needed for a burial.[31]

EPILOGUE

As mentioned in the Introduction, we do not, in the west, talk enough about the eastern empire, which began to come into its own in the fifth century AD.

> Often it is assumed that the part played by Byzantium in history was passive, to be for nearly a thousand years the bulwark of Christendom against the eastern infidel. . . . It is forgotten that throughout its whole existence the empire continually exercised an active influence on the civilisation of the world. . . . Western Europe was perpetually in debt to her. . . . Up to the Latin capture, Constantinople was the unquestioned capital of European civilisation.[1]

It seems strange, therefore, that so little attention is still paid to Byzantium in educational systems. This is partly because the attention of their classical teaching is not unnaturally focused on the periods when there had been great literature – which there was not in the fifth century. Religion also plays a part: for we have to make a great effort, indeed – as most would agree – too great an effort, to understand a period in which religious matters filled such a predominant role. Chauvinism also comes into the matter. We talk so much about petty western kingdoms (such as those of Mercia, Wessex and Northumbria in England) that we forget the point underlined above. But many of us have worried about why the eastern empire, based on Constantinople, survived for so long, when the western empire, based on Italy, did not. An endeavour has been made in this book, as in many others, to answer that question.

I have not tried to exalt the east at the expense of the west; the east was surely, in many ways, a pretty nasty place. But I have tried to explain something about the eastern empire, which is so sadly neglected by our educational system. It surely deserves as much attention as the west, if not more. That, I hope, will be clear, and not least from Chapter 11, which shows how wonderful the architectural achievements of the eastern empire were, even though some of them, nowadays as well as at other times, are far from easy to visit and see. I, of course, have had to deal principally with the earliest part of the Byzantine period (if indeed it is Byzantine at all). But all the better, I feel, because it has made it possible to concentrate on the little known origins and early years of the eastern empire which then continued to last for so many hundreds of years.

Many people like their history to be garnished by relating its relevance to modern times. Such relevance can be justly ascribed to the fifth century AD. For it was the eastern empire, above all, which protected Europe from ruin at the hands of external aggressors; and it was in the fifth century that this empire survived its critical moments, and succeeded in living on to assume its critical protective role. True, the Arab and Turkish outsiders had not yet, by that time, arrived on the scene. But there would have been no Europeans to encounter them and keep them at bay if Constantinople had not, during the fifth century, battled on, and created the Byzantine empire that was to come.

The relevance of all this today lies in the fact that Europe is once again threatened from outside. The exact nature of the threat is much disputed, but most would agree that the next world war will take the form of a war of 'clashes of civilisation', between Europe, or the west, and what lies beyond.[2] Of course the situation will not exactly repeat itself. For the eastern Roman empire, and Byzantium, stood for the Christian Church (however divided) against non-Christians. For that was a highly religious age, which the present epoch is not. The next major war, therefore, will be secular rather than religious. But we can still think gratefully of the east Roman, Byzantine empire which established itself in the fifth century, for in the centuries to come that empire, looked at from a secular point of view, defended the western world against the onrush of other secular powers, based elsewhere.

We should therefore study the fifth century with great care, since it heralded a movement of defence against the outside world which may very well have to be repeated during the years just ahead of us.

It may seem rather artificial to choose a specific century for this book; because, after all, history is continuous and does not pay attention to the beginning and end of hundred-year periods. And yet few will echo that view today, when we are approaching a millennial landmark. For, after all, the beginning and end of a millennium, or a century, do mean something. People are conscious of when these landmarks have been reached, and are determined to make a new start. This is so in AD 2000, and was so in AD 400 (or at whatever moment the new century was recognised). Men and women may, it is true, not have been conscious of the fact, but in reality it was one of the decisive moments in the transition between the ancient and medieval worlds. Without all that occurred the fifth century AD, the

Middle Ages would have been very different. And yet what took place during those hundred years is little known, because the geographical location of what happened and the attitudes of those who made things happen are alien from our modern experience. That is why the effort ought to be made to explain what the fifth century was all about.

Already in 1929 Robert Byron, whose work has on the whole not met with universal scholarly approval, saw the relevance of the Byzantine empire to the modern world; and much of what he said is relevant to the present study of the fifth century.

> The European countries correspond to the city-states of Greece; the range of Anglo-Saxon institutions to that of Roman; Europeanism to Hellenism; and the intellectual effect of the scientific revolution to Christianity.
>
> It may be argued that, far from creating an international spirit, the British empire has done no more than propagate an evil nationalism. During the last half-century, the charge may hold good. But by its work of Europeanisation, of which, indeed, it is only the foremost exponent, it has laid a common ground on which the peoples of the world may find the basis of international concord.
>
> This also, on a lesser territorial scale, did Constantinople accomplish. Within her walls mingled all the races of Eurasia, and all their products, commercial, cultural, philosophical. . . . The internal structure of the Byzantine state bears . . . a singular affinity to that of ourselves.

This is, perhaps, pitching it rather strongly. Fifth-century Byzantium was, in many respects, very different from our own culture. And Robert Byron seems to talk rather too favourably of the British empire, though it still existed when he wrote, which gives additional interest to what he said. But he is quite right to point out that the Byzantine empire was one of our most important forerunners. The first stages of that empire are what has been considered here.

> The first of the eight periods into which the life of the empire is usually divided, lasted from 350 to 518. . . .
>
> The new city, the imperial whim, was proved. Sheltered by the Black Sea, as though beneath an umbrella, from the full torrent of the Asiatic migrations to the south-west, she escaped the disasters that overtook the west, as the great leaders, Alaric, Attila and Theoderic allowed themselves to be diverted by the seductions of

Italy and Spain. . . . The strength of the empire lay in the Levant. . . .

Amid convulsions, abstract and material, the Byzantine empire was formed and tempered. From the barbarian migrations it emerged intact when Europe lay inundated.[3]

APPENDIX 1

CONSTANTINE I THE GREAT AND AFTER

This book is about the fifth century, but I feel that the period should be linked up with Constantine I the Great (306–37) – about whom I wrote a book[1] – to demonstrate the continuity that existed. I have tried to note in the present volume certain of the points of direct contact and influence between Constantine and the fifth century, but something more needs to be said about the role of Constantine in determining the future: or rather, the book to which I referred needs to be quoted, before later developments can be outlined.

First of all, the religious developments to which allusion has been made in Chapter 9 need some reference to Constantine as a prelude.

> Constantine is, of course, best known as the first Christian emperor. . . . He was a Christian of a very peculiar type, a type that would hardly be recognized as Christian at all today. For the God he believed in was a God of power, who had given him victory, and he would have had little sympathy with the idea that Christianity meant love, or charity, or humility. . . . Furthermore, he was utterly confident that he himself was the man of God, God's servant and representative who was constantly in touch with him and was told by him what to do – and how, by doing accordingly, he could avoid divine anger. . . .
>
> The Christian community . . . should be brought in as the ally and close component of the government, and should be amalgamated with it, so as to achieve the *national unity* which the persecution had so conspicuously failed to supply. And there lay Constantine's great failure. For it became clear, very soon, that Christianity was hopelessly divided within itself. . . .
>
> Although an impulsive man, he also had a keen eye for what was politically possible, and his whole reign is an object lesson in how to get Christianity accepted, firmly yet cunningly, without attempting too much speed. [But] his Christianization of the

Figure 37 Colossal head of Constantine I the Great (306–37), Palazzo Capitolino. (Archivi Alinari/Anderson)

Roman world [was] accompanied by an unprecedented outburst of church construction.[2]

What seems rather odd, however, though it did not, apparently, seem odd to the dynastic mind of Constantine I the Great, was the division of the empire which he envisaged in 335, to take place after his death (which

Figure 38 Head generally supposed to represent Constantine I the Great; or one of his sons. (Metropolitan Museum, New York. Archivi Alinari/Anderson)

occurred in 337). The beneficiaries of this solution were mostly his sons. Constantinus junior [II] was to rule in the western provinces, Constans in Italy and Pannonia and north Africa, and Constantius II in the east; although Constantine's step-nephew Delmatius was to rule in eastern Europe, while the easternmost provinces were allotted to Delmatius's brother Hannibalianus.

How did the mind of Constantine work, in making these hopelessly divisive arrangements? This is what I have said on the subject:

> While [his son] Crispus (d. 326) was alive, it is not impossible that Constantine envisaged him as his sole successor, though this solution would have been strenuously resisted by the emperor's wife Fausta, who was pushing her own three sons forward as Crispus's rivals.
>
> After the removal of both Crispus and Fausta, Constantine . . . did nothing to discourage the continued advance of her sons. . . . But why, in that case, did Constantine I not designate his eldest surviving son Constantinus junior (II) as the future sole emperor, such as he was himself? Probably because he did not think that Constantinus junior was capable of the role . . . which was evidently correct. . . . [And the] multiple subdivision [which he instead arranged] at least served the purpose of diminishing the danger of a plot against Constantine I himself, while he was still alive and in charge.
>
> But can he seriously have thought that such a joint arrangement would work? In fact, it failed to work, very quickly and completely and abysmally and explosively.[3]

First of all, Delmatius and Hannibalianus soon died at the hands of the army. Then, in 340, Constantine II was slain at Aquileia by Constans. In 350 Constans was killed in Gaul by the pagan usurper Magnentius.[4] Then, in 353, at Mursa Major (Osijek), Magnentius was suppressed by Constantius II, who re-established his father's sole rule of the empire until his death in 361. During the next three years Julian the Apostate (361–3) and then Jovian (363–4) managed to maintain this imperial unity. Julian carried through many administrative reforms, and fought with dubious success against the Persians.

He is also known as the Apostate because he renounced Christianity in favour of paganism.

> Julian had long been a secret pagan. Reacting violently against the Christian teaching that he had received in a lonely and miserable childhood, he had developed a passionate interest in the art, literature and mythology of Greece and had grown to detest

the new religion which condemned all he loved as pernicious vanity. . . . Now that he was sole Augustus he was able to come out into the open.[5]

But he was killed in 363. He had fought a losing battle against Christianity; and the house of Constantine was extinct. Julian was succeeded by Jovian, a genial and popular young officer (a Christian), who was little more than a nonentity. He signed a disadvantageous treaty with the king of Persia, but then, almost immediately, died, after a reign of less than eight months (363–4).

Nine days later, a unanimous vote of the great officers of the empire, assembled in conclave, elected another Pannonian officer, Valentinian I, as emperor. He was a violent, brutal and uncultivated man, but a capable soldier and a careful administrator, taking a genuine interest in the welfare of the lower classes, to which he himself by origin had belonged.[6] Only a month later he nominated as his fellow-Augustus his brother Valens, who, at the age of thirty-six, was seven years younger than himself. The choice, said A.H.M. Jones,

had very little to commend it, save that Valens' loyalty could be depended upon. Valens was utterly undistinguished, still only a *protector* [bodyguard], and possessed no military ability. He betrayed his consciousness of inferiority by his nervous suspicion of plots and savage punishment of alleged traitors. But he too was a conscientious administrator, careful of the interests of the humble. Like his brother, he was an earnest Christian.

The two brothers parted in Sirmium, Valentinian going on to take charge of Illyricum, Italy, Africa and the Gauls, while Valens returned to rule the eastern prefecture. . . . The two brothers naturally promoted their Pannonian friends. The process had indeed begun under Jovian, who was likewise of Pannonian origin.[7] Although Valentinian was a strong Christian, 'I do not consider', he wrote, 'any rite permitted by our ancestors to be criminal. . . . Everyone [has been] granted a free choice of practising whatever religion his mind determined.'[8]

And, under Valentinian, most 'heretics', too, were tolerated. Valentinian was one of the few emperors who firmly refused to take sides in theological controversies. . . . Valens had a more complicated theological situation to deal with in the east, where opinion was still much divided.[9]

But Valens encountered a crisis in 376. The advancing Huns had caused a panic among the Sarmatian and German tribes of south Russia, vast numbers of whom crossed into the empire, some with imperial permission and some without. The latter became violent, and were joined by Thracian gold-miners. Valens, who was at this time at Antioch, moved up to encounter them at Adrianople (Hadrianopolis; Edirne), where he was heavily defeated and lost his life, although the Germans thereafter failed to take Constantinople itself. The western emperor Gratian,[10] who had come to the western imperial throne in 375 after the death of his father Valentinian I, did not do anything useful to help. But he did recall Theodosius, the son of his father's executed Master of Horse,[11] who became, in 379, the emperor Theodosius I, ruler of the east.[12] For the first two years Theodosius I made Thessalonica (Salonica in Macedonia) his headquarters, and then he moved to Constantinople, where, in 382, after operations that seemed to save Roman honour, he made a treaty of peace with the Visigoths, who henceforward, under their own chiefs, fought as allies of the empire (*foederati*).[13] He also signed a treaty with Persia, by which Armenia was partitioned.

Meanwhile in the west, where Valentinian II (d. 391) was emperor,

Figure 39 Relief of Theodosius I and his family watching the races on the base of his obelisk (originally erected by the Pharaoh Tothmes III of Egypt, *c.* 1504–1436 BC) in the Hippodrome at Constantinople. The inscriptions in Greek and Latin on the base of the blocks compliment the emperor and his city prefect Proclus for setting up the obelisk so quickly. (The Conway Library, Courtauld Institute of Art. Photograph reproduced by permission of Professor A. Bryer)

things were not going very well. Theodosius I had to move there, to deal with two usurpers, Magnus Maximus (383–8) and Eugenius[14] (391–4), the nominee of Valentinian II's Master of Soldiers Arbogast. Theodosius I was called in to deal with both of them: he defeated Magnus Maximus at Siscia (Šišak) and Poetovio (Ptuj), and executed him at Aquileia, and then he defeated Eugenius and Arbogast at the battle of the Frigidus (Vipacco). Less than five months later Theodosius, having reunited the empire, died at Mediolanum (Milan),[15] bequeathing the rulership to his sons, Arcadius, aged seventeen, whom he had left in Constantinople, and Honorius, who was only ten, and was brought to Italy by Theodosius. They were both not only youthful, but feeble; the real ruler of the empire, in the west, was Stilicho, the Master of Soldiers, a friend of the late emperor Theodosius, and in the east Rufinus.

Why did Theodosius take the disastrous decision of leaving the empire to Arcadius in the east, and to Honorius in the west? Granted that he had performed a unique feat by uniting the empire, which was, otherwise, doomed by military and administrative necessity to be divided into two. But why leave it to his very young and incompetent sons? – as we already asked with regard to Constantine I. We may dismiss the view that Theodosius just did not care; he may not have fully deserved the title of 'the Great', which was awarded to him (because of his piety) by ecclesiastical historians, but he was not that kind of cynical fool. On the other hand, like most people, he was a believer in his family, and their keen supporter, and he could back this natural inclination by a conviction that dynastic policy alone was the key to imperial survival. And so, as was stated in Chapter 2, he sanctioned and solidified the already existing division of the Roman world between western and eastern empires; and by the time that this book truly begins, at the onset of the fifth century, the two governments – even if strict legalists still declared that they represented a single unit – were in fact separate, under Honorius at Mediolanum and then Ravenna in the western empire (which was destined to last only until 476), and under his elder brother Arcadius at Constantinople in the east.

APPENDIX 2

AFRICA, SPAIN, GAUL

All these three areas, which had belonged to the western Roman empire, succumbed to the 'barbarians' before Rome itself fell,[1] unlike the provinces of the east, which remained under the imperial control of Constantinople, at least for the time being.

North Africa was one of the culturally and commercially most active parts of the western empire. Based on Carthage, it kept Latin going, and at a time when both Latin and Greek literature were otherwise at rather a low ebb it produced the great Latinist Augustine.

Augustine was also active in stimulating the Church against schismatics, notably the Donatists, who flourished in Africa (Chapter 9). Nevertheless, the country remained prosperous – Alaric's scheme to invade north Africa after his sack of Rome came to nothing – and a decisive stage in the collapse of the western empire was marked when Carthage was conquered in 429 by Gaiseric, king of the Vandals, who found it an easy prey, since the defensive system of the city was suited to nothing more than policing and the suppression of sporadic tribal revolts. Carthage became the capital of Gaiseric and his successors, and in 442 the Vandals were recognised as the masters of north Africa.

Of all the striking events which the fifth century saw in Europe, writes E.A. Thompson, none was of more consequence for the political life of the Mediterranean than this Vandal conquest of north Africa. And this conquest split the Mediterranean into two parts. Once north Africa was lost, the days of the western empire, as a political entity, were numbered. So this is another reason for its fall.[2] The Vandals were also a great threat in the Mediterranean area as a whole.

> Not only did the Vandals have at their disposal the men and material wealth of Africa, which they were to control until the Byzantine reconquest of 533 [Appendix 3], but they set themselves up as the original Barbary pirates. With their fleets they made commerce in the Mediterranean extremely difficult and carried out raids on the south coast of Europe.[3]

129

In 431, 441 and 467 Gaiseric defeated Roman and eastern attempts to overthrow him. And in 455 he temporarily captured Rome. He died in 477.

As for the Iberian peninsula, which produced distinguished Latin writers during the fifth century, after the Visigothic sack of Rome (410), various groups of Germans, led by Ataulf, crossed the Pyrenees – Gaiseric's

Figure 40 Mausoleum of Theoderic, Ravenna. (Archivi Alinari/Anderson)

Vandals heavily defeated the Romans at Carthago Nova (Cartagena) (Chapter 7, n. 1), causing the downfall of the western emperor Majorian (the city having been destroyed by the Vandals in 425) – and the Suebi occupied Emerita (Merida) in southern Spain. The Suebi took root in northern Lusitania (Portugal), where Recharius (445–56) was the first barbarian monarch to embrace Arianism, under the influence of the Visigoths, who overthrew the Suebian monarchy and maintained a protectorate in northern Spain (one source for the Visigoths in Spain is Hydatius of Callaecia [Galicia], who died after 468).

On the death of Theoderic (Theodoric) the Ostrogoth (526), a mass of Gothic tribesmen flocked to the peninsula. In 551 part of southern Spain was reconquered by Justinian I, who for a short time made Carthago Nova (Cartagena) the capital of his empire in Spain.

In Gaul, the Romans settled Visigothic *foederati* (led by Ataulf, officially in the service of the western emperor Honorius) in Gallia Narbonensis (Septimania) in 412 and in western Aquitania. Then, under Wallia, more were settled in western Aquitania in 418. In 443 the Burgundians were installed by Aetius in Sabaudia (which includes Savoy).[4] Both Visigoths and Burgundians, although Arians, sent troops to help Aetius against Attila the Hun, who claimed Gaul, at the battle of the Catalaunian Plains (near Châlons-sur-Marne) (451). But Euric, king of the Visigoths from 466 to 484, rejected the unreal sovereignty of the western Roman empire in 475.

In 481 or 482 Clovis succeeded his father Childeric as leader of a tribe of Franks round Turnacum (Tournai), and before his death in 511 had created a great Frankish kingdom in Gaul, having vanquished the Alamanni, Burgundians and Visigoths (under Alaric II) (507).[5] At Caesarodunum (Tours) he received a delegation from Constantinople in 508, and was apparently invested with the insignia of a Roman consul.[6]

APPENDIX 3

JUSTINIAN I AND BEFORE

Justinian does not come into the present book, because he reigned too late (527–65). But it was he who reaped the fruits of the long, patient proceedings of his predecessors during the fifth century, and who became the most famous Byzantine emperor, representing, it has been truly said, an apogee in the history of Byzantium.

Born in *c.* AD 482 or 483, probably at Tauresium (near Skoplje), he had at first the name of Petrus Sabbatius, but took the name Justinianus on his adoption by the previous emperor Justin I (518–27). This was the most notable thing that Justin I did.

> Justin I was an Illyrian peasant who had risen from the ranks, and was now, at the age of about 65, *comes excubitorum* [Commander of the Bodyguard]: his military career had been respectable but not distinguished, and he possessed neither culture nor administrative experience – his enemies alleged that he was illiterate, and had to use a stencil to sign his name.[1]

He was said, therefore, to be backward and stupid. Unlike Leo (I), Zeno and Anastasius (I), Justin I had won his way to the front in the army.

His reign of nine years would have been of little note in history – for he made no wars and spent no treasure – if he had not been the means of placing on the throne of the east the greatest ruler since the death of Constantine I the Great. Justin had no children himself, but had adopted as his heir his nephew Justinian, son of his deceased brother Sabbatius. And then Justin I rapidly promoted Justinian.

In 522 the latter married Theodora, who on a number of occasions strengthened his resolve.

> Theodora was . . . a Greek of Cyprus. Her father was a keeper in the Constantinople zoo. From an early age the audacity with which she defied the proprieties of a community already thoroughly corrupt, won her the position of Queen of the Half-World. From this she

Figures 41 and 42 Mosaic in the Church of San Vitale, Ravenna, depicting the
Byzantine emperor Justinian I (527–65) and his wife
Theodora, with their staff. They are shown in full imperial
majesty, into which considerable eastern (Persian) elements
have intruded. (Both Archivi Alinari/Anderson)

rose by a higher audacity to be empress of the eastern hemisphere.

The character of her public performances is best left veiled in the verbosity of Gibbon or in the obscurity of Byzantine chroniclers. . . . But Theodora was no mere light-hearted votary of Vanity Fair. She was equally shameless, whether making herself a career as a singer or as a saint. . . . There have been attempts to whitewash Theodora. . . . The hard brilliance of her character gleams through them like Byzantine mosaics. . . .

There can be no doubt that her repentance and retirement into private life was a trap set for Justinian, who used to find her day after day sitting demurely at her spinning wheel in a modest attic. Justinian was then principal adviser and heir-presumptive to his uncle, the worthy Justin [I]; and he risked his whole career when he determined to marry her. . . .

Theodora responded by becoming most rigidly respectable, though insatiably rapacious. She undoubtedly saved Justinian his crown when the lawlessness of the circus factions nearly destroyed the city in the Nika riots [532].[2]

She was, however, a convinced Monophysite (Chapter 9), thus belonging to a sect which Justinian I, after various developments, declared unorthodox (564), though the Monophysites paid no attention to his edict. Justinian actually favoured a *via media*, but he also believed that the greatness of the empire depended on the suppression and extermination of Christian 'heresy', as well as of paganism.[3]

For Justinian I, a well-read student of history, was profoundly conscious of the former grandeur of the Roman empire, and was determined to restore it, by recovering the lost territories of the west.

He began by sending his famous general Belisarius to [north] Africa with a small but efficient force. The Vandals were quickly conquered, and Africa, with its highly important natural wealth, was to remain under Byzantine control for a hundred years thereafter, until it fell to the Moslems.[4]

After Belisarius

had broken the Vandal power in Africa and conquered a new continent for Justinian, [he] consequently became suspect and was recalled. But, in deference to his immense influence with the people, he was accorded a triumph in the style of Old Rome, the first that New Rome had seen.

It must have been a sight worth seeing. For, to the usual display of the treasures of the eastern empire was added the spoil of the Vandals, themselves for generations the spoilers of the ancient world. In this spoil were many historic relics, such as the vessels of the Jewish Temple. Behind it walked Gelimer, the handsome Vandal chief, repeating to himself as the chronicler tells us, 'Vanity of vanities, all is vanity.' While beside him, in plain service uniform, walked Belisarius. The captive chief and the conquering general then knelt before the throne of Justinian and Theodora: the general, before he rose from his knees, obtaining pardon and a pension for his opponent.[5]

The military task in Italy was then entrusted, first to Belisarius, and subsequently to Narses.[6] The campaigns were successful, but costly, devastating and impermanent: in 568 the Lombards had settled in northern Italy, where they remained for two centuries.

Justinian's active interest in the west represented no radical departure from the policy of some Byzantine emperors during the fifth century. Indeed, his expeditions to recover the western provinces, involving the commitment of important resources of his empire, arose from (1) a long background of fifth-century eastern military expeditions to aid the west against internal and external threats, and (2) the extensive interest of both eastern pagan and Christian individuals in western misfortunes and the significance of those misfortunes for the eastern half of the empire.

Justinian also did a great deal to regularise the Law. In 528 a commission was appointed to codify all imperial constitutions, in so far as they were still valid, from Hadrian (117–38) onwards. The first Codex Justinianus was published in 529 (with a revised edition in 534), and the *Digest* became public in 533. Justinian subsequently issued more than 150 *Novels*, dealing with various legal topics.[7] He also reformed the provincial administration and was determined to abolish corruption and extortion. He increased the status and pay of provincial governors. And he also revised the system of appeals, arranging that minor cases should not be sent to the capital.

Since Justinian's wars cost a very large amount, he instituted numerous economies, with the help of his efficient but much disliked financial adviser John of Cappadocia.[8] For example, the public post was cut down, and a strict auditing system controlled municipal and military accounts. Nevertheless, a new land-tax (the *aerikon*) had to be created,[9] and numerous monopolies were set on foot. Justinian I was accused of being avaricious with his own resources, and spendthrift with those of others.

A great deal of money was also spent on a lively building programme throughout the empire, which has been considered the beginning of truly

Byzantine architecture. Even if, in many cases, what really happened was a refurbishment of works started earlier by Anastasius I, fortresses were constructed by Justinian I, and aqueducts and other public structures were restored by him.[10] Among many architectural innovations, his supreme achievement, a 'world wonder', was the reconstruction of the Church of the Holy Wisdom (Santa Sophia, Aya Sofya) at Constantinople, which can still be seen more or less in the form that Justinian gave to it.

> The architecture of Santa Sophia is essentially an architecture of space. The Byzantines seem to have concerned themselves much less about the exterior aspect of their buildings. . . . It was the interior that was all-important. . . . Here the intention was to give an impression of movement by covering the walls with shimmering colours. . . . The decoration owed much of its effect to a subtle use of light. . . .
>
> There must be symmetry, achieved by the perfect realisation of geometric possibilities. There must be a feeling of movement; for movement meant life. Plotinus [205–69/70] had defined beauty as symmetry irradiated by life. The Byzantines agreed with this. And their use of light, and of shade, was intended to make every mosaic, even every bas-relief, shimmer with movement. At the same time the spectator's glance was expected to move. He was not to stare fixedly, but to let his eye wander across and up and down the building or the picture, noting the harmonious sequences of the parts till he could appreciate the whole. A favourite theme of Byzantine philosophy was diversity creating unity.
>
> Santa Sophia was unique: there were no attempts to copy it, at Constantinople or elsewhere. . . . The construction of St Sophia belonged to an age when the Roman idea of empire was still dominant, when Majesty expressed itself in size and magnificence.
>
> The Church of St Sophia . . . was the fourth church on the site. The basilica of Constantine [I] was rebuilt by Constantius [II] with a 'trick' dome which fell [shortly after the] accession of Julian the Apostate [361]. The third church, built by Theodosius [I], was burnt in the Nika riots. The architect of the fourth church was Anthemius of Tralles [Aydin]. . . . Under Anthemius ten thousand workmen finished the building in about six years, by which time it had cost, according to the estimate of Professor Paparigopoulos, about ten million sterling in our values. Such extravagance strained even the resources of Constantinople in the Golden Age. . . .
>
> It is not until one gets inside that one recovers something of the impression that inspired medieval and modern travellers with

Figure 43 The interior of Santa Sophia at Constantinople, as seen by G. Fossati in the sixteenth century. (The Conway Library, Courtauld Institute of Art)

pages of eulogies and ecstasies. . . . Of the original glories of the interior decoration [however] there alone remain the columns and the mosaics. . . .

In Justinian's day the service of the cathedral employed 1,000 people, and its upkeep the rentals of 11,000 shops. There were 100 singing eunuchs and 200 choir boys. There was even a choir of 100 women, a concession to art contrary to orthodoxy. Three hundred musicians in crimson silk played harps, cymbals, dulcimers, mandolines, tambourines, and zithers. . . .

Five years' revenue from Egypt had been expended on the pulpit (*ambon*). . . . In the sacristy were the chariots of Constantine and Helena [his mother], made of solid silver, and such a quantity of gold plate that it took 100 porters to carry it in procession. But of greater value than all was, to medieval eyes, the hundreds of relics, records of every important event in Scripture, from the True Cross and Crown of Thorns down to the Crib of Bethlehem.[11]

From an architectural point of view, Santa Sophia represented, on a vast scale, the concept of rectangular basilica combined with circular mausoleum. (There were also other important Justinianic buildings at Constantinople as well.)[12]

But it was not only at Constantinople that there were significant churches of this period. They were also to be found at Ravenna.

The apse mosaic of Sant'Apollinare in Classe (535–49) shows an allegorical representation of the Transfiguration, the large cross which occupies the central position symbolising the Transfigured Christ, and the sheep close beside it the three Apostles who witnessed the scene.

This type of symbolism belongs to the Semitic world, and it probably came to Italy from Syria along with the Christian faith. . . . It is, indeed, one of the most successful pieces of decoration that have come down to us.[13]

But the greatest construction, or reconstruction, in Justinian I's Italy was San Vitale in the same city.

San Vitale is an essentially Byzantine church with an essentially Byzantine mosaic decoration inside it, even if certain eastern and certain classical elements can be isolated by means of a careful stylistic analysis.

The main apse of San Vitale (526–47) is occupied by a very beautiful composition, showing Christ enthroned upon the orb of heaven. The treatment is basically idealistic and naturalistic, and the colouring is particularly fresh and lovely. The panels at the side of the presbytery, which include portraits of Justinian [I] and Theodora and their courts, on the other hand, are much more eastern in conception.[14]

Sant'Apollinare Nuovo, in the same city of Ravenna, was another Justinianic building, again with superb mosaics.

The scriptural scenes along the nave walls . . . constitute one of the earliest and most complete series of New Testament scenes that survive, and tell the story of Christ's life and passion with great vividness and expression. Classical and eastern ideas are here

Figure 44 Church of S. Apollinare Nuovo, Ravenna, built in 490 by Theoderic in honour of St Martin. (The Photographic Collection, The Warburg Institute)

once more blended. . . .

The lovely processions of saints at a lower level are to be assigned to the third period, that of Justinian I. They were set up soon after 561 when the church was rededicated as an Orthodox instead of an Arian sanctuary.

The character of the ruler who inspired all this magnificence is worth considering. Weak-willed and vacillating as he could often be, Justinian was – with anyone except his wife – an autocrat through and through. He possessed in full measure the faults which are all too frequently associated with absolute power: the vanity, the quickness of temper, the occasional bursts of almost paranoid suspicion, the childish jealousy of anyone (though it was usually Belisarius) who he feared might threaten his prestige.

On the other hand, his energy astonished all who knew him, while his capacity for hard work was apparently without limit. Known within his court as *akoimetos* (the sleepless) he would spend whole days and nights together pondering on affairs of state, attending personally to the minutest details, wearing out whole successions of secretaries and scribes as the sky darkened, then lightened, then darkened again outside the palace windows.

Such, he believed, were the duties imposed by God upon an emperor; and he performed those duties with conscientious dedication and – at least until the very last years of his life – with unfailing efficiency. . . . He must also move out among his people, dazzling them with a majesty and magnificence that reflected the glory of the empire itself. . . . He worked ceaselessly, indefatigably, as few rulers in history have ever worked, for what he believed to be the good of his subjects. . . . More than any other monarch in the history of Byzantium, he stamped the empire with the force of his own character; centuries were to pass before it emerged from his shadow.[15]

A.H.M. Jones, too, offers a fairly favourable opinion of Justinian I.

Whatever may be the verdict on his policy and achievements, there can be no doubt that Justinian was a commanding personality and a most conscientious emperor. He was lucky in being served by a number of able generals and ministers, but he had at least the merit of having picked them out and promoted them, often from very humble posts, and he directed their policy and commanded their unswerving loyalty.

His own abilities were not perhaps of the first order, but he used them to the full in the service of the empire. He was immensely industrious, regularly working far into the night, and his legislation shows that he took an active interest in all departments of government and had a remarkably detailed knowledge of their complexities.

His laws also show that he was deeply concerned for the welfare of his subjects, and strove to give them honest governors, protect them from fiscal extortion and assure them uncorrupt justice.

Justinian had two major passions which overrode all other considerations. He was in the first place a Roman to the core. It was his boast that Latin was his native tongue. . . . His second passion was religion. He was an earnest Christian.[16]

Yet Justinian I, for all his ability, seemed withdrawn, and lacked the common touch. There was also a fearful plague during his reign: although for that he cannot be blamed. But he left the Treasury exhausted, and the economy ruined, and his eastern empire (the only one that had survived) on the verge of collapse. A somewhat cheerless period followed him, even if its miseries have been exaggerated. Nevertheless, it is as a prelude to the remarkable achievements of Justinian that the whole of the fifth century can be regarded, and often has been regarded;[17] though that has often unduly prevented the consideration of the century in its own right.

NOTES

INTRODUCTION

1 Gibbon (*The Decline and Fall of the Roman Empire* [1776–88], Ch. 32) took a gloomy view of the Byzantine empire which, it seemed to him, 'subsisted in a state of premature and perpetual decay'. See also the extreme hostility of W. Lecky, *History of European Morals* (1869). N.H. Baynes, *The Byzantine Empire* (1925), p. 243, which, conceding excessive adherence to 'inherited moulds', objected to the idea of the empire's 'unchanging rigidity'. F.W. Walbank (*The Awful Revolution* [1969], p. 110) called the Byzantine state 'a rump'. But see now Moorcock, *Times Literary Supplement*, 17 November 1945, p. 10. There is much dispute whether the fifth century AD should be called 'Byzantine' or 'proto-Byzantine' or 'late antique'. In fact, however, it should be considered in its own right (see Epilogue), though without too rigid an idea that this (or for that matter any other) century should be regarded as a separate, independent period. Professor Norman Baynes, Sir Steven Runciman, and (a few) other distinguished experts, have done a great deal to put Byzantium on the map.

2 I am particularly well aware of this because I lived for five years at Ankara. I found that in Britain very little was known about Asia Minor, which did not surprise me since I had not heard much about it at school or university. In particular, the extraordinary diversity of the area passed unrecognised, since it looks homogeneous enough on the map. Research on Rome's eastern provinces (led by archaeology) has greatly increased, despite the comparative absence of books; and I hope that this is now beginning to hit Asia Minor. The British Institute at Ankara, which now produces a journal, *Anatolian Archaeology*, is proving very useful in this respect, but I confess that I am not unbiased, since the Institute particularly interests me. The dimensions and complexities of Asia Minor were described by J. Freely, *Companion Guide* (1984), p. 15, who called it 'a vast sub-continent with an enormous variety of topography and scenery'. See also Classical Numismatic Conference on 'Western Asia Minor in Graeco-Roman Times', Berkeley (1996); F.V.T. Arundell, *Discoveries in Asia Minor* (reprint 1975); W.C. Bryce, *Encyclopaedia Britannica* (1971 edn) vol. II, pp. 605, 612; *Journal of Roman Studies*, 86, 1996, pp. 219ff.; K. Ashton (ed.) *Studies in Ancient Coinage from Turkey* (1996); C.S. Lightfoot (ed.), *Recent Turkish Coin Hoards and Numismatic Studies* (1991).

Asia Minor is the principal land-link between Europe and Asia and has often witnessed conflicts between western and eastern civilisation.

The populations of Asia Minor have always been extremely mixed. See M.N. Turfan, *Blue Guide* (1969), pp. 13f.: 'Anatolia (Anadolu) has for the last 9000 years been the homeland of many distinct civilisations. It is a land rich in heritage, home through the ages to peoples of diverse origins, diverse lives, diverse contributions.' How right of him to stress the *diversity* of the peninsula, called by the Turks the 'Land of Civilisations' – which is so easily neglected or brushed aside by its unitary appearance on the map and its modern designation as 'Turkey in Asia'. For the Iron Age population of Asia Minor in general, see P.R. Helm in M. Grant and R. Kitzinger (eds), *Civilization of the Ancient Mediterranean* (1988), I, p. 146; and for Greco-Roman times, S. Lloyd, *Ancient Turkey* (1989), pp. 76ff. See also J. Steele, *Turkey: A Traveller's Historical and Architectural Guide* (1990), S. Mitchell, *Anatolia: Land, Men and Gods in Asia Minor* (1993).

    This is only one, very important, part of the recognition that the Byzantine empire did not consist of Constantinople alone – although it was 'the dazzling crown of the empire' [C. Diehl, *Byzantine Portraits* [1927], pp. 337f.) – but also of provinces. For over against the capital is the rest of the empire. Over against the rottenness of court life are the provincials with their rough, solid virtues – less refined, less elegant, perhaps, but at the same time less corrupt. Over against the paltry minds of the courtiers and traitors are the earnest, sober middle classes, the old provincial nobility – countrified, brave and warlike – and the sturdy eastern peasantry. From their ranks the administration is recruited, the framework of the huge edifice; and they composed the army that again and again carried the imperial standards to victory all over the east. We are granted, it is true, few glimpses of this other Byzantium; the obscure lives of those who constituted it come only too seldom into the full light of history. Nevertheless, they did exist; and they served as an inexhaustible reservoir of strength for the preservation and glory of the Byzantine empire.

3 The misgovernment of Asia Minor by Byzantium is often stressed, but this was not particularly noticeable by the fifth century – or, when it existed, it was not a new phenomenon, and did not, in any case, hamper the continued (or growing) prosperity of many of the towns (see note 4), despite the increased greatness of Constantinople, which held them in check. There were imperial troops to keep order, in many cities (or to keep out the Germans); see R. MacMullen, *Soldier and Civilian in the Later Empire* (1963), pp. 187, 215. The birth-rate seems to have been high in the peninsula.

4 Pausanias, *Guide to Rome*, VII. For the Arcadian Way at Ephesus see G. Koch, *Early Christian Art and Architecture: An Introduction* (1966), p. 65 and fig. 28. There have been recent, rather surprising, fifth-century excavations at the place. Smyrna (Izmir) confronted it with some success. Miletus (Balat) declined in the fourth and fifth centuries, but then recovered, housing many churches. Sardes (Sart) (a major producer of glass) maintained its position until at least the seventh century (see C. Foss, *Ephesus after Antiquity* [1979]). Aphrodisias (Geyre) is an important source of information for the period. For Side (Selimiye or Eski Antalya) see J. Nollé, *Side in Altertum* (1993).

5 The principal part of Cappadocia was a massive, rugged tract of mountainous territory, with some table-land. For the prominence of Isauria, see below, Ch. 7.

6 *Journal of Roman Studies*, 1943, p. 31; see also D. Talbot Rice, *The Byzantines* (1962), p. 39. It is doubtful whether Armenia should be considered part of Asia Minor; but it is worth mentioning that, although partitioned by Theodosius I, in the fifth century it enjoyed a cultural (if not political) Golden Age.

7 A beginning was made to examine this theme in M. Grant, *The Fall of the Roman Empire* (1976, 1990, 1996), Appendix 2.

8 A.H.M. Jones, *The Later Roman Empire 284–602* (1964), p. 957.

9 A. Cameron, *The Mediterranean World in Late Antiquity* (1993), pp. 66f.; see pp. 128, 220 n. 1. Perhaps the last appearance of paganism was as a design on textiles (see Chapter 12). The Church Councils, however, seem nowadays 'somehow irrelevant' (ibid., p. 21). But for the pre-eminence of the super natural in the Byzantine view, see Mango, *Byzantium*, p. 151.
10 *History of the Wars of Justinian*, V, 3, 5f.; see G. Mathew, *Byzantine Aesthetics* (1963), p. 71, and Chapter 4, n. 7.
11 See G. Young, *Constantinople* (1992), p. 28.
12 See P. Brown, *Religion and Society in the Age of St Augustine* (1979), p. 11: 'Nothing is quite what it appears in the late empire'; see also F. Lot, *The End of the Ancient World* (1931), p. 203. Yet the fifth century is 'the birth-hour of our modern civilization' (A.H.T. Clarke, *Fortnightly Review*, 120, 1923, p. 332). It was certainly an acute, memorable period of transition.
13 W.B. Anderson, *Sidonius Apollinaris* (Loeb edn, 1965), p. ix.
14 M. Andreades in N.H. Baynes and H. St L.B. Moss (eds), *Byzantium* (1949), pp. 71f.; G. Mathew, *Byzantine Aesthetics*, p. 64.

1 ROME AND OTHER CITIES

1 *Panegyric* IV (X), 3.3, 6.1, 6.4; M. Grant, *The Emperor Constantine* (1993), p. 116.
2 Herodian II, 11, 9; see W. Ensslin, *Cambridge Ancient History*, XII (1956), p. 374. 'Until Theodosius [I] the emperor's life was a constant chasing from one end of the empire to the other' (p. 202). 'His successors were more sedentary.'
3 See M. Grant, *History of Rome* (1978, 1996), pp. 284f. Furthermore, under Ambrose, Mediolanum (Milan) became the spiritual capital of the western world. The big cities drew on the wealth and population of the smaller centres; see Introduction, n. 3.
4 Cassiodorus, *Chronica*, AD 275, *Scriptores Historiae Augustae (Aurelian)*, 21.9; D.R. Dudley, *Urbs Roma* (1967), pp. 35f., W. Ensslin, *Cambridge Ancient History*; L. Homo, *Essai sur le règne de l'empereur Aurélien* (1904), pp. 221f.; F. Lot, *The End of the Ancient World* (1931), pp. 21f.
5 H. Mattingly in *Cambridge Ancient History*, XII, p. 298.
6 For Mediolanum as a Tetrarchic capital see R. Krautheimer, *Early Christian and Byzantine Architecture* (1965), pp. 516f.
7 A.H.M. Jones, *The Later Roman Empire 284–602* (1964), p. 40.
8 Refs in P. Brown, *Augustine of Hippo* (1967), p. 290.
9 Jerome, *Preface to Ezekiel*, F.A. Wright, *Select Letters of St Jerome* (Loeb edn, 1963), p. x.
10 Pelagius, *Epistula ad Demetriadem*, 30; Brown, *Augustine*, p. 289.
11 H. Dessau, *Inscriptiones Latinae Selectae* (1892–1916), 544; A. Alföldi in *Cambridge Ancient History*, XII, p. 213.
12 Alföldi, *Cambridge Ancient History*, XII, p. 189.
13 See also above, n. 4.
14 It is disputed where Valentinian III was crowned.
15 Ferrandus (d. 546/7), *Vie de Saint Fulgence de Ruspe* (1929); see P. Llewellyn, *Rome in the Dark Ages* (1971, 1993), p. 21. Fabius Fulgentius Planciades wrote on mythology (published at Basel in 1535) and compiled a commentary on Virgil's *Aeneid* in dialogue form. His bishopric of Ruspe seems a little uncertain, see J.A. Butler (transl. and ed.), *Edward Herbert: Pagan Religion* (1996), p. 212, n. 2.
16 Rutilius Namatianus, *Carmen De Reditu Suo*, I, 66.

17 Llewellyn, *Rome in the Dark Ages*. Rich people in Rome included Plinianus and his wife Melania, who sold their vast and widespread estates in *c.* 410. See also Symmachus in the Bibliography.

18 See R. MacMullen, *Soldier and Civilian in the Later Roman Empire* (1963), p. 223, n. 60. But Augusta Trevirorum (Trier: a centre for the making of military uniforms) was devastated four times during the fifth century. See E.M. Wightman, *Roman Trier and the Treviri* (1911, 1970).

19 See F.W. Walbank, *The Awful Revolution* (1969), p. 86. Arelate was the headquarters of the Praetorian Prefect of Gaul. Constantine I the Great resided there. The town remained an important centre, and coins were issued there (e.g. by Romulus Augustulus, the last Roman emperor, 475–6). Archbishop Caesarius of Arelate (470 to 542 or 543) was a famous Churchman.

20 M. Grant, *The Emperor Constantine* (1993), pp. 44, 118.

21 *Scriptores Historiae Augustae, Probus*, 18.8, 21.2; cf. 3.1.

22 Yet the search for Galerius's imperial residence at Sirmium has been elusive. As A. Boethius and J.B. Ward-Perkins (*Etruscan and Roman Architecture* [1970], p. 579) wrote: 'The current excavations at Sirmium have not revealed any certain remains of the imperial palace.' However, Constantine I the Great is supposed to have inhabited Galerius's palace, and to have enlarged it. Sirmium, the capital of Illyricum until the seat of the prefect was moved to Thessalonica (Salonica) in *c.* 442, was often the residence of emperors (Theodosius II lived there for a time) and high officials. It was also the headquarters of an archer cohort and two legions. The town was strategically situated on the Via Egnatia, which was, however, very vulnerable once the Danube line was breached. *Antoniniani* of Gallienus (base silver pieces of two *denarii*) are attributed to Sirmium. A. Alföldi, *Numizmatikai Közlony*, 26–7, 1927–8, pp. 23f.

23 The date of this war, however, is disputed (Grant, *Emperor Constantine*, p. 42).

24 Ibid., pp. 156, 158.

25 Ibid., p. 117. Once Constantinople was established, the second city of the empire was Thessalonica (Salonica), which was the only eastern town, apart from Constantinople, to issue gold coinage during the fifth century. In 442/3 the capital of the prefecture of Illyricum was moved there for protection from the Huns.

26 Ibid., pp. 115f. *Fragmenta Historicorum Graecorum*, IV, 189. Constantine moved his headquarters to Serdica in 317/18, and announced the appointment of his three new Caesars there.

27 See below, Ch. 9. Antioch's theological (now Christian) tradition was immense, and the intellectual ferment continued. The churches were always full, and in spite of corruption there was great wealth – much of it in the hands of ten families; see also Ch. 3, n. 7; and for Alexandria, n. 29 below, and Ch. 3, n. 8.

28 Grant, *Emperor Constantine*, p. 118.

29 C. Foss in C. Mango and H. Dagron, *Constantinople and Its Hinterland* (1995), pp. 181, 183, 187. Nicomedia was conveniently equidistant from the Danube and the Euphrates. Galerius was named Caesar there. Valentinian I and Valens were elevated to the throne at Nicaea (Iznik), from which, however, the ecclesiastical Council of 451 was moved to Chalcedon (Kadiköy). Nor must Egypt be forgotten. Alexandria was a great city in which Christianity pullulated. The country was extremely rich, and abounded with sailors. For its other characteristics, see Ch. 3 n. 8. However, Alexandria was hostile to the Council of Chalcedon, because, there, primacy was granted to Constantinople.

2 THE DIVIDED EMPIRE

1 M. Grant, *The Fall of the Roman Empire* (1976, 1990, 1996), pp. 113f. (references in these notes are not to the original Annenberg School Press edition but to the Collier Books [Macmillan Publishing Company, New York] and Weidenfeld & Nicolson paperback edition [1990]); *The Climax of Rome* (1968), p. 68. Carausius ruled in Britain from *c.* 287 to 293, and was succeeded there by his murderer Allectus, who was slain in *c.* 296/7 by Asclepiodotus, the Praetorian Prefect of Constantius I, the Caesar of Maximian and father of Constantine I the Great. Gratian, the son of Valentinian I, ruled in the west from 375 to 383. Theodosius I, the son of Count Theodosius, was proclaimed Augustus in 379 and ruled first in the east and then in the west, and then (for the last time) over an undivided empire (394–5; see List of Emperors, at end of book).

3 CONSTANTINOPLE

1 G. Young, *Constantinople* (1992), pp. 23f; C. Mango, in C. Mango and G. Dagron, *Constantinople and Its Hinterland* (1995), pp. 5f. Constantine I the Great's decision has been the subject of argument. Did he really intend Constantinople to be the imperial capital? He proceeded with some caution. See M. Grant, *The Emperor Constantine* (1993), Ch. 7, pp. 116ff. For the idea of Constantinople as the 'New Rome', N.H. Baynes, *The Byzantine Empire* (1925), p. 77. R. Krautheimer (*Three Christian Capitals* [1983], pp. 41–67) is believed by some to attribute too much to Constantine. But Constantine certainly established a complex of public buildings in the city he had refounded as Constantinople, see C. Mango, *Le développement urbain de Constantinople: IVe–VIIe siècle*, 2nd edn, 1990. Theodosius I embarked on an ambitious programme of reconstruction and enlargement of the place.

2 Grant, *The Emperor Constantine*, pp. 119f.; see Zosimus, *New History*, II, 31, 35:

> The size of Constantinople was increased until it was by far the greatest city, with the result that many of the succeeding emperors chose to live there, and attracted an unnecessarily large population which came from all over the world – soldiers and officials, traders and other professions.
>
> Therefore, they have surrounded it with new walls much more extensive than those of Constantine [Ch. 11] and allowed the buildings to be so close to each other that the inhabitants, whether at home or in the streets, are crowded for room, and it is dangerous to walk about because of the great number of men and beasts.
>
> And a lot of the sea round about has been turned into land by sinking piles and building houses on them, which by themselves are enough to fill a large city.

Zosimus was a Greek historian who wrote this work, a *New History of the Roman Empire* from Augustus to AD 410. He completed it after 408. He was a pagan.

3 A.H.M. Jones, *The Later Roman Empire 284–602* (1964), pp. 692ff., 703. Detailed discussions of the food and water supply of Constantinople are provided in Mango and Dagron, *Constantinople*, in the same volume, Feissel (pp. 367ff.) deals with immigration to the city, and P. Magdalino (p. 35), with its population (mainly later); the number of the inhabitants of the city after 413 was probably 300,000–400,000. The Church of Constantinople was at first

under the Metropolitan of Heraclea (Ereğli). At the (Robber) Council at Ephesus (449), Constantinople obtained official approval of the territories it had
acquired. In due course, its Patriarch displaced Ephesus, and Pulcheria (following what was already a tradition) built three churches at Constantinople, all
dedicated to the Virgin Mary; see Ch. 8.

4 R.M. Haywood, *The Myth of Rome's Fall* (1960), pp. 126–7.

5 S. Runciman, *Byzantine Civilisation* (1933), pp. 163, 170, 15f.

6 E. Gibbon, *Decline and Fall of the Roman Empire* (1776–88), Ch. 17.

7 Antioch (on which see also Ch. 1, n. 27), although it suffered from serious
earthquakes, and was strategically vulnerable, was very rich, and its experts
were well informed (especially about the Resurrection). In the time of
Valerian (253–60) the imperial camp headquarters had been at Antioch, and
Valens (364–78) ruled there, moving from Constantinople. See references in
A. Cameron, *The Mediterranean World in Late Antiquity* (1993), p. 227, n. 3.

8 For Alexandria, about which there is quite a lot of recent literature (e.g. C.
Haas, *Alexandria in Late Antiquity* [1996]); see also Ch. 1, n. 29. Alexandria had
enjoyed the same distributions as Rome since 332. The city had immense
prestige (see the 'Meet us in Alexandria' training course at Beloit College,
1993; and for the Library D. Delia, *American Historical Review*, 97, pp. 1449ff.).
Alexandria proclaimed the Incarnation with authority, especially as its philosophical school was very important. Jerome criticised the bishop of Jerusalem
in 386–7 for referring to Alexandria rather than Antioch. Cyril of Alexandria
brought about the fall of Nestorius, bishop of Constantinople, in 431, and in
the same reign of Theodosius II Pope Celestinus supported Alexandria
against Constantinople. But the Council of Chalcedon (451) was a defeat
for Alexandria's claim of ecclesiastical supremacy, to the advantage of Constantinople. For the strong nationalism of Egypt and Syria alike, see N.H.
Baynes, *The Byzantine Empire* (1925), p. 42. See also Saad-El-Din (etc.),
Alexandria: the Site and Its History (1996), and the *Chronicles of Alexandria* (A.
Bauer and J. Strzygowski, *Eine Alexandrinische Weltchronik* [1905]).

9 See below, Ch. 11: this was an epoch when many cities were given walls.
Constantinople was also protected from maritime assault by the rapid waters
of the Bosphorus. Theoderic marched on the city in 487, but was diverted.

10 K.S. Painter, in J.P.C. Kent and K.S. Painter, *Wealth of the Roman World AD 300–
700* (1977), p. 77.

4 THE FALL OF ROME

1 I dealt with this subject, to the best of my ability, in *The Fall of the Roman
Empire* (1976, 1996). I would now cite also M. Wes, *Im Westen des römischen
Reichs* (1967), with which I was not familiar; and I have a few points to add
here. Italy was in a miserable state. There were famines, there and elsewhere
(e.g. in Pannonia); the Roman world was constantly on the edge of starvation.
For attitudes to Germans, see G.B. Ludner, *Viator*, VII, 1976. Many Germans
had been inside the empire since the disastrous battle of Adrianople (Edirne)
in 378, and before; see also evidence from graves. The poverty (more widespread even than ever before) was violently attacked by S. Dill, *Roman Society in
the Last Century of the Western Empire* (1898, 1958), pp. 228ff., and taxation by
B.W. Wells, *Sewanee Review*, 1922, pp. 421ff., though it has also been argued
that taxation was not a major cause of the fall of the western empire (but see
Ch. 5, n. 1). Valentinian II had already attacked extortion. Undoubtedly, there
was too much centralisation in the western empire – causing an alienation

from the excessively expensive and demanding state system – although the alternative of town councillors (*decuriones, curiales*: see below) and of regional or local *comitiva*, replacing state service, was not attractive. The lack of natural heirs to the western imperial throne after 458 played a significant part in the fall. And brigandage proliferated. In general, there was too much violence. Moreover, the local aristocracies (although their members occasionally renounced the world, and retired) were not free from blame. 'The nobles', said J.B. Bury (*Quarterly Review*, 192, 1900, pp. 129ff.), 'put their money into land, which depressed industry and drove out the small farmer and created big estates [which destroyed many cities] . . . and thus led to the economic ruin of Italy.' O. Seeck's belief in racial dilution now seems dated: depopulation is doubtful (n. 24), as indeed are purely economic explanations (n. 25), and Marxists have talked too much about slaves as the cause of the fall; had they been much more numerous earlier? E. Gibbon, *Decline and Fall of the Roman Empire*, is illuminating. The *coloni* were the most typical rural population; but there was no simple transition from *colonus* to medieval serf. Agriculture was very important. G. Alföldy, *The Social History of Rome* (rev. edn 1988; 1975, 1985), pp. 190ff., 201ff., doubts if it is correct to describe the *curiales* as middle class; they must not be generalised about (p. 224, n. 222; but see Ch. 5, n. 3).

2 A. Ferrill, *The Fall of the Roman Empire: The Military Explanation* (1983, 1988), pp. 166, 168. The 'humiliation' to which Ferrill refers was the invasion across the Rhine (on the last day of 406). This occurred during the western reign of Honorius, whose reign was dominated by German invasions. On 410, see also E.R. Chamberlin, *The Sack of Rome*, New York (1979); and for horrified reactions by Churchmen see Ch. 4. After sacking the city, Alaric I marched south, and died. What remained of his army settled in Aquitania, see Appendix 2. See now T.S. Burns, *Barbarians within the Gates of Rome* (1994); P. Heather, *Goths and Romans* (1994).

3 A.H.M. Jones, *The Later Roman Empire 284–602* (1964), p. 1025; see R.M. Haywood, *The Myth of Rome's Fall* (1960), p. 156. On Augustine, see also Bibliography.

4 See Gibbon, *Decline and Fall*, Ch. 34.

5 Gibbon (*Decline and Fall*) calls Alaric's successor 'Adolphus'. Haywood, etc., call him Athaulf. He was assassinated in 415.

6 F. Lot, *The End of the Ancient World* (1931), pp. 207f. Jordanes was a Greek historian of the sixth century. He summarised the *Gothic Histories* of Cassiodorus (*c.* 490–*c.* 583) in his *Getica*. Jordanes was probably a Goth. It is uncertain whether he wrote his books in Italy or in Constantinople. See Jordanes, *Histoire des Gothes: aux origines de l'Europe* (translated into French 1995).

7 Procopius, III, iii, 15, see S. Perowne, *The End of the Roman World* (1966), p. 81. Procopius was a Greek historian born at Caesarea in Palestine in about 500. His principal work was his *History of the Wars of Justinian* (see Appendix 3); and he also wrote a virulent *Secret History*. See now A. Cameron, *Procopius* (paperback), 1996, and Bibliography (Greek writers).

8 See J.B. Bury, *History of the Later Roman Empire* (1958 edn), I, p. 299. Valentinian III was said to have been incited by the next emperor, Petronius Maximus (455–6), see n. 11.

9 See also Appendix 2.

10 R.A.G. Carson, *Coins of the Roman Empire* (1990), p. 207.

11 455 by Gaiseric (Appendix 2). For these last twenty years of the western empire see C. Scarre, *Chronicle of the Roman Empire* (1995), pp. 231f.:

> Valentinian III was succeeded by Petronius Maximus, a wealthy senator and leading member of the Italian aristocracy. His riches had bought him the support of the troops, but he was killed just eleven weeks later while trying to flee Rome in the face of a Vandal attack. The Vandals [Appendix 2] had crossed to north Africa in 429 and established a strong kingdom from which they were able to raid the Italian peninsula. In June 455 they captured Rome and spent two weeks sacking the city, leading the empress Licinia Eudoxia (Valentinian's widow) and her two daughters away into captivity. The next emperor was proclaimed not in Italy but in Gaul. This was Avitus, the friend and nominee of the Visigothic king Theoderic II, who was proclaimed emperor in July 455 at Tolosa [Toulouse], where Theoderic had established his court. The following year, however, the Suevian army commander Ricimer rebelled at Ravenna. Avitus marched against him but was captured in battle at Placentia [Piacenza] in October 456. Ricimer neutralised him by making him bishop of Placentia, but Avitus was soon forced to flee back to Gaul and died shortly afterwards. Avitus's overthrow and murder was followed by an eighteen-month interregnum. . . . Majorian, a distinguished senator, was officially installed in December 457. Ricimer at length became troubled by Majorian's growing power and decided to overthrow him. Majorian was returning from Gaul in August 461 when he was captured by Ricimer, tortured and beheaded. Ricimer then installed a harmless senator, Libius Severus, as the emperor Severus III. The authority of Ricimer and his puppet-emperor now barely extended beyond the Italian peninsula, and even there they were harassed by Vandal raids from north Africa. . . . Anthemius was proclaimed emperor in Italy in April 467, but . . . in July 472 Ricimer marched on Rome, captured Anthemius and put him to death. Ricimer appointed a Roman noble Olybrius to succeed Anthemius, but Ricimer himself died in August 472 and Olybrius in November. Effective powers passed to a Burgundian prince, Gundobad, who in March 473 nominated Glycerius his puppet-emperor . . . [but when] in June 474 [the eastern emperor] Zeno dispatched a new candidate, Julius Nepos, to Italy . . . Glycerius fled. . . . But a year later [Julius Nepos] too was overthrown by his army commander Orestes . . . [who] installed his son Romulus Augustulus. But neither Orestes nor Augustulus had any real power. That lay with the German mercenaries who now dominated the Roman armies. In the summer of 476 they staged the final *coup d'état*, demanding one third of the land of Italy for themselves. When Orestes refused their demand he was killed and his son deposed. On 4 September 476 the 16-year-old Romulus Augustulus abdicated imperial office and retired to the Gulf of Naples with a pension. . . . The abdication of Romulus Augustulus was the final act in the demise of a once-great office.

12 The origins of Odoacer (Odovacar) are disputed: see A.M. Rollins, *The Fall of*

Rome: A Reference Guide (1983). Was he a Scirian German? Or was his father a Hun? He is described as tolerant and efficient by Perowne, *End of the World*, p. 95. Although an Arian, he showed deference to the Pope. He was overthrown and murdered by the Ostrogoth Theoderic (Theodoric), on whom see B. Saitta, *La civiltà di Teoderico* (1944); A. Garcia, *Teodorico e Bizanzio* (1994). For the constitutional position of these post-imperial rulers see A.H.M. Jones, *Journal of Roman Studies*, 52, 1962, p. 12, J.F. Matthews, *Journal of Roman Studies*, 58, 1968, pp. 165ff. And for the Goths in general see H. Wolfram, *History of the Goths* (1988); P. Heather, *Goths and Romans 332–489* (1994). See also Ch. 7.

13 Haywood, *Myth of Rome's Fall*, p. 262; see also p. 156.
14 D. Kagan, *The Decline and Fall of the Roman Empire* (1912), pp. viif.
15 Grant, *Fall of the Roman Empire*, p. vii.
16 Ibid., p. xii. Or should one speak of 'transformation' as many (e.g. Germans) do? See L. White (ed.), *The Transformation of the Roman World* (1966); with doubts from Ferrill, *Fall of the Roman Empire*, pp. 160f. At least the Latin language survived.
17 W.E. Kaegi, *Byzantium and the Decline of Rome* (1968), pp. 254f.
18 B. Adams, *The Law of Civilization and Decay* (1879, 1943).
19 P. Llewellyn, *Rome in the Dark Ages* (1971, 1993), pp. 22f.
20 G. Mathew, *Byzantine Aesthetics* (1963), p. 52; see also C. Lucas, *Journal of Roman Studies*, 30, 1940, p. 72.
21 P. Brown, *The World of Late Antiquity* (1971), p. 36.
22 Quoted by Grant, *Fall of the Roman Empire*, pp. 69f., esp. p. 77.
23 Ibid., pp. 22f. A. Cameron (*The Mediterranean World in Late Antiquity AD 395–600* [1993], pp. 45, 47) favours an internal but not a purely economic cause for the Fall of Rome:

> There is enough that is clear to show that the Roman government was not so much faced with discrete [individually distinct] incursions as with slow but steady erosion of Roman culture in the western provinces from within. The process was not of course understood in those terms by contemporary writers, who are inspired by ethnographic and cultural prejudice and tend to paint a lurid picture of Romans versus barbarians. . . .
> Their moral and political explanations are not adequate to explain what was happening on a broader scale. And most of the long-term changes lay outside government control. Yet it was these changes, rather than any political events, which would in the long run detach these areas from effective imperial rule, and particularly so once that control passed from the hands even of a weak western emperor to those of a government in far-away Constantinople.

24 Ibid. p. xii. Perowne, *End of the Roman World*, pp. 94f., like others, stresses depopulation. But this has been questioned (see n. 1). For Arianism, to which Odoacer subscribed, see Chapter 9.
25 But the economic type of solution (see next chapter, in text) is regarded as exaggerated, or erroneous, by Cameron (*Mediterranean World*, p. 241):

> Much of the secondary literature presents the later Roman empire as a crumbling, top-heavy economy with too few producers, too many consumers (the army, the Church, the bureaucracy) and too

heavy or otherwise inadequate system of taxation. This view is
increasingly being revised.

It is 'a dreamy and confused story'. See pp. 82, 91, 93, 97ff., 212f., n. 2. She
goes so far as to describe 476 as a 'non-event', though one cannot expect e.g.
numismatists to agree with her. Others, too, call it 'the manufacture of a
turning point'. Contemporary writers, although prepared to call Rome 'on the
threshold of Old Age', took comfort from previous disasters, from which the
city had recovered. See *Ancient*, 4, Feb. 1997, pp. 22ff.
26 The Pope was now the greatest man in Rome, and indeed in the whole of the
west. The supremacy of the popes, and their protests to Constantinople,
make a long story. For a list of popes, see the end of this book. The Roman
Church, it has been said, was the ghost of the Roman empire sitting on its
grave. See F. Dvornik, *Byzantium and the Roman Primacy* (1964); C. Falconi,
Storia dei Papi, 4 vols (1967–70); C. Rendina, *I Papi: storia e segreti* (1983); and
Chapter 6, nn. 22, 23.
27 Jones, *Later Roman Empire*, pp. 1026f.
28 E.A. Freeman, *Western Europe in the Fifth Century* (1904), pp. 101f.
29 Perowne, *End of the Roman World*, pp. 94f. The depopulation insisted upon by
Perowne has been questioned (see above, n. 1). Perowne quotes T. Hodgkin,
Theoderic the Goth: The Barbarian Champion of Civilization, p. 165.

5 FINANCE AND THE ARMIES

1 M. Grant, *The Fall of the Roman Empire* (1976, 1990, 1996), pp. 53–6, 83, 85f.
Subsidies to German tribes (both by western and eastern imperial governments) cost a lot of money. The extent of contemporary inflation within the
two empires has been much disputed, but it inevitably continued to exist. And
'a time came when the suction of the usurers so wasted the community that
the stream of bullion ceased to flow from the capital to the frontiers' (B.
Adams, *The Law of Civilization and Decay* [1895, 1959], p. 43): he writes about
the consequent impoverishment. Ambrose (*c.* 339–97) and Salvian (*c.* 400–
after 470) attacked the attitude of the rich to the poor (but suspicion of the
poor, as traitorous, also existed): a fatal blow had been struck by the con-
fiscations of vast estates, and resultant centralisation, by Septimius Severus
(193–211). On the whole, the imperial governments were of little help. Their
excessive taxation (in which, when money was lacking, payments had to be in
kind or by personal service) was not new, but caused increased oppression, as
well as brigandage (by those who tried to escape), which created a widespread
lack of security. Anastasius I relieved the tax situation in the east. Although
there were very rich families, cities often fared badly (but not Carthage, which
remained prosperous, although riots occurred; Appendix 2). The bureaucracy
was a drain on local resources, and so were increased donations and bonuses.
Trade and industry declined, and so perhaps did the total western (though
scarcely eastern) population. It is fair to speak of financial exhaustion, even in
the east, and lack of stability. Even eastern senators had to sell their jewellery.
See M. Hendy, *Studies in the Byzantine Monetary Economy AD 300–1450* (1985);
but see also Ch. 4, n. 1. The monks and nuns made a good financial policy
difficult to achieve; see Ch. 3.
2 P. Brown, *The World of Late Antiquity* (1971), pp. 43f.
3 The *curiales* (middle-class town-councillors) were caught between two fires:

their own lower class, who considered them oppressors, and their bosses, who hounded them if receipts seemed insufficient. But see Chapter 4, n. 1.

4 Grant, *Fall of the Roman Empire* pp. 31ff., 35, 37f., 46f.; P. Southern and K.R. Dixon, *The Late Roman Army* (1996). Military conscription, as in earlier times, had to be resorted to in emergencies. Paulinus of Nola (353/4–431) was against it. Major massive recruitment had passed from Italy to the lower Danube. Most soldiers (and officers) were now Germans (*foederati* or otherwise) and some were Huns. Many were mercenaries. Despite donations and bonuses, the soldiers were ill-paid. In consequence, they had to batten on civilians, who were terrified of them. They had to police cities (see Introduction, n. 3), and kept local riots down. Although the numbers of soldiers have been much disputed, they were a good deal more numerous than in earlier times – and, many would say, better at their jobs, although there was some insubordination, and the economy was not sufficiently strong to afford them. It has been said that the soldiers both made, and unmade, the empire (M. Cary, *History of the Roman World* [2nd edn, 1954], pp. 771–81; see also M. Chambers, *The Fall of Rome: Can It Be Explained?* [1963], p. 110). Gallienus (260–8) gave the army a strongly cavalry character, establishing a mobile cavalry army, and Constantine I the Great (306–37) divided the soldiery into a striking and frontier force (for which he was called 'pro-barbarian'), as well as separating the civil government from the army command. Theodosius I was also criticised for 'liberalism' to the army. Military thinking (including the work on engines of war) was largely defensive. Arms workers rioted and went on strike. It is uncertain whether the eastern empire, in the early fifth century, maintained a regular standing fleet. Arcadius (395–408) was sneered at by Synesius (*c.* 370–413) for not being a fighting man; the coins of the period lay great stress on military victory. A. Cameron (*The Mediterranean World in Late Antiquity AD 395–600* [1993], p. 10) sums up her opinion of the late imperial army (which she denies was responsible for the downfall of the western empire):

> Diversified, localised and fragmented, the Roman army, or rather armies, of the fifth and sixth centuries were far different in comparison and equipment from those of earlier days, even if not demonstrably inferior, as is often argued.
>
> Whether the army could now effectively keep out the barbarians, and if not, why not, were questions as much debated by contemporaries as by modern historians.

See R. Collins, 'The Disappearance of the Roman Army' (*Early Medieval Europe, 300–1000*). The army needed to be near the money amassed by the tax-collectors. Cameron stresses the vast extent of the borders it had to defend. Yet Sozomen (d. *c.* AD 450) omitted generalship from an emperor's necessary qualities, since there were others to do the job.

5 R. MacMullen, *Corruption and the Decline of Rome* (1988), p. 204.

6 EAST AND WEST

1 M. Grant, *The Fall of the Roman Empire* (1976, 1990, 1996), pp. 115–18, 121. Gratian reigned in the west from 375 to 383, Magnus Maximus was a Spaniard whose western rising lasted from 383 to 388; he was at first recognised by Theodosius I. Stilicho was murdered in 408, and Rufinus

had been assassinated by Stilicho in 395. There has been a lot of argument about whether, and to what extent, Stilicho was responsible for the bad relations of the west with the east (which centred, in part, over the disputed ownership of Illyricum).

2 G. Downey, *The Late Roman Empire* (1969), p. 72. And, in the east, the Hellenistic tradition was stronger; see Kahrt and Sherwin-White (eds), *Hellenism in the East* (1987). Not that everything was pleasant in the eastern empire: for example there was not only bureaucracy but nepotism (e.g. in favour of the family of the Praetorian Prefect Anthemius). And state supremacy was widely imposed (N.H. Baynes, *The Byzantine Empire* [1925], pp. 240ff., 83).

3 M.T.W. Arnheim, *The Senatorial Aristocracy in the Later Roman Empire* (1972), is illuminating on this subject.

4 R.A.G. Carson, *Coins of the Roman Empire* (1990), pp. 210, 217; see also R.M. Haywood, *The Myth of Rome's Fall* (1958), pp. 165, 159. Attila the Hun posed a severe threat to Constantinople in 447: see G. Young, *Constantinople* (1992), pp. 33f.; see Aquileia Conference 1996 (Attila e gli Unni). Was he bought off by the eastern emperor Theodosius II (n. 8)? Marcian refused to pay him any more (see Ch. 7, n. 5).

5 Gainas had been in charge of the regular eastern army, perhaps under the nominal supreme command of Stilicho (see above, n. 1). This eastern army had for some time been increasingly Gothic (although the predominance of 'barbarians' in the west was regarded as a temporary phenomenon in the east). But we do not know how, by what 'miraculous' means, Gainas was dislodged from Constantinople (though it was said to have been another German, Fravitta, who achieved it, with the help of the Patriarch). 'Clever diplomacy' is the phrase of F. Lot (*The End of the Ancient World* [1931], p. 220) about a later development. For Gainas's helper Tribigild, see E.A. Thompson, *Romans and Barbarians* (1982), p. 269, n. 16.

6 It has been emphasised, however, that these tribes were 'insecurely perched'.

7 See A.H.M. Jones, *The Later Roman Empire 284–602* (1964), pp. 688, 710.

8 Downey, *Late Roman Empire*, p. 81. A lot depends on whether the eastern emperor Theodosius II – who was under severe pressure from the Huns – really did *buy off* Attila, so that he invaded the western instead of the eastern empire (n. 4). It has been suggested that at first Theodosius II toyed with the idea of governing the west himself.

9 Grant, *Fall of the Roman Empire*, pp. 116ff. It is true that the eastern empire was in a more favourable geographical position – and that the situation both of the cities and of the farm-workers was more satisfactory. But there were bureaucrats in the east as well as the west (ibid.; see above, n. 2), and there were about 200,000 *curiales* (*decurions*, town councillors) in the east, and there were compulsions; the social cost of survival was enormous. But the *morale* of the easterners was a great help (see P. Whitting, *Byzantium* [1968], p. 3). They believed that their empire was God-given and God-protected. According to Norman Baynes the fact that the eastern empire *was* a single state (even if excessively centralised – a fact which caused the downfall of the west) was what saved it.

> It may be said broadly that, in language, in literature, in theology and cult, east Rome is Greek and is intensely conscious of that fact: in its Law and its military tradition, in its diplomacy, its fiscal policy and its consistent maintenance of the supremacy of the state it is Roman. . . .

> In the east there is *one* state in which all authority is highly centralised; in western Europe of the Middle Ages there is a welter of small states.
>
> (Baynes, *Byzantine Empire*, pp. 237ff.)

And the easterners, although they too suffered from crushing taxation, seem to have been able to put up with it with greater equanimity (ibid., p. 240). For Gainas, see above, n. 5.

10 For Tribigild, see above, n. 5.

11 See Bibliography, and above, Ch. 4.

12 For Constantine, see M. Grant, *Constantine the Great* (1993), p. 225.

13 S. Perowne, *The End of the Roman World* (1966), pp. 70f.

14 Grant, *Fall of the Roman Empire*, p. 131.

15 Moreover, Italy was continuing to decline; see Ch. 4.

16 Use can be made here of many books, notably A. Christensen, *L'Iran sous les Sassanides* (1944, 1966); R.N. Frye, *The Heritage of Persia* (1963, 1966); P. Freeman and D. Kennedy (eds), *The Defence of the Roman and Byzantine East* (1986), pp. 677ff.; and Wilson and A. McBride, *Rome's Enemies 3: Parthians and Sassanian Persians* (1986). The heroic age of Achaemenid Persia was exalted in the sixth century (notably by Khusro I, who visited Constantinople in 534). There was a great deal of coming and going between the Roman and Persian empires; and late Roman sculpture had Persian affinities. For silver-gilt dishes of Vahahran V and probably Firuz, see J.P.C. Kent and K.S. Painter, *Wealth of the Roman World AD 300–700* (1977), pp. 146, n. 307, 147, n. 308. For other fine Sassanian silver of this period, pp. 149, 152. Vahahran V received help from the Arabs of Hira (south of Kufa) – and the eastern Roman emperor Leo I was also very friendly with an Arab, Imra['al Qays. In Mesopotamia, Leo I refounded the city of Nicephorium-Callinicum (now Raqqa in Syria) as Leontopolis. In general, see H. Elton, *Frontiers of the Roman Empire* (1996).

17 V.C. Bullough, *Journal of Conflict Resolution*, 7, 1963, pp. 55–63. East Roman warfare with Persia often consisted of sieges. One of the prices of peace – 'worth paying for', since the wars were futile (F. Stark, *Rome on the Euphrates* [1967]) – was the division of Armenia in the later fourth century. For Theodosius II's friendly gesture to Yazdagird I, see M. Casa, *B. Gentili Festschrift* (1993). Aelia Eudoxia wrote a poem in 422 commemorating 'victory' over the Persians. But they renewed their attacks on the eastern empire in the time of Anastasius I, under Kavad I (502). Anastasius built Dara (Anastasiupolis) near Nisibis (Nüsaybin) as a strategic base against them (505–7). See J. Curtis, *Ancient Persia* (1980).

18 R.A.G. Carson, *Coins of the Roman Empire* (1990), pp. 226f. Ravenna struck coins for the eastern emperor Zeno (474–91), ibid., p. 264.

19 To what extent could the eastern empire have saved Rome, but failed to? This has been much discussed. See N. Clive and P. Magdalino, *Rome and Byzantium* (1977), p. 29. Theodosius II and Honorius issued joint coinages inscribed GLORIA ROMANORVM. There is no direct evidence in support of the theory that eastern tax revenues propped up the west (A.M. Rollins [ed.], *The Fall of Rome: A Reference Guide* [1983]). And the west could not rely on persistent eastern backing (J.J. Sanders, *History* 48, 1963, p. 17). However, it has been argued that the east gave as much aid as it could (W.N. Bayliss, *The Political Unity of the Roman Empire during the Disintegration of the West AD 395–459*). In 410, when Rome was sacked, three days of mourning were declared at Constantinople; and in 467 the two armies joined forces in a (disastrous) enterprise against

Gaiseric the Vandal. But the delay in appointing the western emperor Anthemius (467–72) was largely due to negotiations with the eastern emperor Leo I, who had probably never recognised Majorian (457–61) officially, although Ricimer made futile attempts to get him to do so (Leo wanted his own nominee, Anthemius, to be appointed). However, efforts to stress the differences between east and west must not be exaggerated (R. MacMullen, *Corruption and the Decline of Rome* [1988], p. 246, n. 75). But our whole knowledge of the period is very inadequate (Jones, *Later Roman Empire* p. 1026).

20 A. Ferrill, *The Fall of the Roman Empire: The Military Explanation* (1986, 1988), pp. 159f. The relations between the Roman and Constantinopolitan Churches had already left much to be desired, and Zeno's *Henotikon* (481/2) accentuated the breach (see next note). See Baynes, *Byzantine Empire*, pp. 82f., and F. Dvornik, *Byzantium and the Roman Primacy* (1964).

21 Ferrill, *Fall of the Roman Empire*. (Nepos had come to the throne by deposing Glycerius, with the backing of the eastern emperor Zeno.) There was another problem as well:

> How could [the east Roman emperors] placate the opposition of Syria and Egypt, passionately espousing heresy, and at the same time maintain communion with the orthodox west? Zeno's *Henoticon* united the eastern churches, but the price was schism with Rome. Throughout the reign of Anastasius I (at heart a Monophysite) the breach was unhealed.
>
> (Baynes, *Byzantine Empire*, p. 82)

22 M. Chambers, *The Fall of Rome* (1963), p. 5. In spite of occasional Byzantine discouragement – Rome was only one faction among many when a delegation visited Anastasius I in 517 – the claims and powers of the Pope increased steadily, as the western government first weakened and then disappeared; see Ch. 4, n. 26, and next note.

23 J. Randers-Pehrson, *Barbarians and Romans* (1983), p. 203. For a list of the popes of this period, see the end of this book.

24 G. Alföldy, *The Social History of Rome* (rev. edn, 1988 [1975]), p. 219). B. Singleton, 'Italy in the Early Christian Period' (lecture, 1997).

7 THE EASTERN EMPERORS

1 In the west, although Honorius was feeble – though not perhaps as bad as he was made out to be (Ch. 4) – and Valentinian III was not very exciting, the latter did at least reign for a long time, and kept the dynasty going. After him, Majorian (475–61) was able, but, in spite of eastern support, suffered a grave defeat from Gaiseric's Vandals (Appendix 2) at Carthago Nova (Cartagena), and was put to death by the German generalissimo Ricimer. The eastern emperor Leo I probably never acknowledged Libius Severus (461–5) in the west, and was slow to recognise Anthemius (467–72). But our sources for the whole period, as indicated elsewhere, are poor.

2 M. Cary in M. Chambers (ed.), *The Fall of Rome* (1963), p. 103.

3 M. Grant, *The Fall of the Roman Empire* (1976, 1990, 1996), pp. 120–3. For the Code of Theodosius II see C. Pharr, *The Theodosian Code* (1952). The reign of Theodosius II has been seen as a stable period of consolidation, despite the emperor's personal weakness. As for the emperor Leo I (457–74), did he

really try to save the west? See Ch. 5. The 'two transient successors' of Valentinian III were Petronius Maximus (455) and Avitus (455–6). Before Attila left the east (to attack the west), he destroyed seventy eastern cities. For his relations with the eastern leader Eutropius (exiled 398), see A. Ferrill, *The Fall of the Roman Empire: The Military Explanation* (1988), p. 177, n. 152.

4 E. Gibbon, *Decline and Fall of the Roman Empire* (1776–88), Ch. 36.

5 'I have iron for Attila, but no gold,' Marcian is reported to have said. He showed some interest in the western empire, but came too late to save it. He was a reformer, but of a somewhat orthodox nature: for example, his measures for tax relief favoured aristocrats. At the Council of Chalcedon (451) he secured the triumph of Constantinople over Alexandria. R.A.G. Carson (*Coins of the Roman Empire* [1990], p. 210) praises Marcian. Cf. Gibbon, *Decline and Fall*.

6 R.M. Haywood, *The Myth of Rome's Fall* (1960), p. 170; cf. A.H.M. Jones, *The Later Roman Empire 284–602* (1964), p. 218.

7 Gibbon, *Decline and Fall*.

8 The eastern emperor Leo I's accession was accompanied by the first formal inauguration procedure, based on military custom. For the Isaurians, and Asia Minor, see also the Introduction.

9 H. Goodacre, *A Handbook of the Byzantine Empire*, Part I, *Arcadius to Leontius*, p. 49. Flavius Aspar (Ardaburius), on whose staff Leo I had been, had established himself as Generalissimo in the east, where he was created *magister militum* (Master of Soldiers), and fought against the Vandals in Africa (431–4), the Persians (441) and Attila (447–50). He reached the height of his power under Marcian, but was brought down by Leo I.

10 Jones, *Later Roman Empire*, pp. 22f. Zeno had to deal with the usurpations of Basiliscus and Leontius (backed by Illus); see Ch. 8, n. 10 – after Leo II had also reigned for, it was said, one week. Theoderic the Ostrogoth, too, marched on Constantinople in 487, but was diverted to the west by encouragement to overthrow Odoacer. Zeno's great service was the solution of the problem of the Isaurians, to whose predominance he put a stop.

11 J.B. Bury, *The Later Roman Empire* (1958 edn), pp. 390, 400.

12 For the *Henotikon*, and Monophysites, see also Ch. 9.

13 J.D. Randers-Pehrson, *Barbarians and Romans* (1983), p. 205. For ecclesiastical controversies, see Ch. 9. See also D. Brukke, *Athanasius and the Policy of Asceticism* (1995).

14 Jones, *Later Roman Empire*, pp. 232ff.

15 J.J. Norwich, *Byzantium: The Early Centuries* (1989), pp. 182f. Anastasius I issued a reformed *aes* (bronze) coinage. He also gave merchants an incentive by reducing the income tax (the 'Gold of Affliction') and abolishing the profits tax (*chrysargyron*). But he had to placate the rebellious anti-Monophysite Goth (?) Vitalian (d. 520).

16 Bury, *Later Roman Empire*, pp. 446f.

17 M. Cary, *History of the Roman World* (2nd edn, 1954), pp. 771–81; cf. M. Chambers, *The Fall of Rome* (1963), pp. 103ff.

18 See above, Ch. 7, n. 18, Ch. 4, n. 12, for Odoacer.

19 See F. Lot, *The End of the Ancient World* (1931), pp. 241f.

20 I. Madach, *The Tragedy of Man* (1962); see also S. Mazzarino, *The End of the Ancient World* (1966, 1959), p. 179.

21 C.W.C. Oman, *The Byzantine Empire* (1892), p. 16. Another powerful German general was Gundobad (d. 516), son of the Burgundian king; see Appendix 2.

8 EMPRESSES

1 M. Grant, *The Severans* (1996), p. 45.

2 The intervening period had witnessed the western reign of the usurper Johannes (423–5), formerly *primicerius notariorum* (Chief Secretary), for whom Aetius raised a large force of Huns.

3 Flavius Constantius Felix, consul in 423, was from 425 Master of Soldiers (both branches of soldiery) in the west and the leading personage at the court of Valentinian III. Boniface (Bonifacius), too, was a western general, who served in north Africa and refused orders to return to Italy. He was believed to have invited the Vandals to cross over to Africa from Spain and help him against the western government of Valentinian III. He died of a wound while trying to suppress Aetius.

4 Placidia built the sanctuary of S. Croce at Ravenna. Whether she was actually buried there in the mausoleum that bears her name has been disputed (see Ch. 11). But coins were issued for her at Ravenna, as well as at Rome and Aquileia. Her head has also been identified on a silver ingot (R.A.G. Carson, *Coins of the Roman Empire* [1990], p. 223). See also S.F. Oost, *Galla Placidia Augusta* (1968).

5 R.A.G. Carson, *Principal Coins of the Romans*, vol. III, *The Dominate AD 294–408* (1981), p. 83, no. 1540.

6 The victory against Attila was won by Aetius, but the battle had been caused 'by the folly of Honoria . . . who in resentment at being compelled to marry the husband [Bassus, p.61] chosen for her by her brother [Honorius], wrote to Attila imploring his protection and sending him her ring' (A.H.M. Jones, *The Later Roman Empire 284–602* [1964], p. 194).

7 R.M. Haywood, *The Myth of Rome's Fall* (1960), pp. 160ff. The 'Theotokos' title of Mary, the mother of Jesus ('Mother of God'), which played a large part in politics (see K. Cooper, *The Virgin and the Bride: Idealised Womanhood in Late Antiquity* [1996]), was recognised by the Council of Ephesus (431). On a mosaic in the Church of Santa Maria Maggiore, Rome, Mary is depicted as a Roman empress. Pulcheria built three churches at Constantinople (including, apparently, St Mary of the Coppermarket [Chalcopratia] [480]), backed the 'two Natures' at the Council of Chalcedon (451), and was heavily involved in Pope Leo I's *Tome* (Ch. 9, n. 23). The Pope wrote to her in the hope of annulling the jurisdiction of Constantinople over the dioceses of Pontus, Asia and Thrace. See also Ch. 7, and n. 4.

8 See also K.G. Holum, *Theodosian Empresses* (1982), pp. 79ff. For Pulcheria's churches, see also Ch. 3, n. 3.

9 For the question whether she (Aelia) should be called 'Eudoxia' or 'Eudocia', see H. Goodacre, *A Handbook of the Coinage of the Byzantine Empire, Part I (Arcadius to Leontius)* (1928), pp. 26f. She was criticised by St John Chrysostom on the grounds of the alleged luxury and insolence of her court. She wrote a poem celebrating a supposed victory over the Persians in 422. She must be distinguished from another Aelia Eudoxia, the wife of Arcadius.

10 C. Diehl, *Byzantine Portraits* (1927), pp. 25f.

11 For coins in the name of Aelia Verina, see Goodacre, *Handbook*, p. 43; Carson, *Principal Coins*, nos. 1628ff. Verina was the sister of Basiliscus, who rose against Zeno (475–6).

12 G. Young, *Constantinople* (1992), pp. 35f. Jones (*Later Roman Empire*, p. 230) also describes the scene.

13 For coins in the name of Ariadne, Goodacre, *Handbook*, p. 47; Carson, *Principal Coins*, pp. 102f., nos. 1657f. There are two versions of the ivory

diptych said to bear her portrait, at Florence and Vienna. For Ariadne see also Ch. 7, n. 13.

14 C. Diehl, *Byzantine Portraits*, pp. 6ff., e.g. there is a relief of Holy Women at Augusta Trevirorum (Trier): see Ch. 12, n. 4. For the role of women in the later empire see H. Foley, *Reflections of Women in Antiquity* (1981), A. Cameron and A. Kuhrt, *Images of Women in Antiquity* (1983), R. Howley and B. Levick (eds), *Women in Antiquity: New Assessments* (1996), G. Clark, *Women in Late Antiquity: Pagan and Christian Life-Styles* (1993), A.E. Hickey, *Women of the Roman Aristocracy as Christian Monastics* (1987), D.E.E. Kleiner and S.B. Matheson, *I Claudia: Women in Ancient Rome* (1996).

9 RELIGION

1 Especially at Athens, Thessalonica, and Rome; and in the civil service.

2 A.H.M. Jones, *The Later Roman Empire 284–602* (1964), pp. 904, 957.

3 It is not known how many pagans there were at Rome (for Sun-worship, see below, n. 6). But Gaza was still predominantly pagan in *c.* 400, and at Carrhae (Altibaşak) paganism still survived. The position of 'Hellenism' as a part-base of late east-Roman and Byzantine culture must not be underestimated. And the Neoplatonists, for example (stressing abstinence), were strong; when Justinian I shut down Athens University, some of them were said to have gone to Persia. There has been a revival of interest in late Roman imperial Neoplatonism. See also now E. Herbert, *Pagan Religion* (ed. J.A. Butler, 1996); T.F. Mathews, *The Clash of Gods* (1994, 1995).

4 This was at the battle of the River Frigidus (Vipacco) in 394, in which Theodosius I defeated the western usurper Eugenius and the Master of Soldiers Arbogast, who committed suicide after the battle. Although nominally a Christian, Eugenius had sympathised with the pagan revival. It was once again in the interests (he hoped) of unity that Theodosius I had issued a stringent edict against paganism (see G. Young, *Constantinople* [1992], p. 32).

5 Augustine favoured the destruction of pagan temples, and Jerome violently attacked the dead pagan Porphyry (of Tyre [Es-Sur], or Batanea [probably Nugra], *c.* AD 232/3–*c.* 305); and John Chrysostom (*c.* 354–407) often spoke against the pagans. See now J.N.D. Kelly, *Golden Mouth* (1996); cf. Orosius, *Histories against the Pagans*. But Proclus (410/12–85: see Bibliography) still hoped for toleration of paganism. It had received a boost during the brief reign of the pagan Julian the Apostate (361–3).

6 We know little about the beliefs of ordinary pagans at this time. But the Olympian gods increasingly failed to satisfy people's aspirations (see n. 2 above). These gods could be regarded as symbols; if so, paganism might be made to look a tolerant form of monotheism. Iamblichus of Syria (2nd century) gave the Sun the place of honour among the 350 deities; for Sunworship see also M. Grant, *The Antonines* (1994), p. 76. See also J.H. Smith, *The Death of Classical Paganism* (1976), p. 3, cf. p. 2. Herbert, *Pagan Religion*, p. 82), wrote as follows:

> The adoration of the Sun, so not only scripture, but Homer, Hesiod and the ancient historians tell us, was both ancient and universal. It was generally thought that the Supreme God had made heaven his home (as immortal things are suitable to immortality). And the pagans could not think of anything more conspicuous or worthy of worship and adoration.

> They therefore lifted their eyes and hands devoutly up to heaven, not only in great adversity or difficulty, but also in prosperity did they direct their prayers there, because they did not know from where else anything good could come.

See on the whole subject, P. Chuvin, *A Chronicle of the Last Pagans* (1990); A. Cameron, *The Mediterranean World in Late Antiquity AD 395–600* (1993), pp. 70, 209 (n. 16, references), and p. 210, n. 26; E.R. Dodds, *Pagan and Christian in an Age of Anxiety* (1965), Ch. 4 (pp. 102ff.); and Anon., *L'intolleranza cristiana nei confronti dei pagani* (1990). The priestess of Ceres appears on the leaf of the ivory diptych of the Nicomachi and Symmachi. The pagan god Asclepius (Aesculapius) and the goddess of health, Hygieia, figure on other diptychs; the pagan Symmachus (*c.* 340–422) was especially strong in Rome; two Nikes (Victories) are to be seen on the sides of the pedestal of the Column of Marcian (450–7); and the Lupercalia was still celebrated at the end of the fifth century, much to the annoyance of the Pope. Pagan designs still continued on textiles (G. Koch, *Early Christian Art and Architecture* [1996], p. 146). For textiles see also below, Ch. 12, no. 29; and for textiles from Masada, BM Exhibition of 1995.

7 Illus, who supported Zeno's enemy the usurper Basiliscus (475–6), was close to the Neoplatonist poet Pamprepius of Panopolis (Achmim).

8 M. Grant, *The Fall of the Roman Empire* (1976, 1990, 1996), p. 170. The Jews came in for very severe attacks from Christian emperors, and St John Chrysostom (*c.* 354–407) has a lot to say against them. See also Cameron, *Mediterranean World*, pp. 140f., 224, n. 42; M. Grant, *The Jews in the Roman World* (1973), pp. 282ff; D. Jacoby in C. Mango and G. Dagron, *Constantinople and Its Hinterland* (1995), p. 232; C. Lieu *et al.*, *Jews among Pagans and Christians in the Later Roman Empire* (1992). Revolts by the Samaritans (distinct from the Jews) started in 484.

9 See F. Lot, *The End of the Ancient World* (1931), p. 47. A lot of violence characterised this process: for example, when the Christians lynched the Neoplatonist Hypatia, daughter of the scientist Theon, in 415.

> [Christian fanatics] dragged her from her carriage, took her to the church called Caesareum, where they completely stripped her, and then murdered her with tiles. After tearing her body in pieces, they took her mangled limbs to a place called Cinaron, and there burnt them.
>
> This affair brought no small opprobrium not only upon Cyril [bishop of Alexandria, d. 444], but also upon the whole Alexandrian Church. And surely nothing can be further from the spirit of Christians than massacre, fights and such-like things.
>
> (Socrates, *Historia Ecclesiastica*, VII, 15, transl. Stevenson)

M. Dzieska, *Hypatia of Alexandria* (1995); J.L.E. Dreyer, *A History of Astronomy from Thales to Kepler*, 2nd edn (1953; 1906): 'the curtain went down for ever on the great stage where Greek science had played its part so well and so long.' He speaks highly of her. Nor was this by any means the last physical attack on pagans; see n. 12 below.

10 N.H. Baynes, *The Byzantine Empire* (1925, 1943), p. 85; Edward Gibbon, *The Decline and Fall of the Roman Empire* (1766–88), Ch. 28. As is well known, Gibbon is very critical of early Christianity, and of ecclesiastical historians; see

W.O. Chadwick, *Conference on Gibbon's Decline and Fall* (January 1976), etc. For the early Christian world-view, references in Cameron, *Mediterranean World*, p. 205, n. 5.

11 That probably accounts, at least in part, for the pomp and splendour of the eucharistic rite. It is not practical to try to differentiate between 'Orthodox' and 'Catholic' in the early Christian world, although the two ways of thinking gradually developed in the east and west respectively. Missionary activity was strong, especially among the 'barbarians' (Cameron, *Mediterranean World*, p. 210, n. 25). She also stresses the close link between church and state (for the modern secondary role of religion, see Introduction).

> We should see the fifth century as a period when some of the basic implications of Christian belief were being hammered out, amid a situation of increasing imperial involvement in the Church, and increasing power and indeed wealth on the Church's side.
>
> The question of how to deal with the passionately held differences between Christians was not, as it tends to be today, just a Church issue: it was at the top of the imperial agenda. . . . While in our own society religion is relegated by the majority to a separate, and usually minor, sphere, in late antiquity (in contrast) not only was religion – both pagan and Christian – at the centre of the stage, but the Christian Church was itself increasingly occupying a leading role in political, economic and social life.
>
> (pp. 25, 65f.)

12 R.M. Haywood, *The Myth of Rome's Fall* (1960), p. 165. The Zuni Indians live south of Gallup, New Mexico. In the ancient world, 'there were always going to be a few hard-liners,' said Henry Chadwick (*Times Literary Supplement*, 22 March 1996, p. 4), as there had been earlier:

> In the north African provinces, especially Numidia, militant bands of dissident peasants, armed with stout clubs, mounted unstoppable charges on the orchestral instruments at pagan festivals [390, 391, Syria, Egypt]. . . .
>
> The consequence for the Church of such strong-arm methods was bitter confrontation, with impassioned hatred and resentment, and in some places formidable counter-attacks.

13 S. Katz, *The Decline of Rome and the Rise of Medieval Europe* (1955), p. 150; cf. M. Chambers, *The Fall of Rome: Can It Be Explained?* (1963), p. 118.
14 G.W.F. Hegel found these disagreements 'tiring'. See now G. Lüdemann, *Heretics* (1996).
15 See Grant, *Fall of the Roman Empire*, 1990 edn, p. 171.
16 W.E. Kaegi, *Byzantium and the Decline of Rome* (1968), p. 235.
17 Baynes, *Byzantine Empire*, pp. 42f.
18 On these sects see T.E. Gregory, *Vox Populi* (1979), pp. 223f. Jesus Christ was seen by many as a magician (P. Brown, *The World of Late Antiquity*, p. 55, fig. 39; J.P.C. Kent and K.S. Painter [eds], *The Wealth of the Roman World AD 300–700*, p. 94, fig. 157).
19 E.E. Kellett, *A Short History of Religions* (1933, 1962), pp. 166ff.
20 R. Krautheimer, *Early Christian and Byzantine Architecture* (1965), pp. 67f. Egypt was hostile to the Council of Chalcedon (451), because priority was given to

Constantinople. See also L.M.R.M. de Lusignan, *Rome et les églises d'orient* (1976).

21 See also M. Grant, *The Climax of Rome* (1968, 1993), p. 244. The worship of images was much stronger in the east than in the west. And Antioch, it has been said, stressed the Resurrection, the west the Cross.

22 Kellett, *Short History*, pp. 236f. More is said about Augustine (and Jerome) in the Bibliography.

23 Grant, *Fall of the Roman Empire*, p. 200. During, or as a result of, 'some delicate linguistic work' (J.G. Hull, *Doctrine and Practices in the Early Church* [1991], p. 234), Constantine I the Great tried to side-track opposition by using the compromise term *homoousios* – 'of like substance' – for the Nature of Jesus (see Lot, *End of the Ancient World*, p. 130). Though no one dared contradict him openly, on the spot, there was passionate opposition to 'two Natures' in Egypt and Palestine; see also J. Stevenson, *Creeds, Councils and Controversies* (1966), p. 337; and there were violent scenes before and during Councils. The exact implications of Mariology (Ch. 8) were also hotly debated. Mary, recently acknowledged as the 'Mother of God', is especially prominent on the mosaics of S. Maria Maggiore at Rome (Ch. 12).

Three major attempts were made, during the fifth century, to establish ecclesiastical, and so political, unity, and all were deadly failures. See Lüdemann, *Heretics*.

The first was the *Tome* of Pope Leo I the Great (448). Rome, observed Paul Johnson,

> was more interested in blocking the evasions and misconstructions of heretics than in evolving an absolutely comprehensive and irrefragable formula of its own. . . . The Greeks regarded the Latins as amateurs in theology and in general as barbarous and ill-educated persons.
>
> (Johnson, *A History of Christianity*, 1976, paperback edn 1978, p. 91)

So Pope Leo I hit back, and 'asserted in the strongest language the permanent distinction of the two Natures in the incarnate Lord' (H. Chadwick, *The Early Church*, 1967, p. 202). His *Tome* can be described as a 'clear, precise, systematic exposition of the Catholic doctrine of the Incarnation and the Union of the divine and human natures in Christ' (R.E. McNally, *Encyclopaedia Britannica*, XIII, 1970 edn, p. 955). But the theme of the 'two Natures' met with a poor reception in the east. In particular, its emphasis upon 'the humbled, human element' in Christ shocked the Greek reader. 'For this attitude threatened to leave God's work of salvation half-done: to condemn human nature itself to the position of an untransformable residue, a bitter dreg at the bottom of the unbounded sea of God's power' (P. Brown, *The World of Late Antiquity*, 1971, p. 145).

The Council of Chalcedon (451), about which a great deal has been written, set out, with scant success, to clear the matter up.

> In 451 [an] unusually large assembly of Churchmen met at Chalcedon, constituting the Fourth Ecumenical Council.
>
> So much has been written about it that no attempt will be made here to assess its decisions. It may only be remarked that they 'described Jesus Christ as complete in his humanity as well as in

his divinity; one and the same Christ in two Natures, without
confusion or change, division or separation; each Nature concur-
ring into one person. . . . But the truth is that the definition of
Chalcedon might be interpreted in different ways. To [Pope] Leo
and the western Church it meant one thing; to the followers of
Cyril [of Alexandria] another; to Antiochians . . . something different. . . .

Politically, the Council was a decisive triumph for Constantinople and a final blow to the pretensions of the See of Alexandria.
. . . [But] in Egypt and Syria there was a solid mass of opinion
loyal to the doctrine of one Nature [Monophysitism], and firmly
opposed to the formula of Chalcedon. . . .

The Christian religion, with its theology which opened such a
wide field for differences of opinion, had introduced into the
empire dangerous discords which were a sore perplexity to the
government.'

(J.B. Bury, *The Later Roman Empire*, 1889, 1958 edn, pp. 357ff.)

Another major attempt to heal the divisions in the Church was made by
Zeno; as A.H.M. Jones indicates, Zeno's *Henotikon* was addressed to the
clergy and people of Egypt:

In 482 [others prefer the date 481] Zeno made an attempt to heal
the doctrinal discord which had rent the Church since the Council
of Chalcedon . . . [the opposition to which] was widespread. . . .
Even the Patriarch of Constantinople, Acacius . . . was not enthusiastic for Chalcedon, and he suggested to Zeno that unity might
be achieved if it could be buried.

An imperial constitution, the *Henotikon* or decree of union, was
accordingly issued in this sense. The emperor . . . set forth a brief
statement of the faith, which mentioned neither the one nor the
two Natures of Christ, and anathematised all who believed or had
believed otherwise now or ever, at Chalcedon or any other Council.

(Jones, *Later Roman Empire*, pp. 227f.)

So all the fifth-century attempts to achieve unity in the Church were entirely
unsuccessful – and the results are still with us today.

24 By attacking Arianism and Arians, the emperors absorbed huge properties and
estates.
25 Constantine I the Great had been baptised on his death-bed by Eusebius,
bishop of Nicomedia (later of Constantinople, 338; d. 341/2), who was an
Arian. The greatest Arian was the Visigothic King Euric (466–84). The sect
had already had an eminent writer in Philostorgius (*c.* 368–430/40).
26. For their founder Mani (216–77) see Grant, *Climax of Rome*, pp. 200ff.
27 J.W.L. Myres, *Journal of Roman Studies*, 50, 1960, p. 36.
28 On John Wesley see Kellett, *Short History*, p. 167, n. 1. Many who consider
themselves Christians today in fact have Manichaean beliefs.
29 Augustine particularly disliked the Donatists; see N. Chadwick, *Times Literary
Supplement*, 22 March 1996.
30 After a temporary setback at the Council of Chalcedon (451), the chief homes
of Monophysitism remained Syria and Egypt. See W. Frend, *A History of the*

Monophysite Movement (1972). Severus of Sozopolis (Apollonia Pontica; Burgas), early sixth-century bishop of Antioch, was the outstanding Monophysite theologian; see Bury, *Later Roman Empire*, I, p. 438, n. 2; P. Brown, *Authority and the Sacred* (1995), pp. 73, 87. Zeno's *Henotikon*, directed towards Egypt, placated many moderate Monophysites, although it antagonised Rome (see n. 23). Anastasius I, deeply interested in religion (he even suggested alterations to the liturgy), got into serious trouble in 512 because he sympathised with Monophysitism. See John Malalas (*c.* 491–578):

> The population of the city crowded together and rioted violently on the grounds that something alien had been added to the Christian faith. There was uproar in the palace which caused the city prefect Plato to run in, flee and hide from the people's anger. The rioters set up a chant, 'A new emperor for the Roman state', and went off to the residence of the ex-Prefect Marinus the Syrian, burnt his house and plundered everything he had, since they could not find him. . . .
> They found an eastern monk in the house whom they seized and killed, and then, carrying his head on a pole, they chanted, 'Here is the enemy of the Trinity'. They went to the residence of Juliana, a patrician of the most illustrious rank, and chanted for her husband, Areobindus, to be emperor of the Roman state.
> (John Malalas, *Chronographia*, transl. Jeffreys, 728)

For Marinus, see Bury, *Later Roman Empire*, I, p. 470.
31 G. Downey, *The Late Roman Empire* (1969), pp. 90–2.
32 Baynes, *Byzantine Empire*, p. 79:

> Nestorius, trained in the historical and critical methods of the school of Antioch, was Patriarch of Constantinople. . . . [He] was accused of dividing the personality of Christ into the divine Word (Logos) and the human Jesus, and at the third Ecumenical Council of Ephesus [431], Cyril [of Alexandria, where he was bishop, 412–44], acting as Papal Legate, secured his condemnation and deposition. Theodosius II after some hesitation yielded to the commanding personality of the Egyptian bishop. Alexandria triumphed afresh. But Rome grew uneasy.

Cyril of Alexandria had continued his predecessor's policy of suppressing paganism (he was said to be guilty of partial responsibility for the death of the pagan Hypatia [see n. 9]). But in 433 cautious concessions on his part helped to heal schisms between Alexandria and Antioch. At the Council of Chalcedon (451) both sides appealed to his statements, but Alexandria did not fare well.
　　In 428 Eutyches at Constantinople had opposed the doctrine of two Natures of Nestorius, but Pope Leo I, whose *Tome* (n. 23 above: suspected by St John Chrysostom and many easterners) stressed the two Natures, pronounced against him – although deploring his condemnation, which then occurred: for Eutyches, at the tough, continuous insistence of Cyril of Alexandria, was accused of Monophysitism – though his teaching lived on, because of his stress on the humanity of Jesus.
33 Dodds, *Pagan and Christian*, p. 67 and n. 1. For Justinian I, see Appendix 3.

34 Grant, *Fall of the Roman Empire*, p. 232, see W.H.C. Frend, *Journal of Roman Studies*, 59, 1969, p. 9. The big estates were sometimes split up if their owners renounced the world. Libanius (314–*c.* 393) had been very hostile to the monks, but St John Chrysostom supported those known as the 'Tall Brothers', and the Monastery of the 'Sleepless Ones' contained no less than four linguistic groups. There were at least 140 monasteries in Judaea, and many more in Syria and Mesopotamia. Monks, augmented by social malcontents and bankrupt fugitives, were influential, over a long period, as advisers of laity and mediators for those affected by bad harvests or plague or personal troubles. Indeed, they helped, it was said, to 'forge the new mass religion of the future'. And, according to the sixth-century historian Procopius of Caesarea (Palestine), their prayers assisted in the defence of the Syrian frontier. For three fifth-century writings on the monks, see C. Mango, *Byzantium* (1980), p. 113.

'What do I do with those fanatical monks?' Theodosius I reportedly said to St Ambrose. For they could also be violent. They were prominent among the militant *circumcelliones* of north Africa; and they surely played a part in the lynching of Hypatia at Alexandria (nn. 9, 12 above); they attacked the 'Sleepless Ones' from Antioch in 426 (the 'Sleepless' Alexander [d. 430] was chased out of Constantinople); and in 466 Sinuthius (Shenoudi, Schenudi) of Atripe (the White Monastery, in the Thebaid; he wrote *Contra Origenistes*) led a band of monastic *vigilantes*. There were many monks in the deserts of Judaea (Y. Hirschfeld, *The Judaean Desert Monasteries in the Byzantine Period* [1992]; for the Monastery of Martyrius see Cameron, *Mediterranean World*, p. 142, pl. 9). Palladius (*c.* 364–*c.* 430) reported that there were 2,000 monks at Alexandria, 5600 male ascetics and hermits at Nitria (Wadi Natrun), 1,200 monks and 12 women's convents on the island of Tabennisi (see also next note). See also individual holy men, e.g. Simeon the Stylite and Daniel the Stylite at Constantinople, (Ch. 11, nn. 31 and 32; see also next note). Holy men played an influential part at the Councils of Ephesus (431) and Chalcedon (451). See now a reference in P. France, *Hermits: The Insights of Solitude* (1996); but for the financial burden that these monks (and the clergy) represented, Jones, *Later Roman Empire*, II, pp. 933f.

35 Basil of Caesarea (Kayseri) in Cappadocia – where monasticism was active – *c.* 330–79. See S. Perowne, *The End of the Roman World* (1966), pp. 127f.; V. Wimbush (ed.), *Ascetic Behaviour in Greco-Roman Antiquity* (1996), and Bibliography.

> Basil the Great . . . sought to found asceticism on a scriptural basis: the ascetic is one who 'practises with a view to perfection and trains himself by means of solitude, renunciation and continence for the attainment of one great prize, union with God'. To Basil the life of the solitary was inactive and unfruitful, and labour in the field or workshop was to form part of the life of prayer.
> The rules of Basil served as a model to St Benedict [*c.* 480–547] when legislating for the monks of the west.
> (Baynes, *Byzantine Empire*, p. 87)

'Pillar saints like Simeon the Stylite [Ch. 11, n. 31]', wrote Henry Chadwick (*Times Literary Supplement*, 22 March 1996, p. 4), 'fulfilled a social role as arbiters or patrons, "facilitators of change", helping to emancipate surrounding residents from attachment to their part polytheistic practices.' There is a relief of Holy Women at Augusta Trevirorum (Trier). See also n. 34 above, and A.E. Hickey, *Women of the Roman Aristocracy as Christian Monastics* (1987).

36 Baynes, *Byzantine Empire*. For the role of the pilgrims, see S. Coleman and J. Elsner, *Pilgrimage: Past and Present in the World Religions* (1995).

37 F.A. Wright and T.A. Sinclair, *A History of Later Latin Literature* (1969), pp. 49f. Paula helped to direct his activities at Bethlehem. There is more said about St Jerome (and St Augustine) in the Bibliography.

38 Ibid., p. 10.

10 LITERATURE

1 K.H. Marshall and I. Mavrogordato, in N.H. Baynes and H. St L.B. Moss (eds), *Byzantium* (1948, 1949), p. 221. Our own literary taste is diametrically opposed to that of literary Byzantines: see C. Mango, *Byzantium* (1980), p. 234.

2 C.E. Stevens, *Oxford Classical Dictionary*, 2nd edn (1970), p. 128. See J.M. Rist, *Augustine* (1994); H. Chadwick, *Augustine* (1986). When I was Professor of Humanity (Latin) at the University of Edinburgh, one of my colleagues in the Faculty of Divinity came to warn me not to give lectures on St Augustine, because he was reserved for the Divinity Faculty.

3 M. Hadas, *A History of Latin Literature* (1952), pp. 439f.

4 Ibid., pp. 438f. See F.A. Wright and T.A. Sinclair, *A History of Later Latin Literature* (1969), pp. 56, 58, 64.

5 Hadas, *History of Latin Literature*, pp. 432, 437f.

6 R.M. Haywood, *The Myth of Rome's Fall* (1960), p. 170.

7 A. Souter, *Oxford Classical Dictionary* (2nd edn, 1970), pp. 562f.

8 See also F.A. Wright, *Jerome: Selected Letters* (Loeb edn, 1963).

11 ARCHITECTURE

1 One must bear in mind that architecture is only an expression of settlement patterns:

> The study of settlement patterns represents a major advance towards understanding the process of change in the western empire, and especially towards circumventing the problems inherent in the literary sources. Much of the evidence so far collected remains incomplete, and in some cases controversial; interpretation is very much a specialist matter.
> (A. Cameron, *The Mediterranean World in Late Antiquity AD 395–600* [1993], p. 45)

She also points out, however (p. 199), that much of the present flow of research on the late imperial eastern provinces is led by archaeology; see Ch. 11. See also S. McReady and F.H. Thompson, *Roman Architecture in the Greek World* (1987, 1990); G. Koch, *Early Christian Art and Architecture: An Introduction* (1996).

2 M. Gough, *The Origins of Christian Art* (1975), p. 62; G. Young, *Constantinople* (1992), p. 55; H.P. L'Orange, *Art Forms and Civil Life in the Late Roman Empire* (1965), pp. 81f., 84, 103; but W. Sas-Zaloziecky, *Die altchristliche Kunst*, p. 24, doubted L'Orange's emphasis on palace origins. A. Bryer (*Byzantium* [1968], p.

29) stressed the ecclesiastical (functional) character of this type of architecture. Koch (*Early Christian Art and Architecture*, p. 29) wrote as follows:

> In the early Christian and Byzantine period 'basilica' denoted a church generally. Today art-historians understand by 'basilica' a church building with the following properties:– it must be longitudinal; it must have several aisles – at least three; the nave must be raised, with a clerestory, an area with windows – the main entrance must be at one narrow end and the sanctuary at the other. . . . It is questionable whether there were already basilicas in the time before Constantine.

See also S. Runciman, *Byzantine Style and Civilization* (1975, 1981), p. 24; Gough, *Origins of Christian Art*, p. 62; Young, *Constantinople*, p. 25.

3   D. Talbot Rice, *Byzantine Art* (1935, 1962, 1968), p. 16.
4   S. Agnese on the Via Nomentana dates from some period after Constantine I's death. The vanished S. Petronilla contained burials of *c.* 400.
5   It is not certain who was actually buried in the 'Mausoleum of Placidia'; the building may have been, originally, a *martyrium* of St Lawrence (S. Lorenzo). At Ravenna there are also various other churches of fifth-century date, e.g. S. Francesco, St Peter Chrysologos and the Cathedral (built before 425). And Galla Placidia (Ch. 8) vowed S. Giovanni Evangelista during a storm (436). The mosaics of Ravenna are noted in the next chapter.
6   Talbot Rice, *Byzantine Art*, pp. 148, 152.
7   J. Vogt, *The Decline of Rome* (1967), pp. 305f. The windows are of alabaster.
8   R. Krautheimer, *Early Christian and Byzantine Architecture* (1965), p. 133; Gough, *Origins of Christian Art*, pp. 94, 96.
9   Talbot Rice, *Byzantine Art*, pp 152, 156. There are also other fifth-century architectural remains in Italy: e.g. M. Small and R.J. Buck, *The Excavations at S. Giovanni di Ruoti*, vol. I: *The Villas and Their Environment* (1994).
10 M. Grant, *The Emperor Constantine* (1993), pp. 199f. The original Church of St Irene at Constantinople may have been Constantinian (see Young, *Constantinople*, pp. 24, 26), and there seems to have been a predecessor of Santa Sophia (Appendix 3, n. 11).
11 Krautheimer, *Early Christian and Byzantine Architecture*, p. 77. For Proconnesian production, N. Asgari in C. Mango and G. Dagron (eds), *Constantinople and Its Hinterland* (1995), pp. 263ff., and brisk exports from the same source, C. Mango, *Byzantium* (1980, 1994), p. 261.
12 Krautheimer, *Early Christian and Byzantine Architecture*, p. 78; see also Sas-Zaloziecky, *Die altichristliche Kunst*, pl. 4; M. Grant, *Art in the Roman Empire* (1995), pp. 80ff. All that survives of the monastery to which the church belonged is a large cistern (Koch, *Early Christian Art*, p. 58).
13 C. Mango, *Byzantine Architecture* (1976), p. 36; S. Hill, *The Early Byzantine Churches of Cilicia and Isauria* (1996), p. 36. The seat of the prefect of Illyricum was moved to Thessalonica from Sirmium in *c.* 442.
14 Krautheimer, *Early Christian and Byzantine Architecture*, pp. 95ff. Probably the church was built shortly after Meryemlik (see below); Hill, *Early Byzantine Churches*, pp. 55ff.
15 Krautheimer, *Early Christian and Byzantine Architecture*, pp. 74ff., fig. 25. A rotunda or mausoleum or throne room was converted into the Church of St George at Thessalonica.
16 Neos Anchialos had been Thebes in Phthiotis. Its harbour-town Pyrasos took

over its name and became a bishopric. The old town was fortified by Justinian I (Appendix 3). Greece had started to recover in the third century AD, and the process was continuing.

17 Cilicia was divided into two parts, Rough (Aspera) and Plain (Campestris, Pedias). Cilicia was often hard to distinguish from Isauria (Hill, *Early Byzantine Churches*, pp. 31f., 55). Cilicia's churches were on the whole faithful to the basilica form (ibid., p. 55). The district was relatively ignored by ancient writers – and recent excavators (ibid., p. xxii). Yet, with Isauria, it was an architectural hothouse and archetype (ibid., pp. 7, 38f.).

18 Gough, *Origins of Christian Art*, pp. 64, 68; Hill (*Early Byzantine Churches*, p. 39) believed in the Cilician dome, and pointed to five cognate 'domed basilicas' in the country.

19 The 'Cave Church' at Meryemlik is a kind of crypt of the huge basilica, which was probably the emperor Zeno's creation. There is also a 'Cupola Church' at Meryemlik. In effect, St Thecla was the patron saint of Rough Cilicia. For her, see S. Lloyd, *History Today*, 11 August 1952, pp. 527–31.

20 Krautheimer, *Early Christian and Byzantine Architecture*, p. 177 and fig. 99. Hill (*Early Byzantine Churches*) does not believe in these Constantinopolitan influences.

21 Gough, *Origins of Christian Art*, p. 64.

22 Hill, *Early Byzantine Churches*, p. 68. The 'East Church' (Koca Kalesi) is the best preserved.

23 Gough, *Origins of Christian Art*, pp. 65f.

24 For a discussion of this point see Hill, *Early Byzantine Churches*, pp. 80, 214.

25 Gough, *Origins of Christian Art*, pp. 177f.

26 J. Freely, *The Companion Guide to Turkey* (1984), p. 221.

27 Gough, *Origins of Christian Art*, pp. 65f.; Hill, *Early Byzantine Churches*, pls 62–74; probably not Coropissus. The dome was probably made of masonry (ibid., p. 150). There is also an Ambulatory Church (ibid., p. 155).

28 Ura and Uzuncaburç may be winter and summer settlements of the same town. Only one church at Olba stands to any height (if indeed it still does) (ibid., pls 112, 113, see also p. 150). There was also a church of this period at Canytela (Kanlidivane), part of Olba (ibid., pls 82, 93). Olba was near Seleucia (Silifke), the metropolis of Isauria. There were fine roads in Cilicia. Lycia also requires to be mentioned: see A.S. Hall (*In Memoriam*), *Studies in the History and Topography of Lycia* (1994).

29 There were also a good many other early churches in the area: notably at Carallia (Hill, *Early Byzantine Churches*, p. 179), Anazarbus (Anavarza): from the time of Theodosius II the metropolis of half of Cilicia, probably influenced by Anatolia more than Syria (ibid., pp. 85, 91). Anemurium (Eski Anamur) (ibid., p. 91), Adrassus (Balabolu), Celenderis (Aydincik) (ibid., p. 99), Flavia (Kadirli) (ibid., p. 179), Yanikhan (this shows links with early *martyria* in the Holy Land: ibid., p. 32, pls 118–26), Akören (in the Taurus foothills) (several churches: ibid., p. 66), Alikilise (ibid., p. 83), Emirzeli (ibid., p. 110), Epiphaneia (Erzin) (ibid., pp. 166f.), Canbazli, Mahras Daği (Kale Pinar) (ibid., pls 95, 96), Elaeusa-Sebaste (Ayaş: though the city itself had declined [ibid., p. 97]).

30 Freely, *Companion Guide to Turkey*, p. 113; see also pp. 105, 108ff., 118. For the area see Cameron, *Mediterranean World*, p. 227, n. 9.

31 Qal'at Sim'an was on the road which connected Antioch and Beroea (Aleppo). The church at Resapha (Rusapha, Sergiopolis, R'safah) in Mesopotamia may have been later (see Sas-Zaloziecky, *Die altichristliche Kunst*, pp. 50f., fig. 21).

Simeon Stylites (390–459) was a saint whose piety bordered on madness. He was expelled from his first monastery for winding a rope of twisted palm leaves so tightly around his body that it ate into his flesh and took three days to be surgically removed. He then moved to the hills beyond Aleppo [Beroea], where, after various mortifications, he chained himself to a rock. This attracted some attention; people were curious to see the fanatic for themselves.

Finding the interruptions disagreeable, Simeon built a nine-foot pillar, climbed to the top and stayed up there for four years. More people than ever came to see him. Every so often Simeon built a higher pillar; the last, on top of which he spent twenty years, was sixty feet high.

By this point he was attracting visitors from as far away as Britain. Accepting that his behaviour precluded solitude, Simeon became an evangelist, bawling the Word from on high. When he died, an enormous cruciform church was built around the final pillar. At the time it was the biggest church in the world.

(Joe Roberts, *The Times*, 6 April 1996, p. 18)

See also Ch. 9, nn. 34, 35, and P. Brown, *Authority and the Sacred*, pp. 66, 76f; D. Kruger, *Symeon the Holy Fool* (1996). St Simeon's pillar was raised in height in order to bring him closer to heaven. His dealings were mostly with lower-class drop-outs, but he also had rich contacts. For the church, see Krautheimer, *Early Christian and Byzantine Architecture*, pp. 111, 113. For a good reconstruction of the four churches which formed the cross, see Sas-Zaloziecky, *Die altchristliche Kunst*, fig. 17, and for a colour picture the paper-back jacket of Koch, *Early Christian Art*. There was an inn below the churches, probably of the late fifth century (or a little later) (Koch, *Early Christian Art*, p. 73). For Syria at this time see W. Ball, *Syria: A Historical and Archaeological Guide* (1996); H. King, *Syria Revealed* (1996); R. Burns, *Monuments of Syria* (1996).

32 Krautheimer, *Early Christian and Byzantine Architecture*, p. 330, n. 26. For a Syrian imitator of St Simeon, namely Daniel the Stylite, see M. Kaplan in Mango and Dagron, *Constantinople*, pp. 196–201, 204, and Mango, *Byzantium*, p. 111. Daniel (d. 493) was born near Samosata (Samsat), and settled at Anaplous, near Constantinople. At the sight of his swollen feet it was said that Basiliscus, the rebel against Zeno (476–7), ceased to be a 'heretic'.

33 Krautheimer, *Early Christian and Byzantine Architecture*, p. 111.

34 Ibid., p. 120. At Gerasa, at least seven churches were constructed during the fifth century. St Theodore deserves special mention.

35 Gough, *Origins of Christian Art*, p. 63. St Jerome also constructed important buildings at Bethlehem, with the help of Paula (see Chapter 9, n. 37).

36 Krautheimer, *Early Christian and Byzantine Architecture*, p. 89. For this man see above, Ch. 9, n. 34.

37 Talbot Rice, *Byzantine Art*, p. 34. There were two small square constructions akin to mausoleums at El Bagawat in the Kharga Oasis. The funerary Chapel of the Exodus there has been attributed to the fourth or fifth century (see P. du Bourguet, *Early Christian Painting* [1965], figs 151–5). See, in general, K. Painter (ed.), *Churches Built in Ancient Times* (1994).

38 The Great Palace at Constantinople (Young, *Constantinople*, pp. 24, 35) is a conspicuous example (though of uncertain date), and the emperor Anastasius

I built a palace at Blachernae in the suburbs of the city. And there was, of course, another at Ravenna, which became a worthy capital of the west under Valentinian III (425–55) and Placidia, when the Church of S. Croce (c. 425), and others, were built. The archbishop's palace at Ravenna, too, is notable, though much restored; and there were other private citizens' palaces at Constantinople (e.g. of Antiochus and Lausus). For such private palaces see Koch, *Early Christian Art*, pp. 68f. There are also remains of an inn at Qal'at Sim'an (see above, n. 26), and a fifth-century inscription about a hostel: that of the deacon Appius at Amida (Diyarbakir).

39 e.g. the Forum of Arcadius, with its high column, begun in 402. For the Arcadian Way see Koch, *Early Christian Art*, p. 65 and fig. 25.

40 Krautheimer, *Early Christian and Byzantine Architecture*, pp. 48f. The walls were not only very strong, but seventeen miles in length; only fragments of the sea-walls survive. Seven of the fifty gates remain in use. The walls date from 413, when Constantine's Walls were demolished. See B. Granville Barker, *The Walls of Constantinople* (1910); A. von Millingen, *Constantinople: The Walls of the City* (1899).

41 J.G. Crow in Mango and Dagron, *Constantinople*, pp. 109f., 112f., 120–4: 'It is clear that, until the death of Marcian [457], there was a very real concern for the security of the Danubian provinces in Thrace, and that this was reflected in an active building programme' (p. 120). See also references in *Anatolian Archaeology I*, 1995, pp 12ff., and J.F. Haddon in Mango and Dagron, *Constantinople*, p. 144, n. 3; and for a neighbouring encampment, p. 154. For Procopius (sixth century) and Gibbon on the subject, see Crow, pp. 124f. For the deliberate aesthetic appeal, Koch, *Early Christian Art*, pp. 66f.

42 Young, *Constantinople*, p. 33.

43 H.P. L'Orange, *Art Forms and Civic Life in the Late Roman Empire* (1965), p. 131.

44 Crow in Mango and Dagron, *Constantinople*, p. 121, n. 36; J. Crow and A. Ricci, *Anatolian Archaeology*, Research Reports 1996, pp. 16f. (*The Times*, 2 January 1997). Bargala in Macedonia (near Stip) was relocated to a new defensible position in the fifth century.

45 The new walls at Thessalonica were of the time of Theodosius II and Marcian (Crow in Mango and Dagron, *Constantinople*, pp. 120, 132) and J.F. Haddon, in ibid., p. 154.

46 For the Chersonese (Gallipoli) walls, see Crow in ibid., p. 124 (and n. 46); see also Crow and Ricci, *Anatolian Archaeology*, p. 16; G. Greatrex in Mango and Dagron, *Constantinople*, pp. 125ff. City walls were also erected at Carthage, to keep out the Huns. Early Byzantine cities were normally walled.

12 THE HUMAN AND DIVINE FORM

1 M. Grant, *The Climax of Rome* (1968, 1996), pp. 96f.

2 Archaeological Museum, Istanbul; J.D. Randers-Pehrson, *Barbarians and Romans* (1983), pl. 37; S. Vryonis, *Byzantium and Europe* (1967), pl. 14; M. Gough, *The Origins of Christian Art* (1975), p. 115, fig. 98; C. Scarre, *Chronicle of the Roman Emperors* (1995), pp. 223, 227. Was statuary an almost forgotten art, or was there a sort of revival under Arcadius and Theodosius II? See W. Sas-Zaloziecky, *Byzantinische Kunst* (1963), p. 74; G. Koch, *Early Christian Art and Architecture* (1996), p. 127. There was (though it no longer exists) an equestrian statue of Theodosius II (K.G. Holum, *Theodosian Empresses* [1982], p. 110 and n. 127 [references]). The bronze military statue of an emperor at Barletta is omitted here because, although attributions are often uncertain, it may well be

earlier (and represent Valentinian I). See N. Hannestad, *Tradition in Late Antique Sculpture* (1994).

3 Private collection, Rome; Holum, *Theodosian Empresses*, p. 38.

4 Museum of the History of Art, Vienna; D. Talbot Rice, *Byzantine Art* (1935, 1965), p. 399, fig. 363 (but is this really the minister and consul Eutropius?). There is also an early fifth-century statue of an official at the Archaeological Museum in Istanbul (Koch, *Early Christian Art*, pl. 29.2). J.M.C. Toynbee (*The Art of the Romans* [1965], p. 42) wrote as follows about other portraits:

> The characteristics of the portraiture of non-imperial persons during the fifth century are summarised in two outstanding works. One is a colossal head found at Ostia, with enormous, deep-set, far-seeing eyes that wholly dominate the face. . . . A thick wreath of heavy, stylised curls overhangs the brow, across which are cut three equally stylised furrows. . . . The expression is rapt, as of one who has little concern with this world.
>
> (H.P. L'Orange, *Studien zur Geschichte des spätantiken Porträts* [1933], pls 221, 223)

Professor Toynbee then proceeds to quote a second head (*Art of the Romans*, pls 216–18), found at Ephesus and now at Vienna (see start of note), which may, however (although this is uncertain), date from after 500. 'This', she says, 'is the likeness of a prophet or contemplative. As we look at it, we are transported right out of the world of ancient humanism into that of medieval spirituality.'

The base of the Column of Theodosius I at Constantinople shows imperial reliefs of a slightly earlier date (M. Grant, *FMR* [Franco Maria Ricci], 20, 1989, pp. 19ff). This already displays the hieratic style which was becoming fashionable. But we should remain cautious about seeing a continuity between *imperial cult* and early Christian art.

As for non-imperial themes, a relief at Augusta Trevirorum (Trier), showing Holy Women (see Ch. 8, n. 15), is worth mentioning; and other Victories on the sides of the Column of Marcian at Constantinople (a pagan theme; see Ch. 9, n. 6), to which a lot came in from elsewhere. Aphrodisias (Geyre), for example, was active and sent a lot of its products to Constantinople. See also S. Walker, *Greek and Roman Portraits* (1995); and D.M. Brinkerhoff, *A Collection of Sculpture in Classical and Early Christian Antioch* (1970).

5 Koch, *Early Christian Art*, pp. 133ff.

6 S. Williams and G. Frick, *Theodosius: The Empire at Bay* (1994), p. 17.

7 J.P.C. Kent and K.S. Painter, *The Wealth of the Roman World: Gold and Silver, AD 300–700* (1977), p. 186. The *trabea* was a robe of state. For Justinian I, see Appendix 3. There were also reliefs on the Ravenna Sarcophagus in that city's cathedral (first half of fifth century); for sarcophagi see below, n. 31. And there were metal reliefs. But the marble reliefs on the Throne of the Archbishop Maximian at Ravenna may be later. (There is also a fine relief in wood on the door of S. Sabina's Church in Rome.)

8 Gough, *Origins of Christian Art*, p. 134. The earliest consular diptych is that of Probus (408) (ibid., p. 124, fig. 100, cf. p. 120). For the 'diptych of the Nicomachi and Symmachi', ibid., p. 127. For the picture of Honorius on one diptych, Williams and Frick, *Theodosius*, pl. 14. There is also an ivory plaque of him in Aosta Cathedral.

In addition, there were engraved ivory boxes (Gough, *Origins of Christian*

Art, p. 196) – used as caskets for relics in the Middle Ages (Koch, *Early Christian Art*, p. 135).

9 Kent and Painter, *Wealth*, p. 57.

10 J. Vogt, *The Decline of Rome* (1965), pp. 305f. The mosaic cycle from the Church of the Holy Apostles at Constantinople is only known from much later descriptions. It is, as stated elsewhere, very uncertain whether the mosaics in the Great Palace at Constantinople belong to the fifth century (see Ch. 11, n. 33). There are, however, fine fifth-century mosaics at Ravenna (notably in the Mausoleum of Galla Placidia, where the predominant colour is blue), and there is a mosaic of the Good Shepherd at Aquileia. As regards the technique of the mosaic, mathematical ratios of colours were carefully observed; and one can note the gradual change in the attitude of artists and patrons from a taste for naturalistic realism to a preference for the fantastic, unreal and hieratic.

11 S. Runciman, *Byzantine Style and Civilization* (1975, 1981), pp. 25, 27.

12 Gough, *Origins of Christian Art*, pp. 86, 88, 91.

13 H. Neumayer, *Byzantine Mosaics* (1964), pl. 1; see also pl. 2 (*c.* 450).

14 Gough, *Op.cit.*, p. 93.

15 Neumayer, *Byzantine Mosaics*, pl. 20.

16 Gough, *Op.cit.*, p. 85 (*c.* 406).

17 R. Krautheimer, *Early Christian and Byzantine Architecture* (1965), p. 55; see also Gough, *Origins of Christian Art*, fig. 72; Saints Onesiphorus and Porphyrius. The 'mosaic vision of the heavenly Jerusalem in the Dome epitomises the art of later Antiquity' (R.C. Gordon, *Times Literary Supplement*, 6 July 1996, p. 27).

18 Krautheimer, *Early Christian and Byzantine Architecture*, p. 55.

19 Pavement mosaics have been revealed at Constantinople when the foundations of the Town Hall were being constructed (P. du Bourguet, *Early Christian Painting* [1971], pp. 149ff.).

20 Gough, *Origins of Christian Art*, pp. 73f., 76. These mosaics at Mopsuestia (Misis) are not earlier than the late fifth century (S. Hill, *The Early Byzantine Churches of Cilicia and Isauria*, p. 235).

21 Gough, *Origins of Christian Art*, p. 77. The emperor Zeno favoured animals and birds because, as a native of Isauria, he regarded St Thecla (Ch. 11) as his patron saint. Other mosaics of the period have come to light at El-Tabgah (the Heptapegon [du Bourguet, *Early Christian Painting*, figs 161–2 – Loaves and Fishes]) and on a tomb at Tabarca (Thabraca: in Tunisia, ibid., figs 158ff.).

22 Gough, *Origins of Christian Art*, pp. 77, 166. Panel mosaics (*opus sectile*, 'cut work') also existed. The materials used were precious kinds of marble and porphyry of various colours, and for walls also coloured glass panels, which were cut into different forms. Geometrical and floral patterns and figures were composed with them (Koch, *Early Christian Art*, pp. 97f.). But glass of this period is insufficiently researched: J.J. Henderson and M.M. Mango, in E. Mango and G. Dagron (eds), *Constantinople*, p. 333 (and n. 1); see also Toynbee, *Art of the Romans*, pp. 141ff. Mosaics of this kind appear in various fifth-century churches (Koch, *Early Christian Art*, p. 98). One of them was at Ephesus.

23 du Bourguet, *Early Christian Painting*, pp. 3, 5, 7 (early fifth century). Paintings often imitate expensive panel mosaics (Koch, *Early Christian Art*).

24 du Bourguet, *Op.cit.*, figs 172–5, 171. There were also monumental paintings in the Church of St Peter and St Marcellinus in Rome: Christ is shown

between Peter and Paul. 'Icons' occur in the sixth or seventh centuries (Koch, *Early Christian Art*, p. 103).

25 Sas-Zaloziecky, *Byzantinische Kunst*, p. 91. For the Quedlinburg Itala, Koch, *Early Christian Art*, p. 104 (he points to the probability of earlier examples, now lost). But the present location of the Quedlinburg Treasure, and its various parts, remains uncertain, because of disputes (see J. Langton, *Sunday Times*, 7 April 1996, p. 7).

26 Kent and Painter, *Wealth*, p. 160.

27 For items from the Coleraine silver hoard, see ibid., pp. 123, 125. For a silver reliquary at the Louvre, Koch, *Early Christian Art*, pl. 28, no. 3 (cf. the reliquary at the Museo dell'Arcivescovado, Ravenna, pl. 27, no. 1). It is uncertain whether the Carthage hoard is of this date (or is it fourth century?). For imperial stamps, ibid., p. 80, and for gold bars, R.A.G. Carson, *Coins of the Roman Empire* (1990), p. 30, n. 20 (references). For gold finger(signet)-rings, Kent and Painter, *Wealth*, p. 6. For jewellery in general, H. Tait, *Jewellery through Seven Thousand Years* (1976); H. Tait (ed.), *Seven Thousand Years of Jewellery* (1989, 1995); J. Ogden, *Ancient Jewellery* (1992); A. Catinescu (ed.), *Ancient Jewellery and Archaeology* (1996); D. Williams and J. Ogden, *Jewellery of the Classical World* (1994). For silverware see M. Grant, *Art in the Roman Empire* (1995), pp. 116ff.; Kent and Painter, *Wealth*. Silver was prominent in Britain: and in general it fulfilled a significant role in Roman diplomacy and commerce.

28 Kent and Painter, *Wealth*, p. 160. See also P. Grierson and M. Blackburn, *Medieval European Coinage*, vol. I: *The Early Middle Ages* (1956).

29 Silks were also extensively used for hanging, though they have not survived. They were imported; silk-worms were not introduced into the Byzantine empire until 552. For pagan designs on textiles see above, Ch. 9, n. 6. Contemporary glass-work should also be mentioned: see E.M. Stern, *Roman Mold-Blown Glass* (1995); BM exhibition of 1995, 'Glass of the Caesars'; D.B. Harden, *Glass of the Caesars* (1987).

30 Koch, *Early Christian Art*, pp. 144, 146.

31 Ibid., p. 113, cf. above, n. 7. See also M. Koortbajian, *Myth, Meaning and Memory on Roman Sarcophagi* (1995). The various types of sarcophagus are enumerated by Koch, (*Early Christian Art*, pp. 109–12). He also illustrates what is described as a 'pseudo-sarcophagus'. He points out that Ravenna styles (some taken from Rome) are different from those of Constantinople. But it remains difficult to tie down many, or any, sarcophagi to the fifth century. Yet sarcophagi had already become a very significant portion of Roman imperial art (Grant, *Climax of Rome*, pp. 25f.; Koortbajian, *Myth*), and they were taken over by the Christians, who added a second row of niches to make room for their Biblical themes (E. Strong, *Art in Ancient Rome*, II [1929], p. 188). There has lately been much comment on the (earlier) sarcophagus of Junius Bassus.

EPILOGUE

1 S. Runciman, *Byzantine Civilisation* (1933), p. 277.

2 S. Huntington (*Foreign Affairs*, 1993) sees a coming clash between the west and Islam. Yet the adherents of that religion are, at present at least, deeply divided. As to the medieval role of Byzantium, however, it is possible to be more definite: 'had not the citadel held the isthmus between the continents, the wave of Islam would have swept Europe in the infancy of Christian civilization, and might well have supplanted it. . . . Christianity

might have been crushed in its cradle' (G. Young, *Constantinople* [1992], p. 64). It is possible to translate this into secular terms, and to think of the medieval countries of Europe, or, more specifically, western Europe, rather than only of the Christian religion, as having been saved by Byzantium. The fifth century is the first decisive period in the medieval history of the European countries.

3 R. Byron, *The Byzantine Achievement* (1929, 1987), pp. 28, 78f. See M. Moorcock, *Byzantium Endures* (paperback 1992).

APPENDIX 1 CONSTANTINE I THE GREAT AND AFTER

1 M. Grant, *The Emperor Constantine* (1993), p. 64.

2 Ibid., pp. 221ff.; see R.A.G. Carson, *Principal Coins of the Romans*, vol. III: *The Dominate AD 294–498* (1971), p. 61, no. 1334.

3 Grant, *Constantine*, pp. 217f. Constantine's eldest son Crispus was executed at Pola (Pula) in 326 by order of his father, on evidence provided by Constantine's second wife, Flavia Maxima Fausta, whom Constantine subsequently put to death as well, at Augusta Trevirorum (Trier).

4 J.M.C. Toynbee, *The Art of the Romans* (1965), p. 41. Flavius Magnus Magnentius (350–3) was proclaimed emperor at Augustodunum (Autun). For the possibly Constantinian origin of the Church of St Irene at Constantinople, see Ch. 11, n. 10.

5 A.H.M. Jones, *The Later Roman Empire 284–602* (1964), pp. 120f.

6 For the *defensor civitatis*, appointed with this purpose, ibid., pp. 144f.

7 Ibid., p. 139. The *protectores divini lateris*, imperial bodyguard, seem to have been founded by Gallienus (260–8). By the time of Diocletian (284–305) there was a corps of *protectores* who accompanied the emperor. Subsequently they more or less ranked as officer cadets.

8 Ibid., p. 150.

9 Ibid., pp. 150f.

10 Gratian was overthrown by Magnus Maximus and murdered at Lugdunum (Lyon) in 383.

11 Constantine I the Great (306–37) had placed his field army, or central striking force, under the command of a Master of Infantry and Master of Horse (*magistri peditum, equitum*). Subsequently, the generalissimo of the day controlled both, becoming Master of Soldiers (*magister militum*).

12 Dacia and Macedonia at this time belonged to the eastern region (Dacia was now on the south bank of the lower Danube).

13 The *foederati* were regarded by some as partly responsible for the subsequent downfall of the western Roman empire. For them, see also Appendix 2, n. 4.

14 Eugenius was a professor of rhetoric at Rome, and a friend of Symmachus. He was nominally a Christian, but sympathised with paganism and restored the Altar of Victory in the Roman senate-house.

15 The building programmes of the period after Constantine I are disputable. The first Santa Sophia and the first Church of the Holy Apostles at Constantinople were probably mainly due to Constantius II (337–61); see (for the former), C. Mango, *Byzantinische Zeitschrift*, 82, 1990, pp. 51–61. But the theories about the origins of Santa Sophia are varied: see M. Gough, *The Origins of Christian Art* (1973), p. 149; and G. Koch, *Early Christian Art and Architecture: An Introduction* (1996), p. 52.

APPENDIX 2 AFRICA, SPAIN, GAUL

1 For the loss of these three territories by the western empire, see many secondary sources, including J.P.C. Kent and K.S. Painter, *Wealth of the Roman World: Gold and Silver, AD 300–700*, p. 117. Cf. Chapter 10, n. 1.

2 For Africa, see B.H. Warmington, *The North African Provinces from Diocletian to the Vandal Conquest* (1954); D.S. Mattingly, *Tripolitania* (1995). It was believed that in 420 the Roman general Bonifatius (Boniface; d. 432; see also Ch. 8, n. 2) had invited the Vandals to cross over from Spain and help him against the western Roman imperial government. The loss of (still prosperous, though occasionally riot-ridden) Carthage (J.G. Pedley [ed.], *New Light on Ancient Carthage* [1990], *Carthage: A Mosaic of Ancient Tunisia* [1987], A.B.A. Ben Khader and D. Sören [eds], *Carthage* [1990], and for recent excavations S. Lancel, *Carthage: A History* [1994, 1992]) was a major disaster for the western empire. And there were also many desert lands in north Africa, where the *circumcelliones* (whether religious or social revolutionaries or not) had been or had become perilous brigands. Imperial efforts to overthrow the Vandals in Africa failed, and their fleet (unique among the Germans) was a perpetual danger; N.H. Baynes, *Journal of Roman Studies*, 19, 1929, pp. 230ff. See also W.H.C. Frend, *Transactions of the Royal Historical Society*, 5, 1955, pp. 61ff.; C. Courtois, *Journal of Roman Studies*, 46, 1956, pp. 161ff. Obviously the *fossatum Africae*, in the south of the north African province, was no help against the Vandals coming from Europe (Spain).

3 R.M. Haywood, *The Myth of Rome's Fall* (1960), p. 160. Africa: C. Courtois, *Les Vandales et Afrique* (1953). A. Cameron (*The Mediterranean World in Late Antiquity, AD 395–600* [1993], p. 37 [cf. p. 231, n. 9]) has this to say about Gaiseric and his Vandals:

> By the late 420s . . . the Vandals under Gaiseric crossed the Straits of Gibraltar into north Africa, reached Augustine's See at Hippo [Regius; near Annaba] by 430, received a hasty land settlement in Numidia in 435, and took Carthage, the capital, in 439.
>
> Despite the abortive attempts of the eastern emperor, Theodosius II, to send a fleet to control them in AD 441, Vandal rule over most of north Africa, including Africa Proconsularis, Byzacena [from the Gulf of Hammamet to the Gulf of Gabes] and most of Numidia and Tripolitania [Tripolitana], received *de facto* recognition in 442.
>
> By 455 Gaiseric had taken over Corsica, Sardinia and the Balearics, and on the death of Valentinian III in that year even entered and sacked Rome, taking Sicily in 468; the further naval expedition sent by the eastern emperor Leo [I; and Majorian from the west] in the 460s [Ch. 7, n. 10] was an ignominious failure, and north Africa remained in Vandal control until the expedition of Belisarius in AD 533.
>
> Though it now seems that Vandal Africa was less isolated economically from the rest of the empire than has traditionally been supposed, the speed and ease with which one of the richest and most urbanized provinces, supplier of grain to Rome, was lost is sufficient indicator of the degrees of change which the northern barbarians were to cause from now on.

See also Ch. 9, n. 29; Ch. 8, n. 1; and Ch. 7, nn. 3, 4, 19 on Gaiseric. North Africa was particularly favourable to monastic life and dissociation; see Ch. 9.

4 The *foederati* were Germans admitted to the Roman empire in groups, very often to serve as soldiers. See E.A. Thompson, *Journal of Roman Studies*, 46, 1956, pp. 65ff., on the policy of settling them in Gaul. Late fourth-century and fifth-century graves sometimes show Roman and German burials side by side. For the imitation of eastern and western imperial coinage by the Ostrogoths, Visigoths, Vandals and Burgundians, see R.A.G. Carson, *Coins of the Roman Empire* (1990), pp. 18, 243. It has been suggested that Aetius was too interested in Gaul – at the expense of Italy and Africa and other western countries – see J.B. Moss, *Historia*, 22, 1973, p. 712; A. Ferrill, *The Fall of Rome: The Military Explanation* (1988), p. 168. In 486 the last western Roman stronghold in Gaul (Noviodunum), under Syagrius, fell to the Franks, on whom see H. Fischer, *Catholic Historical Review*, n.s. 4, 1924–5, pp. 536ff. The Burgundians issued copies of the gold and silver coins of Anastasius I (492–518), as the Visigoths had imitated those of Honorius (395–423). See T.J. Haarhoff, *Schools of Gaul* (2nd edn, 1958); R.W. Mathisen, *Roman Aristocrats in Barbarian Gaul* (1993); F. Funck-Brentano, *A History of Gaul: Celtic, Roman and Frankish Rule* (1993); J. Drinkwater and H. Elton (eds), *Fifth Century Gaul: A Crisis of Identity* (1992, 1994).

5 Alaric II was king of the Visigoths from 485 to 507; Wallia had been king from 415 to 418. See H. Wolfram, *History of the Goths* (1990), etc. The Alamanni were a loose confederacy of German tribes which in the fifth century had settled in Alsace and northern Switzerland.

6 We are told this by St Gregory of Caesarodunum (Tours), the Gallo-Roman historian of the Franks, *c.* 540–94. In 417 the *civitas Vasatica* in Aquitania (Cossio) had been handed over to the Germans by a gang of slaves, according to Paulinus of Pella (born 377/8). See also R. van Dam, *Saints and Their Miracles in Late Antique Gaul* (1995).

A Cameron (*The Mediterranean World in Late Antiquity AD 395–600* [1993], p. 40) writes about Clovis as follows (see also pp. 245f., n. 32 and p. 208, nn. 38, 39 in Drinkwater and Elton, *Fifth Century Gaul*):

> The longest lasting of the German kingdoms was that of the Franks, established by their king Clovis (481–511) after their momentous defeat of the Visigoths at Vouillé [10 miles from Poitiers] in AD 507 and lasting until AD 751. Although it was the Franks who gave their name to modern France, Clovis's descendants are usually known as the Merovingians.
>
> They found a vivid chronicler in the late sixth-century Bishop Gregory of Tours [Caesarodunum], whose History of the Franks is our main source, remarkable not least for its unrestrained cataloguing of the bloodthirsty doings of the Frankish royal family. Gregory provides a colourful account of the conversion and baptism of Clovis himself. . . . More than 3,000 of his army were baptised at the same time.

Gaul was deeply religious (van Dam, *Saints*), but suffered from a very severe tax burden (see Sidonius Apollinaris). Southern Gaul had possibly been the country of origin of a square ivory box in the British Museum: M. Gough, *The Origins of Christian Art* (1973), p. 130.

Britain produced a fifth-century usurper, Constantine III. Or rather, wherever he was born, he was acclaimed emperor by the army in Britain in 407, crossed over to Gaul, where he defeated German invaders, including the Goth Sarus sent against him by Stilicho. Constantine III sent his son Constans to win over Spain, and obtained recognition from Honorius (409), who however sent Constantius (III) and Ulfilas against him. After the defeat of his general Edobicus, Constantine III capitulated at Arelate (Constantina, Arles), and Honorius allowed him to be put to death. 'It is doubtful', writes C.E. Stevens (*Oxford Classical Dictionary*, 2nd edn, 1970), 'whether after AD 410 there was ever a Roman army there again. . . . In the struggle of Celt and Teuton, Roman Britain disappeared almost completely (the precise extent of survival is very controversial).' For the loss of Britain to the Romans see W. Reece, *World Archaeology*, 12, 1980, pp. 77ff.; A.S.E. Cleary, *The Ending of Roman Britain* (1989), the country (or at least its south-eastern part) became Anglo-Saxon.

Britain (or Ireland) was also the place of origin of the 'heretic' Pelagius (d. after 419; see Chapter 9). See S. Hill and S. Ireland, *Roman Britain* (1996). There is much literature too, about King Arthur, e.g. G. Ashe, *The Discovery of King Arthur* (1985), and *Arthuriana*. Viroconium (Wroxeter) was still being reconstructed in the later fifth century, and excavations at Tintagel date ruins to the fifth century. See also *The Times*, 23 August 1996; M. Haig, *The Art of Roman Britain* (1996).

APPENDIX 3 JUSTINIAN I AND BEFORE

1 A.H.M. Jones, *The Later Roman Empire 284–602* (1964), p. 267.
2 C.W.C. Oman, *The Byzantine Empire* (1892), p. 6. See G. Young, *Constantinople* (1992), p. 38. Theodora, who had a portrait-statue of which the excellence was praised by the sixth-century historian Procopius (on whom see, however, G.A. Williamson [transl.], *The Secret History* [Loeb edn, 1966, 1981]; A. Cameron, *Procopius* [paperback 1996]), was a colourful figure about whom much can be said. Her marriage caused many scandals, fully recorded by Gibbon. She has been accused of feeling it more important to conciliate the east than Rome. The Nika riots (532), when she proved tough enough to rescue her husband Justinian I, were staged by the Blue and Green 'factions', of which the existence was a concession by the autocracy to the old city-state ideal. See also C. Diehl, *Byzantine Portraits* (1927), pp. 49ff.; R. Browning, *Justinian and Theodora* (1987).
3 Justinian's closure of the University of Athens has been described as the 'death-blow of pagan philosophy' (N.H. Baynes, *The Byzantine Empire* [1925], p. 86). Justinian's overall aim was to bring pagan Athens and Christian Jerusalem together. He also acted vigorously against the Manichaeans (Ch. 9) and his reign saw the end of the Montanists (ibid., n. 33).
4 R.M. Haywood, *The Myth of Rome's Fall* (1960), p. 164. For Africa see also Appendix 2. The reconquest of Africa by Justinian I increased its prosperity. For Spain, see Appendix 2 (Carthago Nova [Cartagena] was briefly a Byzantine capital). But Gaul, over which Clovis had ruled (481–511), remained beyond his reach. Justinian's army in the west mostly consisted of mercenaries and foreigners. The resources of the east were inadequate for the gigantic task of reconquest, which Justinian, preoccupied by religion, underestimated. By 565 it was clear that the empire could not be reunited. The war in Italy, full of events (including five captures of half-burnt Rome), dragged on until 561. Justinian's statesmanlike enemy Baduila (Totila, 551–62) replaced the head of the living Justinian on his coins by that of the long-dead Anastasius I (491–518), or of

himself. Baduila's successor was Theia. In 534 there was the last western consul (541 in the east). Parts of Italy remained in Byzantine hands until the eleventh century.tinian, there had been dissension in the Byzantine high command in Italy. Belisarius was insufficiently backed by the emperor. Narses was more subtle, but did not have enough ships. Justinian was highly conscious of his historic mission (see *Novel*, 30, 11). Yet, not only was his conquest of Italy not permanent, but its immediate effects were not encouraging, for the old Italian landed aristocracy was destroyed, and 'Rome degenerated', said Henry Chadwick (*Times Literary Supplement*, 22 March 1996, p. 5) 'into a city of collapsing ruins [see above] with a riff-raff population of yobbos held in contempt elsewhere.'

5 Young, *Constantinople*, pp. 54f.

6 See now L.H. Fauber, *Narses: Hammer of the Goths* (1996).

7 W.E. Kaegi, *Byzantium and the Decline of Rome* (1968), pp. 238f. The question whether Justinian I was genuinely interested in Law, and the extent to which his efforts rested on preliminary work, has been much discussed. Why was the Code of Theodosius II neglected or dropped? Justinian's *Corpus* was standard in the east, but not in the west until the twelfth century. It was in Latin, which was now much rarer than Greek, though still the imperial language. The 'House of Laws', at the time, was Berytus (Beirut). Yet the legal publications of Justinian at Constantinople have been hailed as proof of that city's claims to be 'the connecting link between the ancient and medieval civilizations' (Young, *Constantinople*, p. 32; cf above, Ch. 3).

8 John of Cappadocia became *praefectus praetorio* (Praetorian Prefect) of the east, although he was of humble origin and had never received a liberal education. He was reappointed, holding office (except for a brief period) from 531 to 541, when he fell victim to a plot by Theodora. For a criticism of his many administrative reforms see Jones, *Later Roman Empire*, p. 283, cf. pp. 351, 834. He possessed a bodyguard of several thousand men (Procopius, *Bellum Persicum* I [*History of the Wars of Justinian*], XXV.7; Jones, *Later Roman Empire*, p. 866). John advised Justinian I against the western war.

9 Justinian I got involved in an obstinate struggle with the large landowners. He was said to have introduced twenty-six new taxes (no doubt largely on the advice of John of Cappadocia; see previous note).

10 Neos Anchialos (Thebes in Phthiotis), for example, was fortified under Justinian I. Anazarbus (Anavarza) was rebuilt after earthquakes in the reigns of Justin I and Justinian I (Procopius, *Secret History*, XVIII.10; S. Hill, *The Early Byzantine Churches of Cilicia and Isauria* [1996], p. 9).

11 Young, *Constantinople*, pp. 41ff., 47ff. The domes and semi-domes of Santa Sophia are its most striking features. Justinian I's chief architect of the church, Anthemius (d. 534), was a mathematician and inventor. After the rebuilding was completed, Justinian is supposed to have said: 'Glory be to God, who has found me worthy to finish so great a work, and to excel thee, O Solomon' (see Young, *Constantinople*, p. 42). The first Santa Sophia had probably been built by Constantius II (see Appendix 1, n. 15), and the ceiling fell in during the reign of Julian (361–3). See also N. Mainstone, *Hagia Sophia* (paperback 1997).

12 Justinian I enlarged St Irene at Constantinople – reputedly the earliest domed basilica in the city – in 532 or soon after (for its previous history see Ch. 11, n. 10). Sts Sergius and Bacchus dates from 523 to 537 (?). The Church of St Polyeuctus (c. 524–7, now excavated), which Santa Sophia (see n. 11) may have been erected to outdo, was constructed by a wealthy nobleman (Anicia

Juliana): C. Mango, *Byzantium* (1980, 1994), p. 262; R.M. Harrison, *A Temple for Byzantium* (1989); Hill, *Early Byzantine Churches*, fig. 62. Cf. S. Runciman, *Byzantine Style and Civilisation* (1975), pp. 50ff., 99, 210. The first Church of the Holy Apostles in the same city was probably erected by Constantius II.

13 D. Talbot Rice, *Byzantine Art* (1955, 1962), pp. 164, 167. Sant'Apollinare in Classe was built by Theoderic for the Arians but rededicated in Justinianic times (549) for the Orthodox (Catholic) Church. It is in many ways a straightforward basilica, but careful examination shows breaches with the earlier basilica tradition. Sant'Apollinare in Classe is remarkable for its atmosphere of rhythm and light and colour (heightened by nationalistic yet symbolical mosaics).

14 Ibid., pp. 158ff. San Vitale was begun in 525 and consecrated in 548. It possessed a memorable plan of three concentric octagons, and is notable for its delicately coloured marbles and superb mosaics, including an excellent portrait of Maximian (archbishop of Ravenna 545–53), whose famous throne, adorned with plaques, has been ascribed to a variety of Egyptian (and other) carvers of various dates. Eastern features, too, have been discerned in the mosaic figures of the emperor Justinian I and his wife Theodora; indeed many of the mosaics, amid the multiple meanings that they embody, reflect successive waves of eastern influences. It has been disputed whether the principal artist came from Constantinople (the churches of which the west surely copied) or was an Italian, or at least a westerner. San Vitale (which contained precious objects) must have been very expensive.

15 J.J. Norwich, *Byzantium: The Early Centuries* (1989), pp. 263f., 266.

16 Jones, *Later Roman Empire*, pp. 269f. (see also now J. Moorhead, *Justinian: The Mediterranean World* [1994]). Sant'Apollinare Nuovo, though in many respects less impressive than Sant'Apollinare in Classe, nevertheless has a remarkable atmosphere of blended light and colour, displayed in its frontal, Asiatic (Syrian) non-naturalistic, symbolic mosaics, including a remarkable procession of male and female saints, and one of the earliest and most complete New Testament scenes.

17 See now J.A.S. Evans, *The Age of Justinian* (1996); cf. J.W. Barker, *Justinian and the Later Roman Empire* (1966).

NOTES TO BIBLIOGRAPHY

1 P. Brown, *Religion and Society in the Age of St Augustine*; cf. his articles, listed in *Augustine of Hippo* (1967), p. 436. See also B. Stock, *Augustine the Reader*, Harvard University Press, 1996, and Chapter 10 (notes 2, 3, 4). For other recent works on St Augustine, see Viella Catalogue no. 16 (1997), nos. 997–1004.

2 See P. Brown, *Augustine of Hippo* (1967) for his biography.

3 M. Hadas, *A History of Latin Literature* (1952), pp. 430ff.

4 G. Downey, *The Late Roman Empire* (1969), p. 76.

5 Daedalus Book Catalogue (1995), introducing a new translation. Cf. also D. Slavitt (tr.), *The Fables of Avianus* (1993).

6 S. Perowne, *The End of the Roman World* (1966), p. 137.

7 M.C. Howatson, *Oxford Companion to Classical Literature* (1937, 1989), p. 342.

8 J. Vogt, *The Decline of Rome* (1965), pp. 177f.

9 W.H.C. Frend, *Journal of Roman Studies*, LIX, 1969, p. 8.

10 Salvian, IV, 30; cf. M. Hadas, *A History of Latin Literature* (1952), p. 444; J. Badewein, *Geschichtstheologie und Sozialkritik im Werk Salvians von Marseille* (1980).

11 J.D. Randers-Pehrson, *Barbarians and Romans* (1983), pp. 251, 258; cf. J. Harries, *Sidonius Apollinaris and the Fall of Rome* (1944).
12 C.W.C. Oman, *The Story of the Byzantine Empire* (1892), pp. 52f.
13 Cf. now C. Siorvanes, *Proclus* (1996).
14 SLR, *Oxford Classical Dictionary*, 1970 edn, p. 1005.
15 Cf. J. Bregman, *Synesius of Cyrene: Philosopher-Bishop* (1982).

LISTS

1 ROMAN EMPERORS

31 BC–AD 14	Augustus
AD 14–37	Tiberius
37–41	Gaius (Caligula)
41–54	Claudius
54–68	Nero
68–9	Galba
69	Otho
69	Vitellius
69–79	Vespasian
79–81	Titus
81–96	Domitian
96–8	Nerva
98–117	Trajan
117–38	Hadrian
138–61	Antoninus Pius
161–80	{ Marcus Aurelius
161–9	{ Lucius Verus
180–92	Commodus
193	Pertinax
193	Didius Julianus
193–211	Septimius Severus
211–17	{ Caracalla
211–12	{ Geta
217–18	Macrinus
218–22	Elagabalus
222–35	Severus Alexander
235–8	Maximinus I
238	{ Gordianus I Africanus
238	{ Gordianus II Africanus

238	{ Balbinus
238	{ Pupienus
238–44	Gordianus III
244–9	Philippus
249–51	Trajanus Decius
251–3	Trebonianus Gallus
253	Aemilianus
253–9/60	{ Valerian
253–68	{ Gallienus
268–70	Claudius II Gothicus
270	Quintillus
270–5	Aurelian
275–6	Tacitus
276	Florian
276–82	Probus
282–3	Carus
283–4	{ Carinus
283–4	{ Numerian
284–305	{ Diocletian
286–305	{ Maximian
305–6	Constantius I
305–11	(Galerius
306–12	{ Maxentius
306–13	(Maximinus II Daia
312–37	{ Constantine I the Great
312–24	{ Licinius I
337–40	(Constantine II
337–50	{ Constans
337–61	(Constantius II
361–3	Julian the Apostate
363–4	Jovian

Division of empire

Western

364–75	Valentinian I
375–83	Gratian
383–92	Valentinian II
392–5	Theodosius I
395–423	Honorius
423–5	Johannes
425–55	Valentinian III
455	Petronius Maximus

180

455–6	Avitus
456–7	*Interregnum*
457–61	Majorian
461–5	Libius Severus
465–7	*Interregnum*
467–72	Anthemius
472	Olybrius
473–4	Glycerius
474–5	Julius Nepos
475–6	Romulus Augustulus

Eastern

376–8	Valens
378–95	Theodosius I
395–408	Arcadius
408–50	Theodosius II
450–7	Marcian
457–74	Leo I
474	Leo II and Zeno
474–91	Zeno
491–518	Anastasius I

2 POPES (FIFTH CENTURY)

398–401	Anastasius I
402–17	Innocentius
417–18	Zosimus
418–22	Bonifacius
422–33	Celestinus
433–40	Sixtus III
440–61	Leo I
461–8	Hilarius
468–83	Simplicius
483–92	Felix III
492–6	Gelasius II
496–8	Anastasius II
498–514	Symmachus

3 EVENTS

395–408	ascendancy of Stilicho in west
396–401	Alans ruled over east Balkans

400	Gainas in power at Constantinople
401–17	tribune mosaics at Church of S. Pudenziana, Rome
402	western capital moved from Mediolanum (Milan) to Ravenna
402, 403	Alaric I, king of the Visigoths, defeated by Stilicho
c. 404	death of Claudian
after 405	death of Prudentius
406 (last day)	Germans cross Rhine
407	Constantine III crosses from Britain to European mainland
408	earthquakes at Constantinople
410	sack of Rome by Alaric I
c. 410	end of Roman army in Britain
411	death of Constantine III
413	Great Wall of Constantinople
?414	death of Anthemius, Praetorian Prefect in east
415	lynching of Hypatia at Alexandria
415	death of Ataulf, king of Visigoths; succeeded by Wallia
417	Placidia married Constantius (later III)
418	Visigoths establish capital at Tolosa (Toulouse)
after 419	death of Pelagius (banished 417/18)
420	death of St Jerome
422	peace of eastern empire with Persians
422–31	Church of S. Sabina at Rome
423	Aelia Eudoxia (II, or Eudocia: Athenais) made Augusta
425	Galla Placidia appealed to eastern emperor
425	University of Constantinople established
c. 425	Church of S. Croce at Ravenna
428	accession of Gaiseric, king of the Vandals
428–31	Nestorius bishop of Constantinople
429 (411)	Donatist dispute simmered down
430	death of St Augustine
431	first ('Robber') Council of Ephesus
432	death of Boniface
437	Honoria made Augusta
c. 440	'Mausoleum of Galla Placidia' at Ravenna
c. 444	death of Cyril, bishop of Alexandria
447	earthquake at Constantinople
448	*Tome* of Pope Leo I
449	Second Council of Ephesus
c. 450	Church of S. Pietro in Vincoli in Rome
c. 450	Church of St John at Ephesus
c. 450	Baptistery of Neon (or the Orthodox; S. Giovanni in Fonte) at Ravenna

451	battle of Catalaunian Plains
451	Council of Chalcedon (Kadiköy)
452	invasion of Italy by Attila, king of the Huns
453	death of Attila
453	death of Pulcheria
454	death of Aetius
455	sack of Rome by Gaiseric
456	Ricimer, German generalissimo in the west, compels Avitus to abdicate
460	death of Aelia Eudoxia (II, or Eudocia: Athenais)
463	Church of St John Studios, Constantinople
466–84	Euric, independent Visigothic monarch
468–83	Church of S. Maria Maggiore (Basilica Liberiana), Rome
468–83	Church of S. Stefano Rotondo, Rome
?before 469	Long Walls of Thrace
c. 470	Church of S. Vittore in Ciel d'Oro, Mediolanum (Milan)
c. 470	Church of Acheiropoietos, Thessalonica (Salonica)
after 470	death of Salvian
472	death of Ricimer
474	accession of Gundobad (Burgundian)
475	Orestes elevates his son Romulus Augustulus as last western emperor
476	fall of Rome: Odoacer becomes king of Italy
476–7	revolt of Basiliscus in east
477	death of Gaiseric
481/2	*Henotikon* of eastern emperor Zeno
481/2	accession of Clovis, king of Franks
483/4	Aelia Verina released by Illus from exile
484–8	revolt of Leontius in east
485–507	Alaric II, king of Visigoths
486	Noviodunum (Pommiers), last imperial stronghold in Gaul, under Syagrius, fell to the Franks
488	death of Illus
491	Ariadne directs eastern succession
493	death of Odoacer, succeeded by Theoderic the Ostrogoth
496	Indian embassy to Constantinople

SELECT BIBLIOGRAPHY

The works of ancient writers listed here are limited to those writers who lived in the fifth century AD.

1 LATIN

AUGUSTINE (Aurelius Augustinus), born and trained in Latin at Thagaste (Soukh-Aras, Algeria), AD 354–430. Wrote *Confessions* (*c.* 397–400), *De Doctrina Christiana*, *De Trinitate* (399–419), *De Civitate Dei* (*The City of God*, 413–26), *Retractationes* (427). Augustine, comments P. Brown,

> marks the end of classical thought. For an ancient Greek, ethics had consisted of telling a man . . . what he would do, and hence, what he could achieve. Augustine, in the *City of God*, told him for what he must live in hope. It is a profound change.[1]
>
> (P. Brown, *Religion and Society in the Age of St Augustine*)

See Brown's articles, listed in *Augustine of Hippo* (1967), p. 436. See also B. Stock, *Augustine the Reader* (1996), and Ch. 10, nn. 2, 3, 4. For other recent works on St Augustine, see Viella Catalogue no. 16 (1997), nos. 997–1004.

Augustine's social observation, not only of the upper classes, is very keen and rich; and 'true life', he said, is 'nothing but the comedy of the human race'. R.M. Haywood adds that he

> never visited the eastern part of the empire. He had an excellent Latin training in the little school in the town of Thagaste [Soukh-Aras], and then as a university student at Carthage and at Rome.
>
> He tells us plainly that Greek left him cold in his student days. In his maturer years as bishop and theologian he feared that he must get his Greek in hand, partly because of some patronizing remarks in a letter from Jerome about his lack of background. His Greek was poor, but he finally became reasonably competent at it.[2]
>
> (R.M. Haywood, *The Myth of Rome's Fall*, 1960)

Augustine's determination to stamp out 'heresy' is further defined by M. Hadas:

If there is a single purpose which dominates [all the numerous works of St Augustine] it is the desire to defeat heresy, and the demands of Augustine's orthodoxy are very rigorous. In regard to the Bible, for example, he believed and his belief was only strengthened with time – that the Biblical chronology was perfectly accurate, that the events recorded were real, actually and not symbolically, that the Biblical history carried so much greater authority that it could not be checked by profane history.

Only through the Church, which was the sole heir of this revelation, could salvation be attained, and the Church could admit of no deviation. . . . All subsequent development in Christianity, Protestant as well as Catholic, is in effect a disputation on Augustinianism.[3]

(M. Hadas, *A History of Latin Literature* [1952], pp. 430ff.)

See also Chapters 9, 10, and cf. Haywood, *Myth of Rome's Fall*

The fate of Rome, St Augustine maintained, illustrated the different ways of life of the two communities that existed side by side in the Roman world, the City of Man and the City of God; the catastrophe demonstrated the inevitable consequences of these ways of life. . . . St Augustine's task was to study and compare two types of communities which differed fundamentally. . . .

But modern readers of *The City of God* are not always aware that the fall of Rome did not make the same impression on the thought of the citizens in the east that it did in the west. Naturally the significance of the catastrophe itself was felt in the east, but no scholar or churchman there ever wrote a similar treatise on the Two Cities.[4]

(G. Downey, *The Late Roman Empire* [1969], p. 76)

AVIANUS (or Avienus); of unknown origin, early fifth-century AD Roman fabulist. He dedicated his forty-two fables, in elegiac metre, to Macrobius. 'The lively and instructive Fables of this . . . Roman writer', it has been said,

enjoyed significant popularity in Europe throughout the Middle Ages. . . . The Fables of Avianus show a world in flux, in which humour and cunning constitute the only saving grace for humans. . . . Writing at a time when the Roman world was being transformed by Christianity, Avianus appears to voice doubt about human-kind's ability to deal with change. . . . He shows a preference for learning how to survive, and for the underdog.[5]

(Daedalus Book Catalogue [1995])

See also D. Slavitt (tr.), *The Fables of Avianus* [1993]).

CLAUDIAN. From Alexandria, *c.* 370–*c.* 404. Poet of the classical tradition. He came to Italy before 395, and turned from his native Greek to Latin. His later works include panegyrics on the consulates of Honorius (396, 398, 404), and Stilicho (400; in two books: a third celebrates Stilicho's entry into Rome), and *On the Gothic War* (402). His medieval fame largely depended on his earlier *Rape of Proserpine*. He employed his mastery of rhetoric and inventions for inferior themes, and the smoothness of his impeccable diction (as well as his invective) becomes tedious. He was an unabashed pagan. See O.A.W. Dilke, *Claudian: Poet of Declining Empire and Morals* (1969).

COMMODIANUS (Lucius Aelius Aurelius). It is uncertain whether he lived in the third, fourth or fifth century. *Instructiones*, and *Carmen Apologeticum*.

DRACONTIUS (Blossius Aemilius). End fifth century. Lived at Carthage. Wrote many secular and Christian poems, including *De Laudibus Dei* in three books of hexameters.

FULGENTIUS (Fabius Planciades). From Thelepte (Medinet el-Kdima) in Byzacena, north Africa, *c.* 437–532. Wrote numerous works, providing comfort for the African Catholics, and much read in the Middle Ages.

HYDATIUS. Born in the fourth century, died after 468. Probably bishop of Aquae Flaviae (Chaves), Gallaecia (now northern Portugal). Wrote continuation of *Ecclesiastical History* of Eusebius of Caesarea in Palestine (Strato's Tower) (*c.* 260–340) to 468.

JEROME (Eusebius Hieronymus). Born at Stridon, Dalmatia, *c.* 348–420. Wrote *Chronicle*, *De Viris Illustribus* (392), *Vulgate* (translation of Bible) and *Letters*.
This is what Stewart Perowne said about him:

> If we view sanctity in the guise of a kind of beautified sweetness – as was the fashion during a large part of the nineteenth century – then we must confess that Jerome would not figure in the establishment.
>
> But the folk of the Middle Ages and the epoch that succeeded them liked their saints to be tough. And Jerome, the darling of Roman drawing-rooms, the scintillating talker and scholar, who might have been excused for being a smooth man, he it was who was to prove himself as hardy as the sons of thunder, and to take the kingdom of heaven, as it were, by storm.[6]
>
> (S. Perowne, *The End of the Roman World* [1966], p. 137)

A good deal is also said about Jerome elsewhere (Ch. 9, nn. 37, 38; Ch. 10, n. 4).

MACROBIUS (known to his contemporaries as Theodosius, Praetorian Prefect of Italy in 439). He wrote the *Saturnalia*, a historically valuable dialogue in seven books dedicated to his son. He was also the author of the Neoplatonist 'Dream of Scipio' (*Somnium Scipionis*). 'A quotation from Macrobius', writes M.C. Howatson, 'was the sole contribution to the conversation made by the otherwise silent Samuel Johnson (1709–84), on his first evening at Pembroke College, Oxford.'[7]
(M.C. Howatson, *Oxford Companion to Classical Literature* [1937, 1989], p. 342)

NOTITIA DIGNITATUM. The major, if sometimes disputable, source for the late Roman army and provinces. On this work, known from a copy, it seems appropriate to quote J. Vogt:

We happen to possess a list, intended for official use, of all the military and civil offices of the empire. . . . This manual, a source of quite exceptional value both for the military system and for the court and administration of the late Roman empire, has long been the object of searching scrutiny, especially from the time the latest edition of the text was published, by Otto Seeck in 1876. . . .

The *Notitia* was drawn up shortly after 395 for the administrative head of the western division of the empire, although certain details about officials and troops were revised in subsequent years. The section in the east reflects the situation as it was not long after 395. On the other hand, many items in the section dealing with the western division of the empire have been brought up to a date *c.* 425, although there are admittedly some omissions and discrepancies. . . . Yet . . . the information contained in the *Notitia* . . . is an insufficient guide to the exact effective strength of the units.[8]

(J. Vogt, *The Decline of Rome* [1965], pp. 177f.)

OROSIUS (Paulus). From Spain. Fled from the Vandals in 414 and became a pupil of Augustine. Among other works, he wrote *Histories against the Pagans*, up to 417.

PAULINUS OF NOLA (Meropius Pontius Paulinus). Born at Burdigala (Bordeaux) *c.* 353–4, d. 411. Became bishop of Nola, Campania, where he had settled, renouncing much of his wealth in order to do so. Wrote more than thirty poems, creating new genres of wedding-hymn and sacred elegy, and sixty letters.

His unending quest for friendship furthered the growth of close ties between the leading western ecclesiastics, whether their sees or monasteries were situated in northern Gaul, Italy, Africa or Bethlehem.

Those intellectual links were valuable in an age of increasing theological debate, and their existence also encouraged the development of a close episcopal network throughout the west at the very moment when the western provinces of the empire were being overrun by the barbarians.[9]

(W.H.C. Frend, *Journal of Roman Studies*, 59, 1969, p. 8)

PRUDENTIUS (Aurelius Clemens). From Spain (Tarraconensis), 348 until after 405. The greatest Christian Latin poet. Wrote hymns and didactic works.

RUTILIUS NAMATIANUS (Rutilius Claudius Namatianus). Probably born at Tolosa (Toulouse). Early fifth century. Pagan. Wrote poem on coastal scenery of Etruria and contemporary events. Frank and tolerant.

SALVIAN. Probably born at Augusta Trevirorum (Trier). *c.* 400 until after 470. In 425 he joined the monastery of Honoratus on the island of Lérins (S. Honorat), and *c.* 439 became presbyter at Massilia (Marseille). Extant, from among his writings, are nine letters, a tract against avarice, and an eight-book work *On the Governance of God* (*De Gubernatione Dei*), 440. Salvian saw the German invaders as an instrument of divine wrath against the decadent western empire. Speaking on behalf of those with few possessions, he denounced inherited wealth. According to M. Hadas, Salvian paints 'an appalling picture of administrative corruption, oppression of the poor by the rich, a frenzied appetite for pleasure'. He exaggeratedly contrasts Christian laxity with the high morality of the barbarians. 'The Roman commonwealth', he writes, 'is dead, and even where it seems still to be alive it is drawing its last breath. . . . It dies and yet it smiles.'[10]

(Salvian, IV, 30; see M. Hadas, *A History of Latin Literature* [1952], p. 444)

SIDONIUS APOLLINARIS (Gaius Sollius Apollinaris Sidonius). Born at Lugdunum (Lyon). *c.* 430–79 or 480s. Wrote youthful poems and three poetical panegyrics, and nine books of letters.

> Sidonius Apollinaris was optimistic when he pronounced his glowing panegyric honouring his father-in-law, the emperor Avitus (455–6), and received the warm plaudits of the admiring Roman senators. . . .
> Sidonius lived for about another quarter of a century (we lose track of him around the year 479), but in that period he had to become adept at political tight-rope walking just to survive. . . . Sidonius used his own power [as bishop] with discretion, to resolve personal disputes or to help members of his flock caught in the press of circumstance. Otherwise, his efforts were probably confined to the business of keeping channels of communication open, with the hope that such channels would be useful at some future date.[11]
>
> (J.D. Randers-Pehrson, *Barbarians and Romans* [1983], pp. 251, 258; C.f. J. Harries, *Sidonius Apollinaris and the Fall of Rome* [1944])

He has also been described, however, as very critical of the western Roman empire.

SULPICIUS SEVERUS. Born in Aquitania (Gaul). *c.* 360–420. Wrote a *Life of St Martin of Tours*, the model of future Latin hagiography, and a universal chronicle to AD 400. In honour of St Martin, he renounced his wealth, and went to live in Gaul.

SYMMACHUS (Quintus Aurelius). *c.* 340–402. The most prominent and powerful opponent of Christianity, as many an incident (including his famous oratorical duel with Ambrose) showed. Symmachus was the owner of numerous properties. During the last period of his life he composed the greater part of the letters that have come down to us. He also wrote speeches (fragments preserved). Some regard him as the original source for 476 as the year of the final fall.

2 GREEK

This was a period, as has been said, when Greek was gaining ground, at the expense of Latin, as the language of the Roman empire. And yet the most important authors of the day wrote in Latin: one need think only of Augustine and Jerome. Nevertheless, in the east, culture was vigorous, once again under Christian influence. But the greatest eastern artistic talent went not into literature but into architecture (though the west, too, was not lacking in this; Ch. 11). Yet there were also a few distinguished Greek writers, as well as a considerable number of second- and third-rate ones, and they are listed here (not all their works are preserved).

ACACIUS. Joint author of Zeno's *Henotikon* (481/2).

CYRIL OF ALEXANDRIA, where he was bishop. Died *c.* 444. 'A man of unbounded ambition, of great skill in intrigue, totally indifferent to the means he used to gain his ends, in fact as un-Christlike a prelate as it would be easy to find.' His voluminous output included twenty books (1–10 extant in full) refuting the pagan former emperor Julian the Apostate. In Egypt, he continued his predecessor Theophilus's suppression of paganism, Judaism and 'heresy'. Edward Gibbon was very hostile to him.

EUNAPIUS. Born at Sardes (Sart) in Lydia. *c.* 345–*c.* 420. Anti-Christian history covering the years 270 to 404; and *Lives of the Sophists*, earlier (*c.* 396).

JOHN CHRYSOSTOM, *c.* 354–407. Educated at Antioch; bishop of Constantinople. Eloquent, forceful preacher in the Antiochene style, often attacking pagans. He also played a great part in the origination of the liturgy. His career and activities give a valuable display of how the power network operated. He supported the monks known as the 'Tall Brothers'. But his ascetic habits helped to make him unpopular, and he was deposed by the Synod of the Oak (403), exiled (for censuring the court of Aelia Eudoxia I), and then exiled again. His *De Sacerdotio* gives his conception of clerical duties. John Chrysostom, said C.W.C. Oman,

> was a man of saintly life and apostolic fervour, but rash and inconsiderate alike in speech and action. His charity and eloquence made him the idol of the populace of the imperial city, but his austere manners and autocratic methods of dealing with his subordinates had made him many foes among the clergy. The patriarch's enemies were secretly supported by the empress, who had taken offence at the outspoken way in which John habitually denounced the luxury and insolence of her court. She . . . at last induced the emperor [Arcadius] to allow the saintly patriarch to be deposed by a hastily summoned council, the 'Synod of the Oak'. . . . Another council . . . condemned John Chrysostom, and on Easter Day, AD 404, seized the patriarch in his cathedral by armed force, and banished him to Asia. . . . [Then] the exiled John was banished to a dreary mountain fastness in Cappadocia, and afterwards condemned to a still more remote prison at Pityus [Pitzunda] on the Euxine [Black Sea]. He died on his way thither.[12]

LEO I. Eastern emperor (457–74). Promulgated *Tome.*

LEO I. Pope. Sermons and letters.

MARINUS. See Proclus.

MARK THE DEACON. Bishop of Gaza. Wrote anti-Manichaean *Life of Porphyry* (*c.* 420), now lost.

189

NONNUS. From Panopolis (Achmim) in Egypt. Fifth century? Wrote 48-book epic *The Dionysiaca*, also probably a hexameter version of St John's Gospel.

OLYMPIODORUS. From Thebes (Medinet Habu) in Egypt. Before 380 until after 425. Although he describes himself as a 'poet by profession', he was the writer of a 22-book *History* (or memoirs) from 407 to 415 (now lost). 'The varied talents of Olympiodorus of Thebes', wrote J.F. Matthews, 'made him a figure of interest to students of his age. . . .' For Olympiodorus, the decline of the western empire was a contemporary event, subject like any other to the consequences of political incompetence and the operations of chance. He spoke to the classes in whose hands it had rested to influence events, by choosing between practical alternatives. That they had failed was a contingent, not a pre-ordained, matter: they had failed through a combination of ill luck, prejudice (not always their own), political ineptitude and dissension.

PALLADIOS. *c.* 364–431/2). A monk in Egypt and Palestine; became bishop of Helenopolis (formerly Drepanum, Bithynia). Wrote *Historia Lausiaca*, about the early Egyptian monks, and *Dialogue on the Life of St John Chrysostom* (*c.* 405).

PETER MONGUS. Joint author of Zeno's *Henotikon* (481/2).

PHILOSTORGIUS. *c.* 368–430/40. From Cappadocia; worked in Constantinople. An Arian. Continued the *Historia Ecclesiastica* of Eusebius (*c.* 260–340) until at least 425. His work is imperfectly preserved; epitomised by Photius (ninth century).

PRISCUS. Fifth century. From Panium (Thrace). Wrote 7-book *Byzantine History*, including events from 433 to 472 (now lost, but extensive excerpts are preserved in later writers).

PROCLUS. 410/12–85. From Lycia (?). Wealthy. Became Head of the Academy in Athens (his successor was Marinus, who wrote a Life of him). Author of *Elements of Theology, Platonic Theology, Elements of Physics*, commentaries on various writers, *Hymns* (translated into French by H.D. Saffrey, 1994), and perhaps *Chrestomathia*. He exercised a charismatic influence over a group of people, and was the last systematiser of the Greek philosophical inheritance. He called Christianity 'the barbarian philosophy'.[13]

SOCRATES (SCHOLASTICUS). From Constantinople. *c.* 380–450. Lawyer, continued the *Historia Ecclesiastica* of Eusebius of Caesarea (*c.* 260–340), dealing with the years 305–439. The chief source of Sozomen and Theodoret (*qq.v.*).

SOZOMEN. From Constantinople. Died *c.* 450. Lawyer. Wrote *History of the Church 324–430*. 'His conclusion', says S.L.R., 'has perhaps been lost. [The work] depends heavily upon Socrates [Scholasticus] (whom it never mentions), is similar in outlook and content, less critical but more stylish. Sozomen has some additional information, particularly for monasticism.'[14]

SYNESIUS. From Cyrene. *c.* 370–413. Pupil of the philosopher Hypatia at Alexandria. Bishop of Ptolemais (Tolmeta) in Cyrenaica. Wrote nine hymns, 156 letters and rhetorical discourses. His oratory was famous. His *De Regno* is highly political, but allegorical and discursive. He possessed a relationship to the land-owning aristocracy of Cyrenaica.[15]

THEODORET. *c.* 393–466. Became a monk and then bishop of Cyrrhus (Kuros), Syria. Wrote *Graecarum Affectionum Curatio, Church History* (from Constantine to 428), *Religious History,* works on biblical exegesis and theological controversy, and letters. Opposed Cyril of Alexandria. His culture was Greek, though his flock mostly only knew Syriac.

ZENO. Eastern emperor (474–91). Promulgated *Henotikon* (481/2). Authors: Acacius and Peter Mongus (*qq.v.*).

3 MODERN

Alföldy, G. *The Social History of Rome,* 1985, rev. edn 1988

Arnheim, M.T.W. *The Senatorial Aristocracy of the Later Roman Empire,* Oxford University Press, 1972

Arnott, P. *The Byzantines and Their World,* St Martin's Press, New York, 1973

Ash, J. *A Byzantine Journey,* Random House, New York, 1996

Bark, W.C. *Origins of the Medieval World,* Stanford University Press, 1958, Doubleday Anchor, New York, 1960

Baynes, N.H. *The Byzantine Empire,* Oxford University Press, 1925

Baynes, N.H. and Moss, H. St L.B. *Byzantium,* Clarendon Press, Oxford, 1949

Boak, A.E.R. *Manpower Shortage and the Fall of the Roman Empire in the West,* Michigan University Press, 1955

Brandon, S.G.F. *Religion in Ancient History,* Allen & Unwin, 1969, 1973

Brown, P. *The World of Late Antiquity,* Thames & Hudson, 1971

——*Religion and Society in the Age of St Augustine,* Faber & Faber, 1972

——*The Making of Late Antiquity,* Harvard University Press, Cambridge, Mass., 1978, 1996

——*The Cult of the Saints,* SCM Press, 1981

——*Society and the Holy in Late Antiquity,* California University Press, 1982

——*Authority and the Sacred,* Cambridge University Press, 1995

Burns, T.S. *Barbarians within the Gates of Rome,* Indiana University Press, Bloomington and Indianapolis, 1994

Bury, J.B. *The History of the Later Roman Empire,* 2 vols, Dover Publications Inc., New York, 1889, 1923, 1958

Byron, R. *The Byzantine Achievement,* Routledge & Kegan Paul, 1927, 1987

Cameron, A. *The Later Roman Empire AD 281–430,* Fontana, 1993

——*The Mediterranean World in Late Antiquity AD 395–600,* Routledge, 1993

Cameron, A., Long, S. and Sherry, L. *Barbarians and Politics at the Court of Arcadius,* California University Press, Berkeley, 1993

Carson, R.A.G. *The Principal Coins of the Romans,* vol. III, *The Dominate AD 294–498,* British Museum Publications, 1971

——*Coins of the Roman Empire,* Routledge, 1990

Chadwick, H. *The Early Church,* Penguin, 1967, 1978

Chambers, M. *The Fall of Rome: Can It Be Explained?,* Holt, Rienhart & Winston, New York, 1963, 1970

Christ, K. (ed.) *Der Untergang des römischen Reiches* (Weg der Forschung), 1971

Chuvin, P. *A Chronicle of the Last Pagans,* Harvard University Press, Cambridge, Mass., 1990

Cochrane, C.N. *Christianity and Classical Culture*, Oxford University Press, 1940, Galaxy, New York, 1957

Coleman, S. and Elsner, J. *Pilgrimage*, Harvard University Press, Cambridge, Mass., 1995

Collins, R. *Early Medieval Europe 200–1000*, Macmillan Education, Basingstoke, 1991

Coster, C.H. *Late Roman Studies*, Harvard University Press, Cambridge, Mass., 1968

Davies, J.G. *The Early Christian Church*, Barnes & Noble, New York, 1946

Deichmann, F.W. *Archaeologia Christiana*, Rome, 1983 (Italian, translated from German)

De Lusignan, L.M.R.M. *Rome et les églises d'Orient*, Paris, 1976

Demandt, A. *Der Fall Roms*, Munich, 1984

Demougeot, E. *La formation de l'Europe et les invasions barbares*, Paris, 1969

Dill, S. *Roman Society in the Last Century of the Western Empire*, Meridian, New York; rev. edn, 1958 (1898)

Dixon, K.R. and Southern, P. *The Late Roman Army*, 1996

Dodds, E.R. *Pagan and Christian in an Age of Anxiety*, Cambridge University Press, 1965

Downey, G. *The Late Roman Empire*, Holt, Rienhart & Winston (Harcourt Brace Jovanovich), 1969

du Bourguet, P. *Early Christian Painting*, Weidenfeld & Nicolson, 1971

Dvornik, F. *Byzantium and the Roman Primacy*, Fordham University Press, 1966 (1964)

Elsner, J. *Art and the Roman Viewer: The Transformation of Art from the Pagan World to Christianity*, Cambridge University Press, 1996

Elton, H. *Warfare in Roman Europe A.D. 350–425*, Oxford, 1995

Ferrero, G. *Le donne dei Cesari*, Milan, 1925

Ferrill, A. *The Fall of the Roman Empire: The Military Explanation*, Thames & Hudson, rev. edn 1988 (1983)

Ferrua, A. *The Unknown Catacomb*, Gedder & Grosset, Yale, 1995

Frend, W.H.C. *The Rise of Christianity*, Fortress Press, 1985

——*The Early Church: From the Beginnings to 461*, SCM Press, 1991 (1965)

Gibbon, E. *The Decline and Fall of the Roman Empire* (1776–88) [There was an Everyman edition in 1993, and in 1996 there was a Penguin Classic and Library of America edition, with an introduction by David Womersley.]

Goffart, W. *Barbarians and Romans AD 418–584: The Techniques of Accommodation*, Princeton University Press, 1987 (1980)

Goodacre, H. *A Handbook of the Coinage of the Byzantine Empire, Part I, Arcadius to Leontius*, Spink, 1928

Gordon, C.D. *The Age of Attila*, University of Michigan Press, 1960

Gough, M. *The Origins of Christian Art*, Thames & Hudson, 1973

Grabar, A. *Byzantium: From the Death of Theodosius to the Rise of Islam*, London, 1966

——*L'art de la fin de l'antiquité et du moyen age*, 3 vols, Paris, 1968

Grant, M. *The Dawn of the Middle Ages*, Weidenfeld & Nicolson, 1981

——*The Fall of the Roman Empire*, Weidenfeld & Nicolson, rev. edn, 1990 (Annenberg School Press, Radnor, Pennsylvania, 1976) and 1996 (Weidenfeld & Nicolson)

Hamblen, L. *Attila et les Huns*, Paris, 1972

Haywood, R.M. *The Myth of Rome's Fall*, Alvin Redman, 1960

Hestiasis: *Studi di tarda antichità offerti as. Calderone*, I, VIII, Vienna, 1988–91

Hild, F., Hellenkemper, H. and Hellenkemper, G. *Reallexikon zur Byzantinischen Kunst*, IV, 1894

Hill, S. *The Early Byzantine Churches of Cilicia and Isauria*, Byzantine and Ottoman Monographs, Birmingham, 1996

Holum, K.G. *Theodosian Empresses*, University of California Press, Berkeley, 1982

Hordern, P. and Purcell, N. *The Mediterranean World: Man and Environment in Antiquity and the Middle Ages*, Oxford University Press, 1993

Hubert, J., Porcher, J. and Volbach, W.F. *Europe of the Invasions*, Braziller, New York, 1969

Hussey, J.M. *The Byzantine World*, Hutchinson, London, 1957, 1961

Jacobini, A. and Zanini, E. *Arte sacra e arte profana a Bisanzio*, Milan, 1995

Johnson, A. and Scott, G.W. *Byzantium*, BBC, 1968

Johnson, P. *A History of Christianity*, Penguin, 1978 (Weidenfeld & Nicolson, 1976)

Jones, A.H.M. *The Later Roman Empire 284–602*, 2 vols, Blackwell, Oxford, 1964
——*The Decline of the Ancient World*, Longman, 1966

Kaegi, W.E. *Byzantium and the Decline of Rome*, Princeton University Press, 1968

Kagan, D. (ed.) *The End of the Roman Empire: Decline or Transformation*, 3rd edn, Yale University Press, 1992 (rev. edn Lexington, Mass., 1978)

Kellett, E.E. *A Short History of Religions*, Gollancz, 1933, Pelican, Harmondsworth, 1962

Kent, J.P.C. and Painter, K.S. *Wealth of the Roman World AD 300–700: Gold and Silver*, British Museum Publications Ltd, 1977

Kitzinger, E. *Byzantine Art in the Making*, Harvard University Press, Cambridge, Mass., 1977

Koch, G. *Early Christian Art and Architecture: An Introduction*, SCM Press, 1996

Krautheimer, R. *Early Christian and Byzantine Architecture*, Pelican, Harmondsworth, 1965

Lane Fox, R. *Pagans and Christians*, New York, 1987

Lazaret, V.M. *Istoria Vizantiskoi Zhiropisi*, Iskustvo, Moscow, 2 vols, 1941–8

Le Goff, J. *Medieval Civilisation 400–1500*, Oxford University Press, 1988

Liddell, R. *Byzantium and Istanbul*, Cape, 1956

Liebesschutz, J.H.W.G. *Barbarians and Bishops: Army, Church and State in the Age of Arcadius and Chrysostom*, vol. II, Oxford University Press, 1990, 1994

Littlewood, A.R. (ed.) *Originality in Byzantine Literature, Art and Music*, Oxbow, 1995

Llewellyn, P. *Rome in the Dark Ages*, Constable, 1993 (Faber & Faber, 1971)

L'Orange, H.P. *Art Forms and Civic Life in the Late Roman Empire*, Princeton University Press, 1965

Lot, F. *The End of the Ancient World*, Routledge & Kegan Paul, 1931, 1966

Loverance, R. *Byzantium*, British Museum Press, London, 1988, 1994

Maclagen, M. *The City of Constantinople*, Thames & Hudson, 1968

MacMullen, R. *Soldier and Civilian in the Late Roman Empire*, Harvard University Press, Cambridge, Mass., 1963

Maenchen-Helfen, O.J. *The World of the Huns*, University of California Press, Berkeley, 1973

Mango, C. *Art of the Byzantine Empire 312–1453*, Englewood Cliffs, N.J., 1972

Mango, C. *Byzantium: The Empire of New Rome*, Weidenfeld & Nicolson, 1980, Phoenix paperback, 1994

Mango, C. and Dagron, G. (eds) *Constantinople and Its Hinterland* (Society for the Promotion of Byzantine Studies), Variorum, London, 1995

Mathew, G. *Byzantine Aesthetics*, Murray, 1963

Matthews, J. *Western Aristocracies and Imperial Court AD 364–425*, Clarendon Press, Oxford, 1975

——*The Clash of the Gods: A Reinterpretation of Early Christian Art*, Princeton University Press, 1995

Mazzarino, S. *The End of the Ancient World*, Faber & Faber, 1966

Milburn, R. *Early Christian Art and Architecture*, University of California Press, Berkeley, 1988

de Montesquieu, C.L. *Considerations on the Causes of the Greatness of the Romans and Their Decline*, Cornell University Press, Ithaca, 1969 (1734)

Musset, L. *The Germanic Invasions: The Making of Europe; 400–600 AD*, Pennsylvania State University Press, University Park, 1975

Neumayer, H. *Byzantine Mosaics*, Methuen, 1964 (1963)

Norwich, J.J. *Byzantium: The Early Centuries*, Knopf, New York, 1989

Oman, C.W.C. *The Byzantine Empire*, Fisher Unwin, 1892

Painter, K.S. (ed.) *Churches Built in Ancient Times*, 1994

Palanque, J.R. *Le bas-empire*, Paris, 1971

Parry, A. (ed.) *Studies in Fifth-Century Thought and Literature*, Yale University Press, New Haven, 1972

Paschoud, F. *Roma Aeterna* (Bibliotheca Helvetica Romana, vol. 7), Rome, 1967

Pelikan, J. *The Excellent Empire: The Fall of Rome and the Triumph of the Church*, Harper & Row, San Francisco, 1987

Pereira, M. *Istanbul: Aspects of a City*, Bles, 1968

Perowne, S. *The End of the Roman World*, Hodder & Stoughton, 1966

Piganiol, A. *L'empire chrétien*, Paris, rev. edn, 1972 (1947)

Randars-Pehrson, J.D. *Barbarians and Romans: The Birth-Struggle of Europe AD 400–700*, University of Oklahoma Press, Norman, 1983

Randsborg, K. *The First Millennium AD in Europe and the Mediterranean*, Cambridge University Press, 1991

Rehm, W. *Der Untergang Roms in abendländischen Denken* (Das Erbe der Alten vol. 18), Leipzig, 1930

Remondon, R. *La crise de l'empire romain: de Marc-Aurèle à Anastase*, Paris, 1964

Rodley, E. *Byzantine Art and Architecture: An Introduction*, Cambridge University Press, 1994

Rollins, A.M. *The Fall of Rome: A Reference Guide*, McFarland, Jefferson, 1983

Rousseau, P. *Ascetics, Authority and the Church*, Oxford University Press, 1979

Runciman, S. *Byzantine Civilisation*, Arnold, 1933

——*Byzantine Style and Civilization*, Penguin, 1975, 1981

Sas-Zaloziecky, W. *Die altchristliche Kunst*, Frankfurt-am-Main, 1963

Scarre, C. *Chronicle of the Roman Emperors*, Thames & Hudson, 1995

Seeck, O. *Geschichte des Untergangs der antiken Welt*, Stuttgart, 1910–14

Singleton, B. *Italy in the Early Christian Period*, Cambridge University Press, 1996

Smith, J.H. *The Death of Classical Paganism*, Scribner, New York, 1976

Sordi, M. *The Christians and the Roman Empire*, Routledge, 1994

Stein, E. *Geschichte des spätrömischen Reichs, I, vom römischen zum byzantinischen Staate* (284–476 n. Chr.), Vienna, 1928 (translated as *Histoire du bas-empire* (ed. J.R. Palanque, Paris, 1949, 1968)

Stevenson, J. *Creeds, Council and Controversies*, SPCK, rev. edn, 1989 (original edn 1966)

Talbot Rice, D. *Byzantine Art*, Oxford University Press, 1935, Pelican, rev. edn, 1952, 1968 (1954)

———*The Byzantines*, Thames & Hudson, 1962

Temple, R. (ed.) *Early Christian and Byzantine Art*, Element, 1990

Thompson, E.A. *A History of Attila and the Huns*, Oxford University Press, 1948, Greenwood Press, Westpoint, 1975 (rev. edn as *The Huns*, Blackwell, 1996)

———*Romans and Barbarians: The Decline of the Western Empire*, University of Wisconsin Press, Madison, 1982

Vasiliev, A.A. *History of the Byzantine Empire*, 2 vols, University of Wisconsin Press, Madison, 1961

Vogt, J. *Kulturwelt und Barbaren: Zum Menschheitsbild der spätantiken Gesellschaft*, Wiesbaden, 1967

———*The Decline of Rome*, Weidenfeld & Nicolson, 1967 (1965)

Vryonis, S. *Byzantium and Europe*, Thames & Hudson, 1967

Walbank, F.W. *The Awful Revolution*, Liverpool University Press, 1969

Wallace-Hadrill, J.M. *The Barbarian West AD 400–1000*, 5th edn, Blackwell, 1985 (original edn, Hutchinson, 1952)

Weitzmann, K. (ed.) *The Age of Spirituality*, New York, 1979

Wes, M.A. (ed.) *The Transformation of the Roman World: Gibbon's Problem after Two Centuries*, University of California Press, Berkeley, 1966

Wharton, A.J. *Refiguring the Post-Classical City*, Cambridge University Press, 1996

Whitton, M. *The Making of Orthodox Byzantium*, Macmillan, 1996

Womersley, D. *The Transformation or the Decline and Fall of the Roman Empire*, Cambridge University Press, 1989

Yoffee, N. and Cowgill, C.L. *The Collapse of Ancient States and Civilizations*, University of Arizona Press, Tucson, 1988

Young, G. *Constantinople*, Barnes & Noble, New York, 1992

Zosso, F. and Zingg, C. *Les empereurs romains 27 av. J.C.–476 ap. J.C.*, Paris, 1994

INDEX

The index covers all chapters, the appendices, and the Latin and Greek authors in the bibliography. The notes are not covered. Maps and illustrations are indicated by page references in italics.